W9-BZJ-402

STORY BY
JOËLLE JONES
& JAMIE S. RICH

ART BY
JOËLLE JONES

COLORS BY
LAURA ALLRED

LETTERS BY
CRANK!

Killer™

PRODUCTION TECH
CHRISTIANNE GOUDREAU

DESIGNER
KAT LARSON

ASSISTANT EDITORS
**SHANTEL LaROCQUE
& JEMIAH JEFFERSON**

EDITOR
SCOTT ALLIE

PRESIDENT AND PUBLISHER
MIKE RICHARDSON

Published by Dark Horse Books
A division of Dark Horse Comics, Inc.
10956 SE Main Street
Milwaukie, OR 97222

First edition: September 2015
ISBN 978-1-61655-757-7

5 7 9 10 8 6
Printed in China

International Licensing: (503) 905-2377
Comic Shop Locator Service: (888) 266-4226

Lady Killer™ © 2015 Joëlle Jones and Jamie S. Rich. Dark Horse Books® and the Dark Horse logo are registered trademarks of Dark Horse Comics, Inc. All rights reserved. No portion of this publication may be reproduced or transmitted, in any form or by any means, without the express written permission of Dark Horse Comics, Inc. Names, characters, places, and incidents featured in this publication either are the product of the author's imagination or are used fictitiously. Any resemblance to actual persons (living or dead), events, institutions, or locales, without satiric intent, is coincidental.

This volume collects *Lady Killer* #1–#5.

Executive Vice President NEIL HANKERSON Chief Financial Officer TOM WEDDLE Vice President of Publishing RANDY STRADLEY Vice President of Book Trade Sales MICHAEL MARTENS Editor in Chief SCOTT ALLIE Vice President of Marketing MATT PARKINSON Vice President of Product Development DAVID SCROGGY Vice President of Information Technology DALE LaFOUNTAIN Senior Director of Print, Design, and Production DARLENE VOGEL General Counsel KEN LIZZI Editorial Director DAVEY ESTRADA Senior Books Editor CHRIS WARNER Executive Editor DIANA SCHUTZ Director of Print and Development CARY GRAZZINI Art Director LIA RIBACCHI Director of Scheduling CARA NIECE Director of Digital Publishing MARK BERNARDI

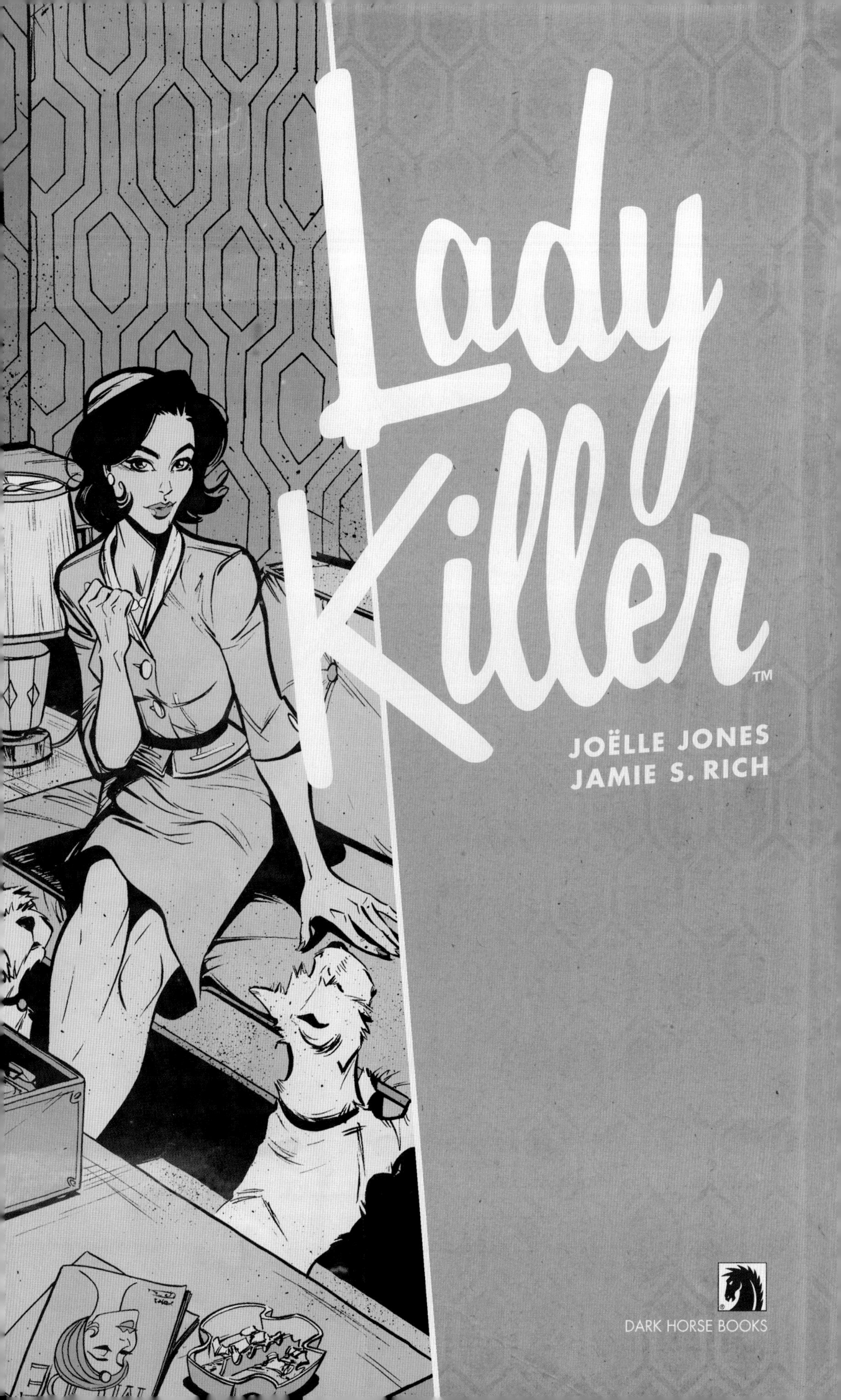

Lady Killer™

JOËLLE JONES
JAMIE S. RICH

DARK HORSE BOOKS

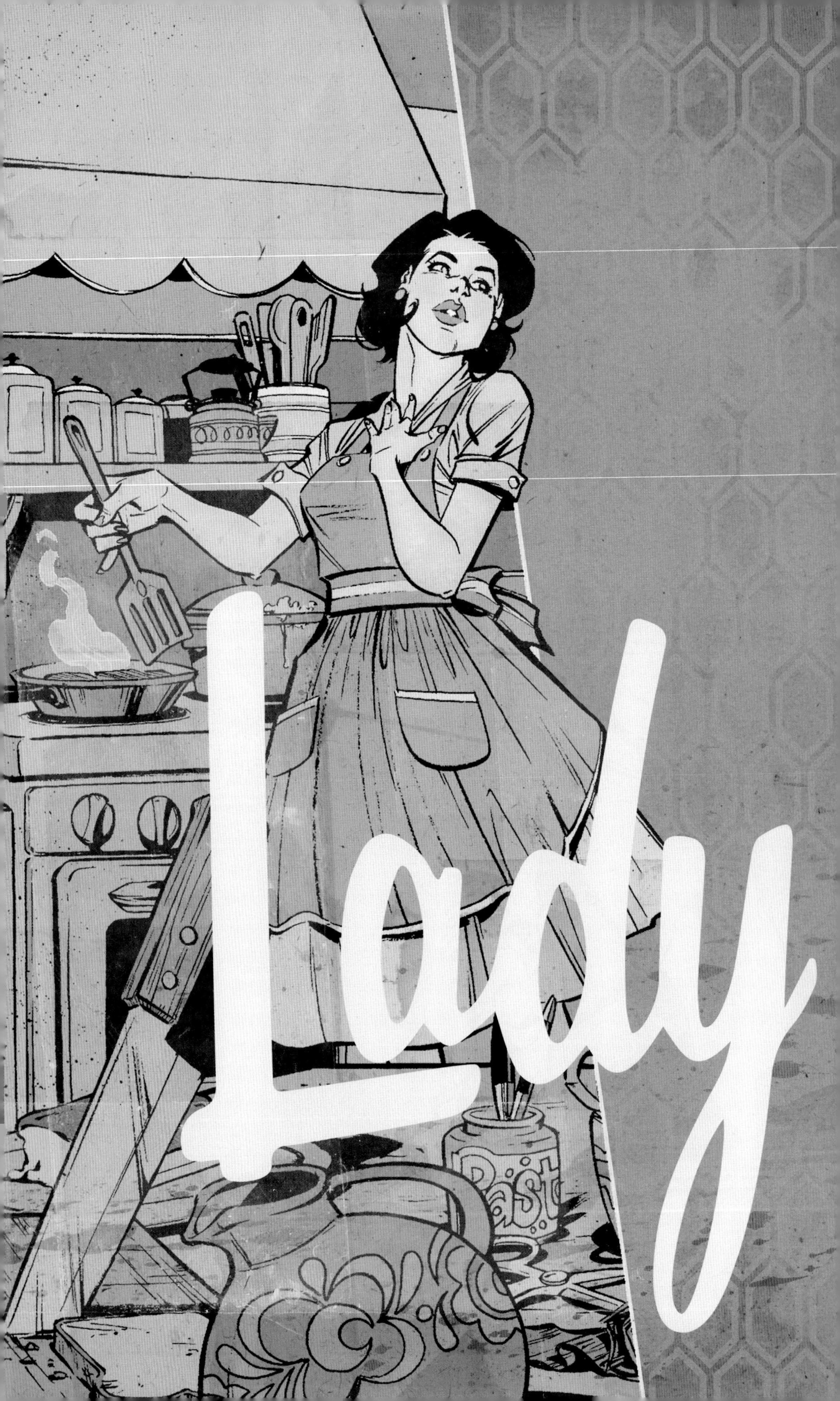
Lady
Paste

INTRODUCTION

JOSIE SCHULLER HAS TWO OF THE TRAITS THAT I ADMIRE MOST IN A PERSON: she knows how to host a boffo cocktail party, and she can kill someone with her bare hands.

I have some experience with pretty women and knives. I write a series of thrillers that feature a beautiful female serial killer named Gretchen Lowell. The books aren't about Gretchen; they're about the detective who is obsessed with her. He's the protagonist. But most people think of them as the Gretchen Lowell books. Some people love her. Some people hate her. But everyone wants to talk about her. Eventually the conversation comes around to a question I get asked a lot: *A girl serial killer? How did you ever come up with that?*

It's true that the majority of serial killers are men. Men are more likely to kill strangers. Women are more likely to kill people we

know. Men, when they kill, make a mess. We suffocate our infants and poison our husbands. There's less to clean up.

It took me a while to realize that what people really wanted to know was not how did I come up with the idea of a female serial killer, but how did I come up with the idea of a female serial killer who kills like a man.

Bloodshed is, apparently, unladylike. We expect women—nurturing, kind, loving women—to avoid violence, even, apparently, when we're murdering someone.

Josie, like Gretchen, isn't afraid of blood. What woman would be?

We bleed for a week every month. Seriously. Look around. Some of the women you see right now are bleeding. Are they freaking out? Are they running around all hysterical? No. I'm guessing they're just going about their day, maybe wondering why you're staring at them. Have you ever seen a woman give birth? Talk about violent. You know the John Hurt scene in *Alien*? Childbirth makes that look tame.

Your mother shared her blood with you. She brought you into the world. And she let you live. I mean it. Because, take it from me, at some point your mother thought about killing you. It might have been in the week or two after the plus showed up on the pee stick. Or maybe later, in the dead of night, when you'd been crying for five hours. Maybe she held a pillow an inch above your pert, perfect little nose. More likely, the thought just flickered in her mind and she jumped back, horrified by it. But it was there. Get a few drinks in her and she'll tell you.

Women are powerful creatures. What with the bleeding and the life-and-death decisions.

Yet most of the female archetypes reflected back to us by pop culture are weak. They don't come close to passing the Bechdel test. They are plagued by self-doubt. They have no agency. Clearly this resonates with us, or it wouldn't be such a dietary mainstay.

Lady Killer goes after these social conventions with wit and panache. You could say it eviscerates them.

Midcentury America was all about style. That's what happens when you shackle people to social norms: everything becomes about appearances. Josie may look like the perfect homemaker. She's Pan Am—stewardess pretty, the perfect wife and doting mother. But she's pretending. In her secret life, she is an assassin. She is self-determined. She is self-reliant. She is highly capable. Which of these things is more socially dangerous?

We should all have such good Ginsu skills. Clearly it builds confidence.

I bet you know a few women who are secret assassins. Don't look. They'll see you watching.

I'll leave you with this thought: maybe the reason we all picture serial killers as schlubby, middle-aged white guys is because they are the ones who get caught.

Happy reading.

CHELSEA CAIN
2015

Chelsea Cain is the author of the New York Times *best-selling Archie Sheridan thriller series, including* Heartsick, Sweetheart, Evil at Heart, The Night Season, Kill You Twice, *and* Let Me Go. *Stephen King included two of her books in his top ten favorite books of the year, and NPR named* Heartsick *one of the best 100 thrillers ever written. In 2014, Chelsea launched the Kick Lannigan series with* One Kick, *which received raves in* People *magazine,* Entertainment Weekly, *the* New York Times, *and* BuzzFeed. *Both Cain's Archie Sheridan and Kick Lannigan series are currently in development for television.*

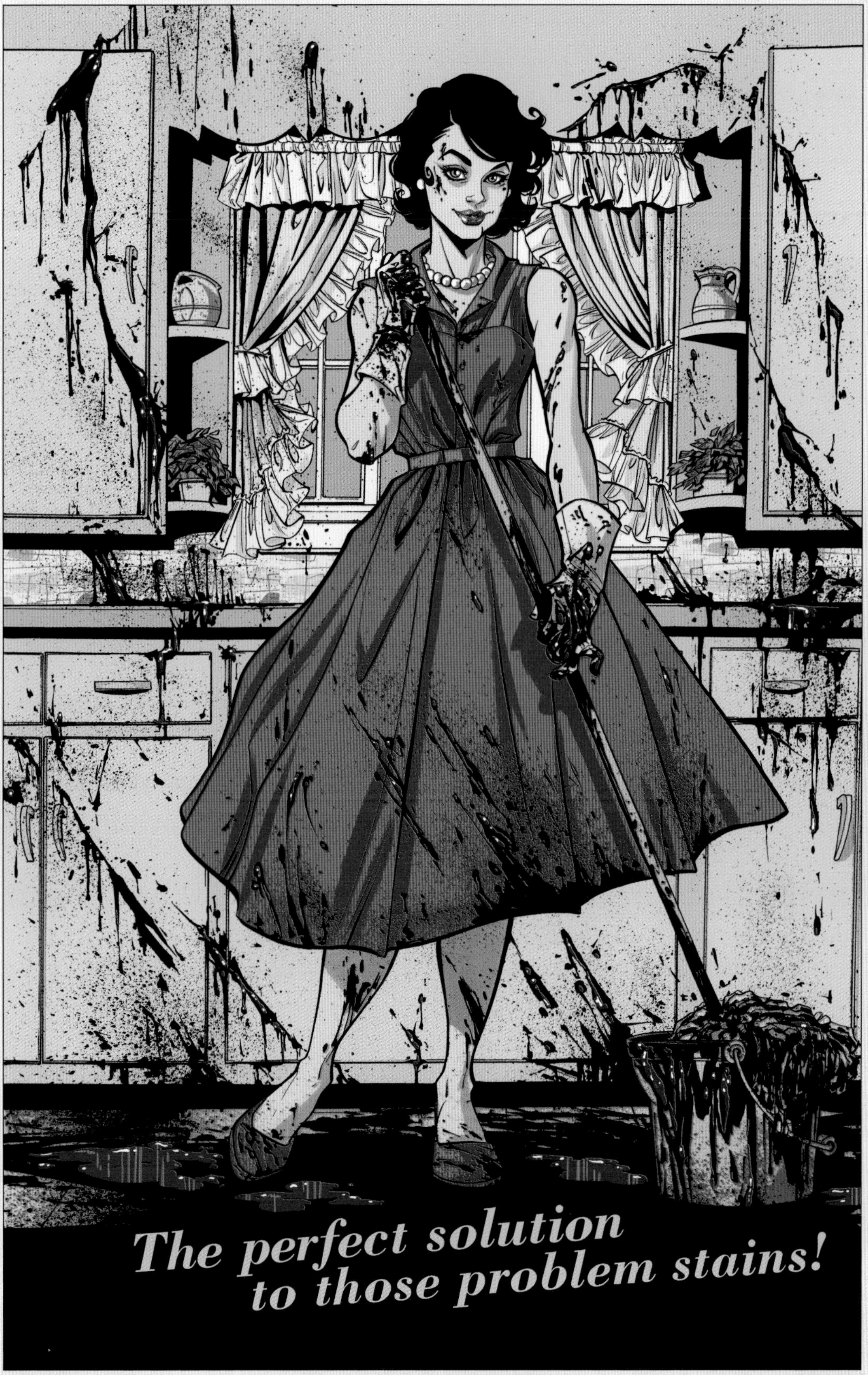
The perfect solution
to those problem stains!

CHAPTER ONE

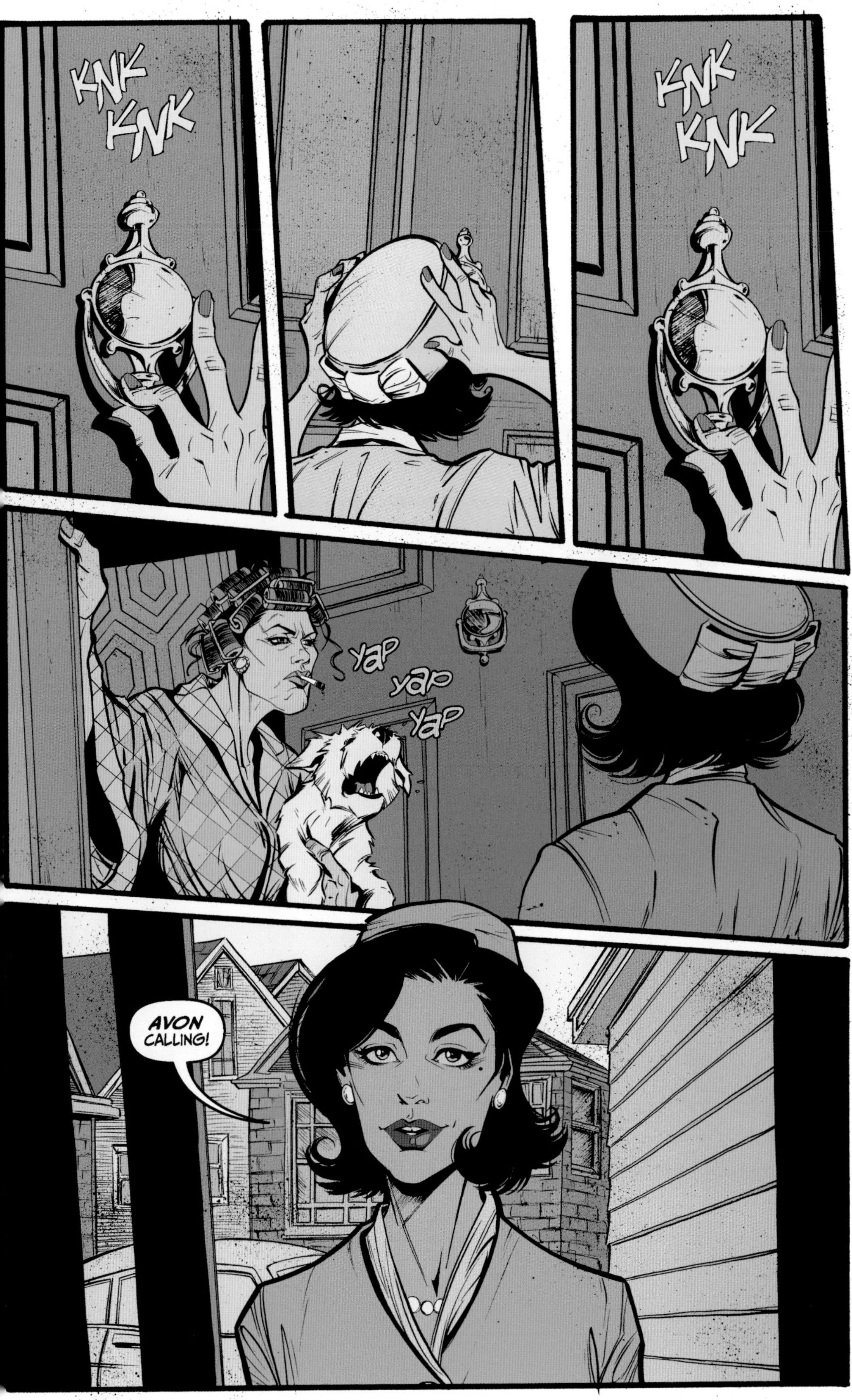
KNK KNK
KNK KNK
YAP YAP YAP
AVON CALLING!

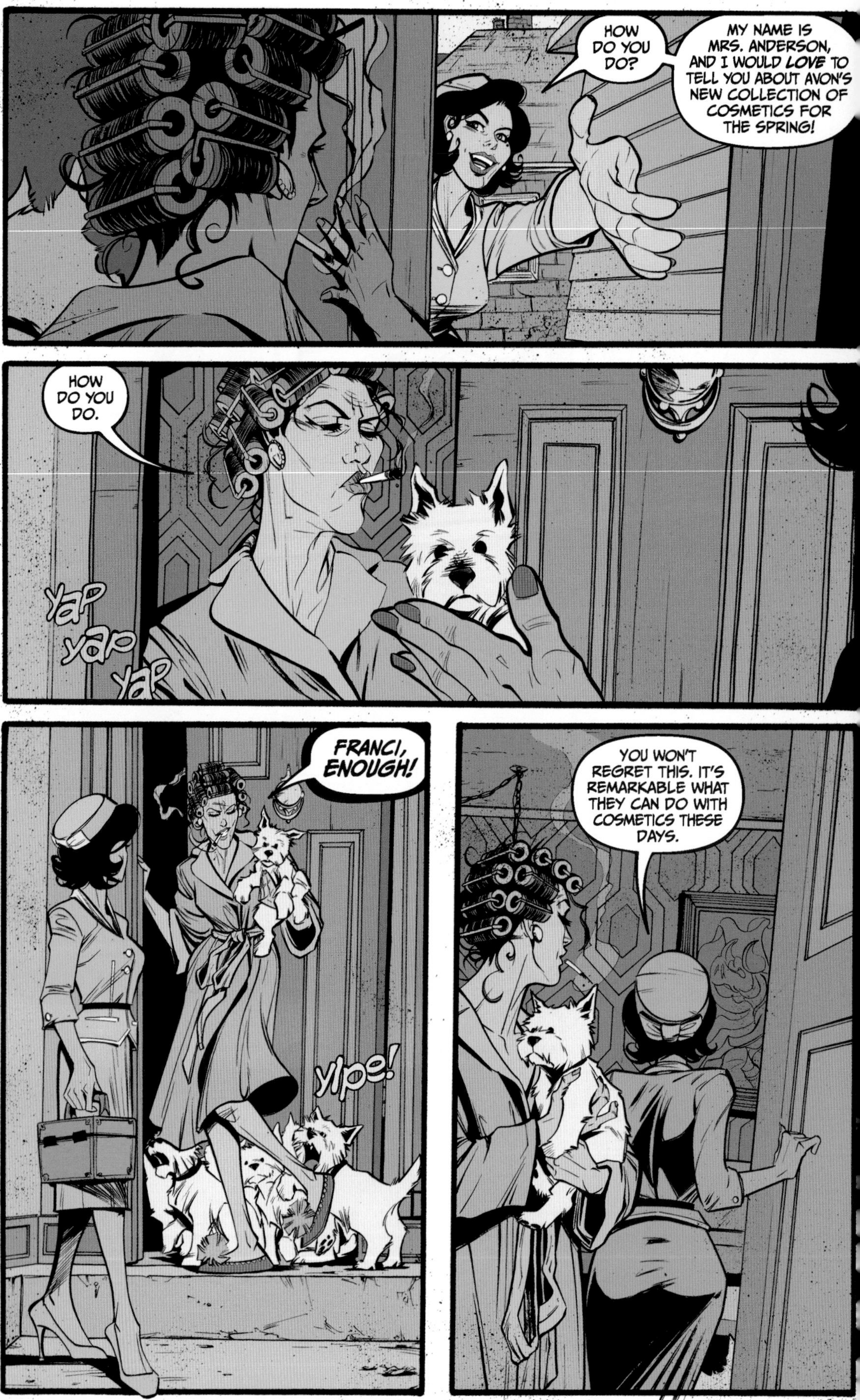
HOW DO YOU DO?
MY NAME IS MRS. ANDERSON, AND I WOULD **LOVE** TO TELL YOU ABOUT AVON'S NEW COLLECTION OF COSMETICS FOR THE SPRING!
HOW DO YOU DO.
YAP YAP YAP
FRANCI, ENOUGH!
YIPE!
YOU WON'T REGRET THIS. IT'S REMARKABLE WHAT THEY CAN DO WITH COSMETICS THESE DAYS.

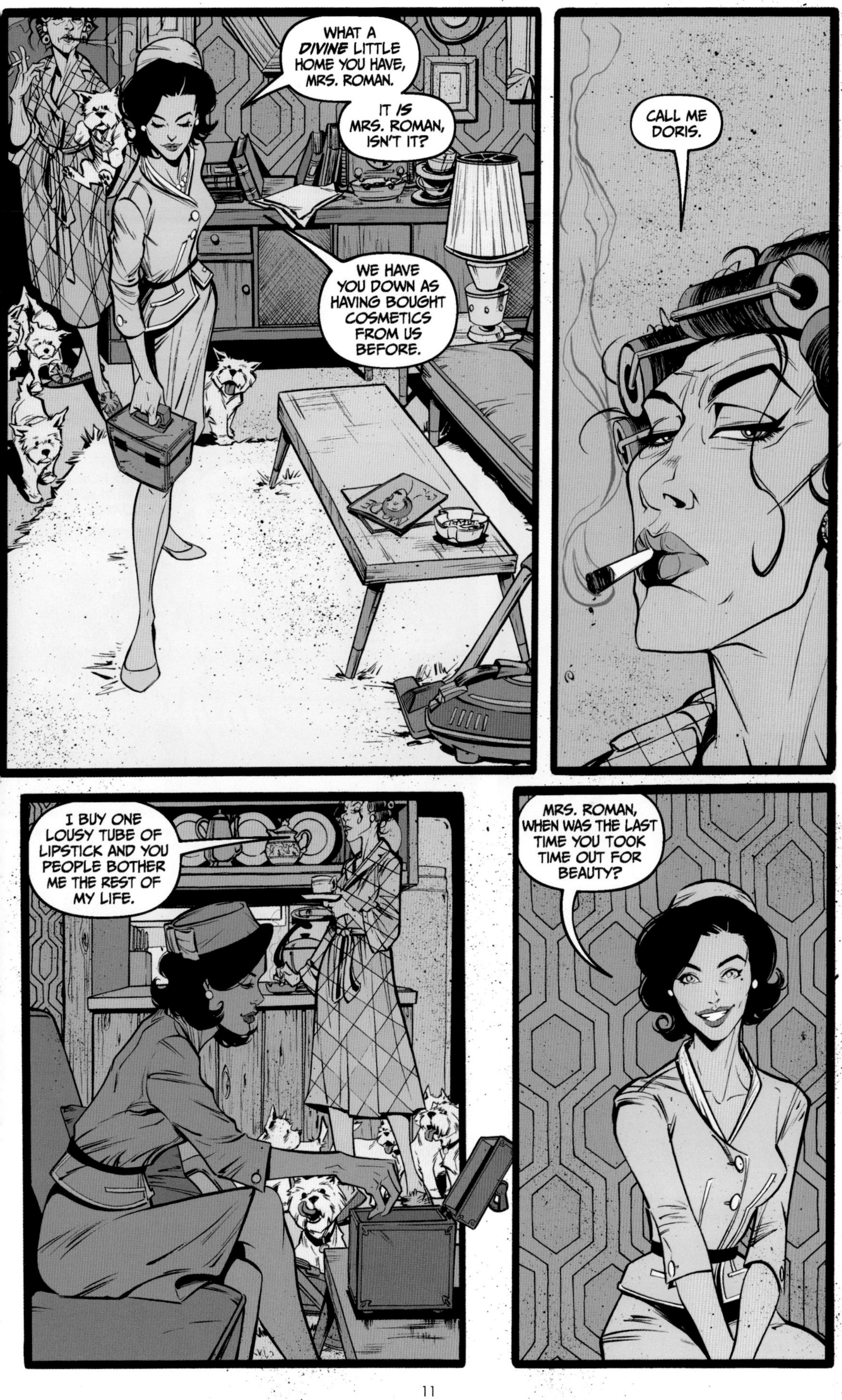
WHAT A *DIVINE* LITTLE HOME YOU HAVE, MRS. ROMAN.
IT *IS* MRS. ROMAN, ISN'T IT?
WE HAVE YOU DOWN AS HAVING BOUGHT COSMETICS FROM US BEFORE.
CALL ME DORIS.
I BUY ONE LOUSY TUBE OF LIPSTICK AND YOU PEOPLE BOTHER ME THE REST OF MY LIFE.
MRS. ROMAN, WHEN WAS THE LAST TIME YOU TOOK TIME OUT FOR BEAUTY?

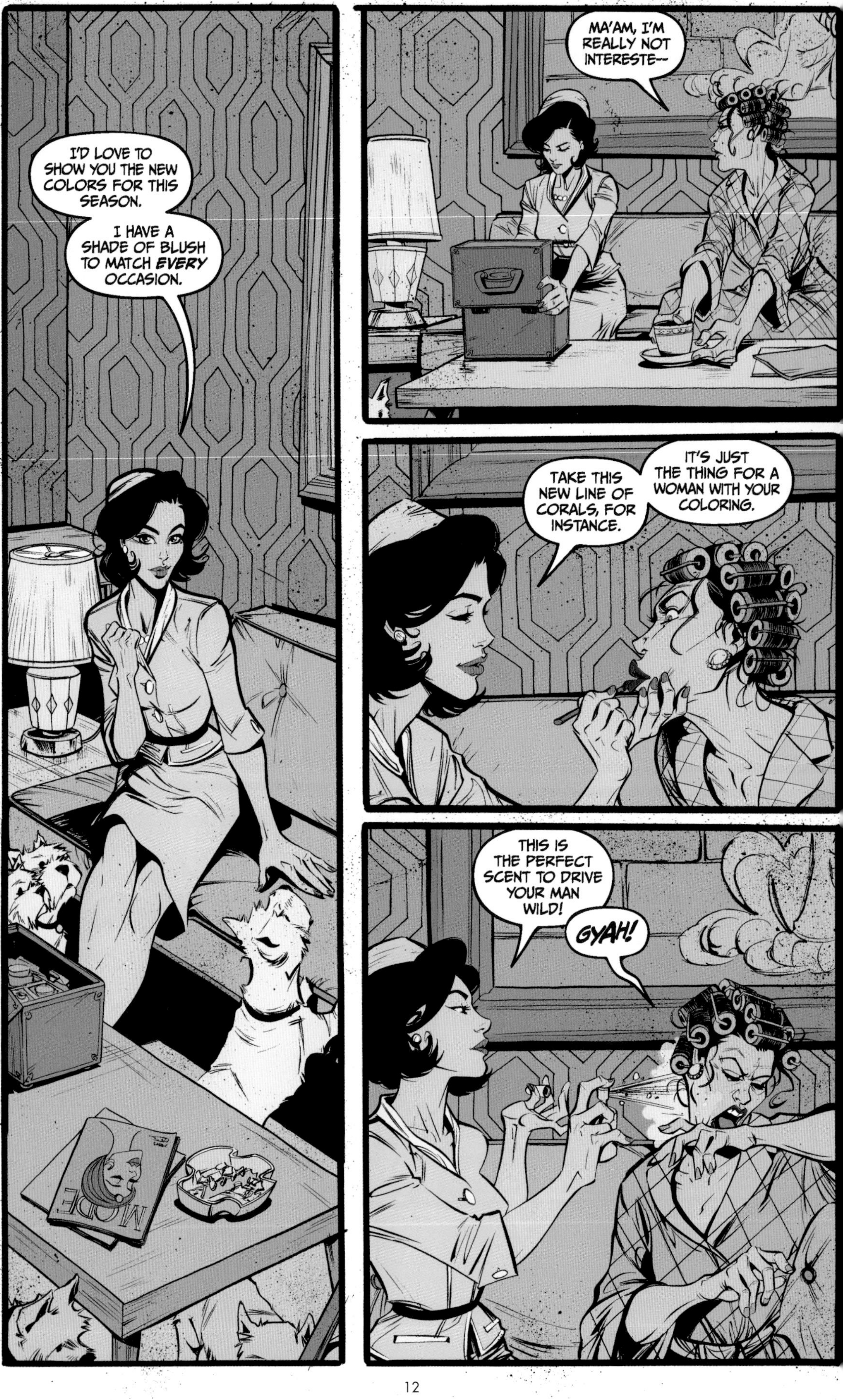
I'D LOVE TO SHOW YOU THE NEW COLORS FOR THIS SEASON.
I HAVE A SHADE OF BLUSH TO MATCH *EVERY* OCCASION.
MODE
MA'AM, I'M REALLY NOT INTERESTE--
TAKE THIS NEW LINE OF CORALS, FOR INSTANCE.
IT'S JUST THE THING FOR A WOMAN WITH YOUR COLORING.
THIS IS THE PERFECT SCENT TO DRIVE YOUR MAN WILD!
GYAH!

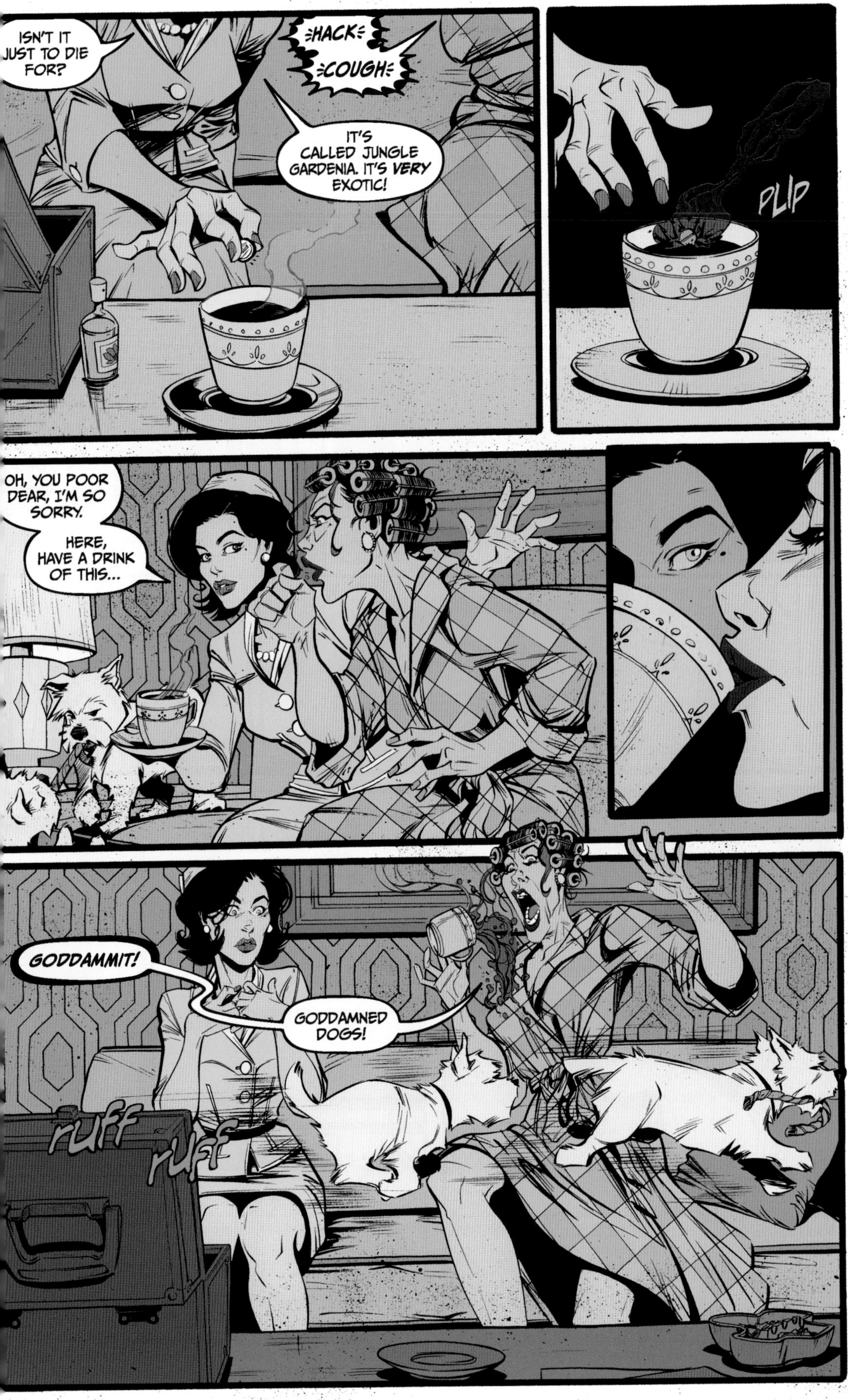
ISN'T IT JUST TO DIE FOR?
HACK
COUGH
IT'S CALLED JUNGLE GARDENIA. IT'S VERY EXOTIC!
PLIP
OH, YOU POOR DEAR, I'M SO SORRY.
HERE, HAVE A DRINK OF THIS...
GODDAMMIT!
GODDAMNED DOGS!
ruff
ruff

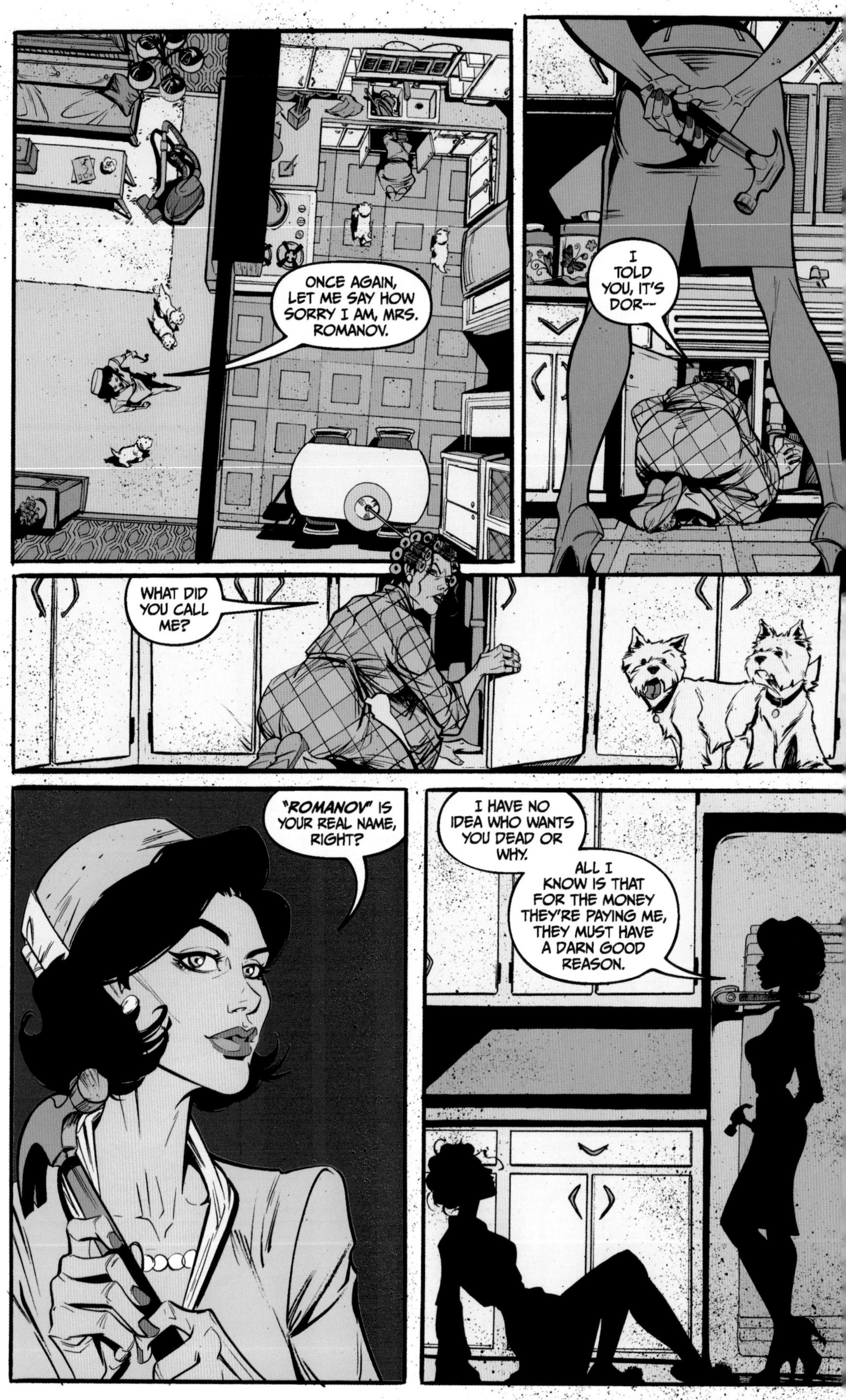
ONCE AGAIN, LET ME SAY HOW SORRY I AM, MRS. ROMANOV.
I TOLD YOU, IT'S DOR--
WHAT DID YOU CALL ME?
"ROMANOV" IS YOUR REAL NAME, RIGHT?
I HAVE NO IDEA WHO WANTS YOU DEAD OR WHY.
ALL I KNOW IS THAT FOR THE MONEY THEY'RE PAYING ME, THEY MUST HAVE A DARN GOOD REASON.

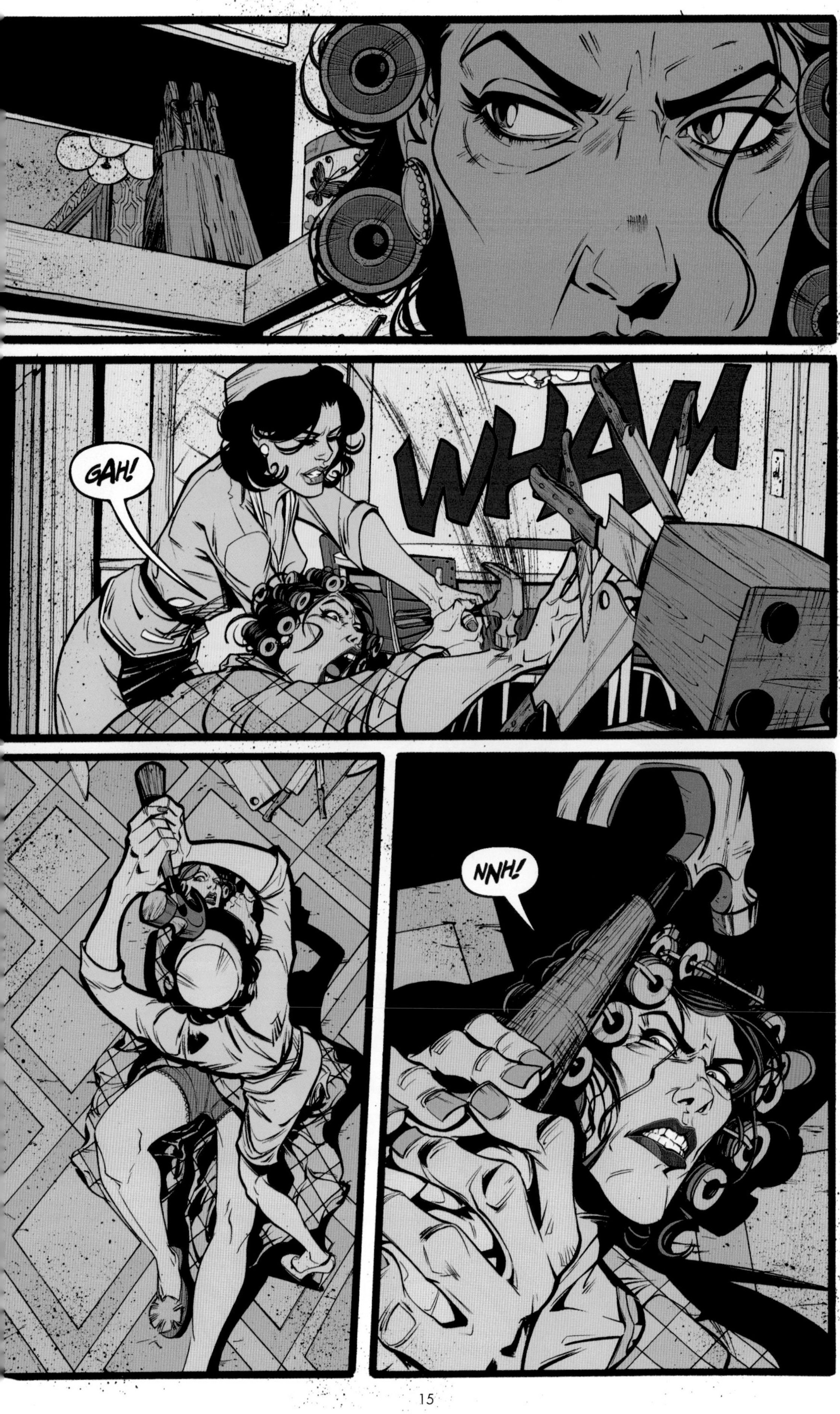
WHAM
GAH!
NNH!

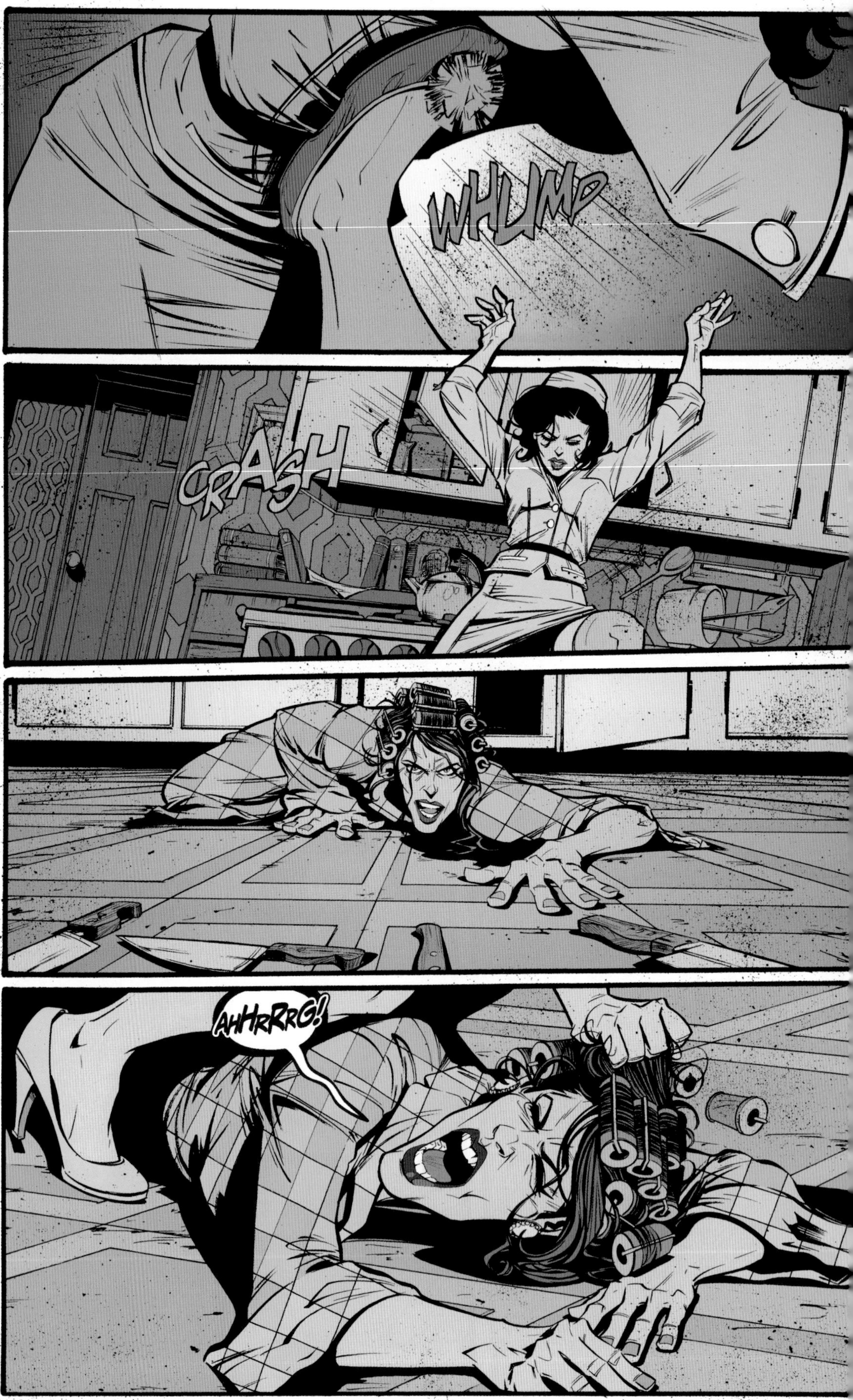
WHUMP
CRASH
AHHRRRG!

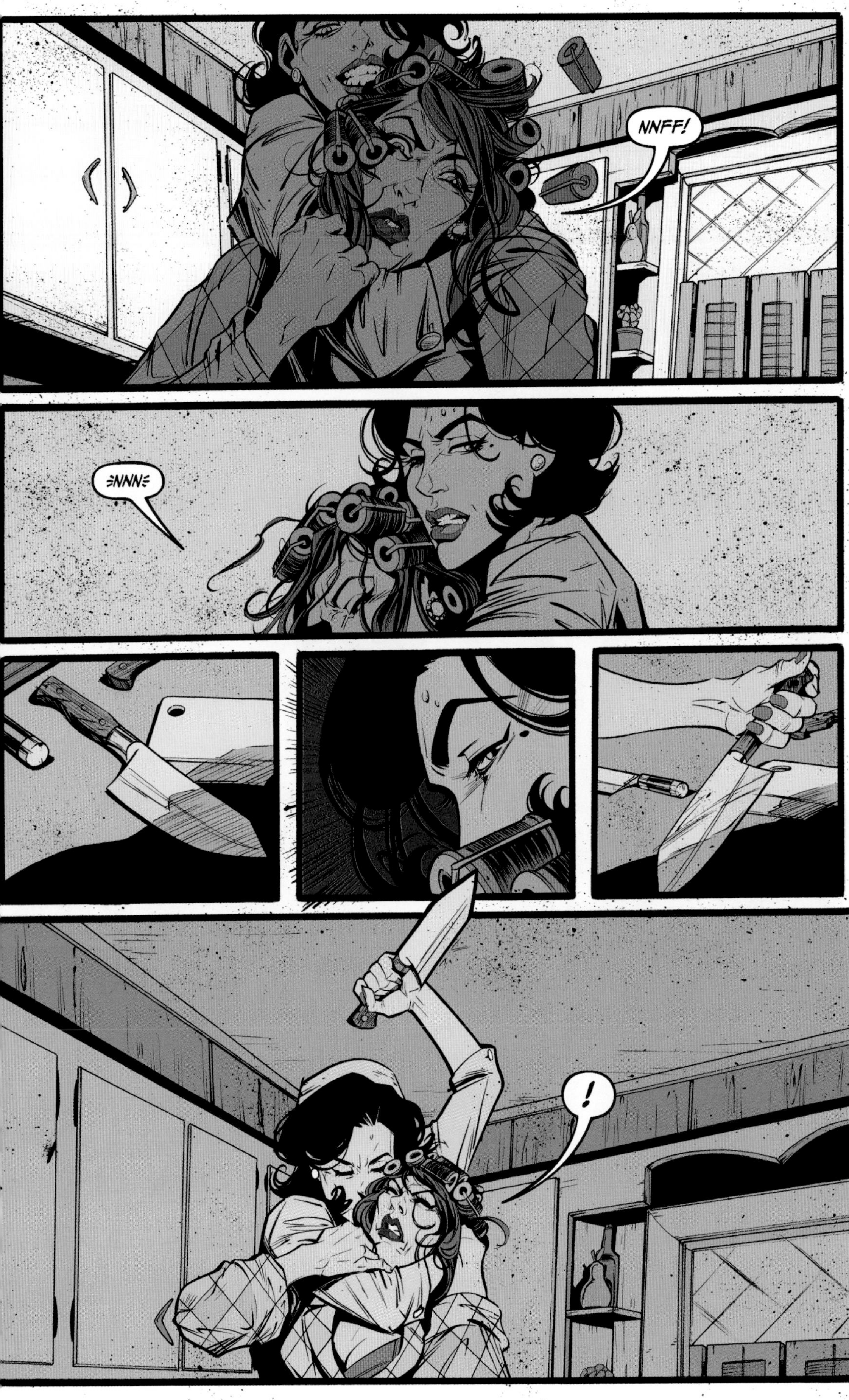
NNFF!
NNN
!

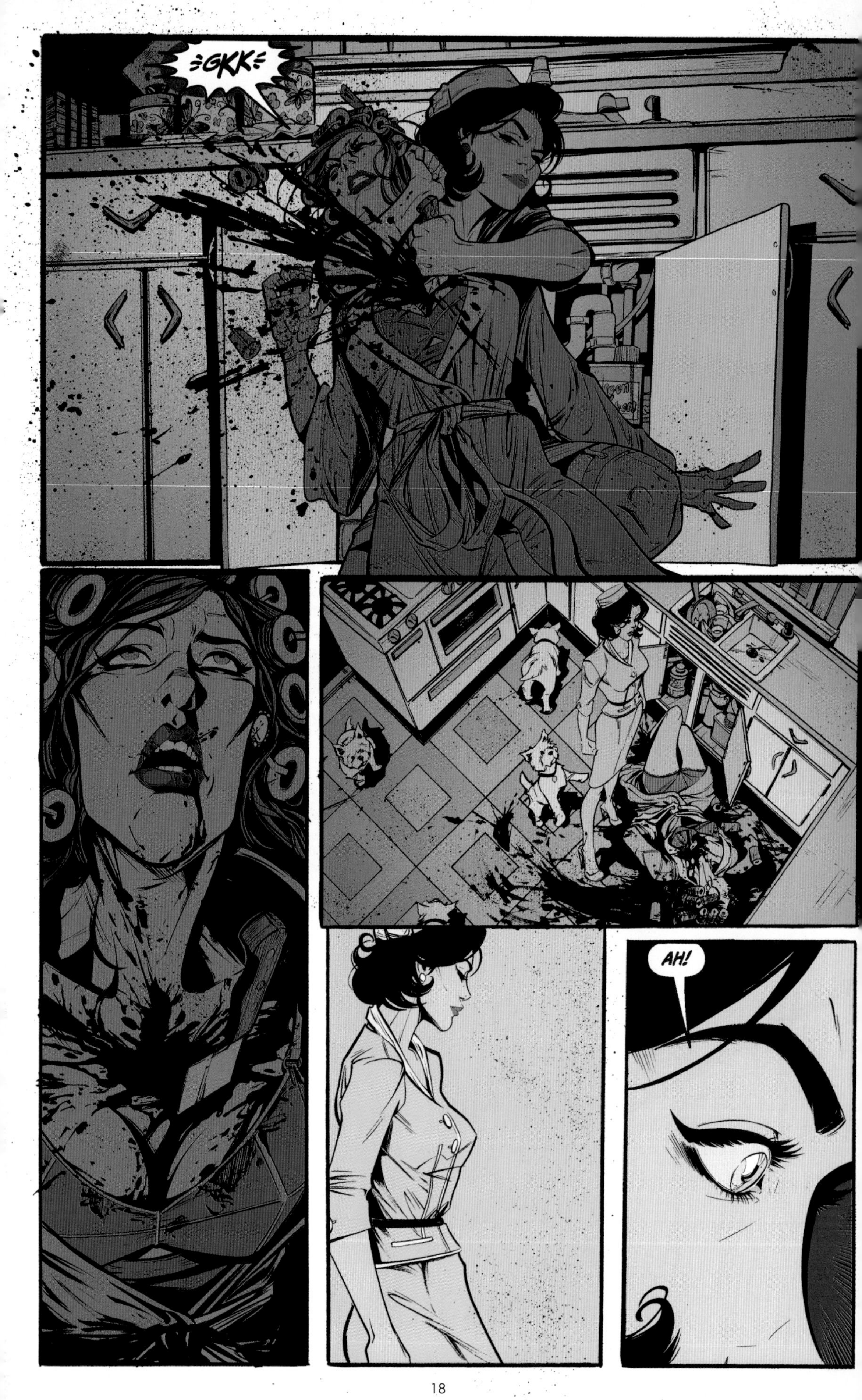
GKK
AH!

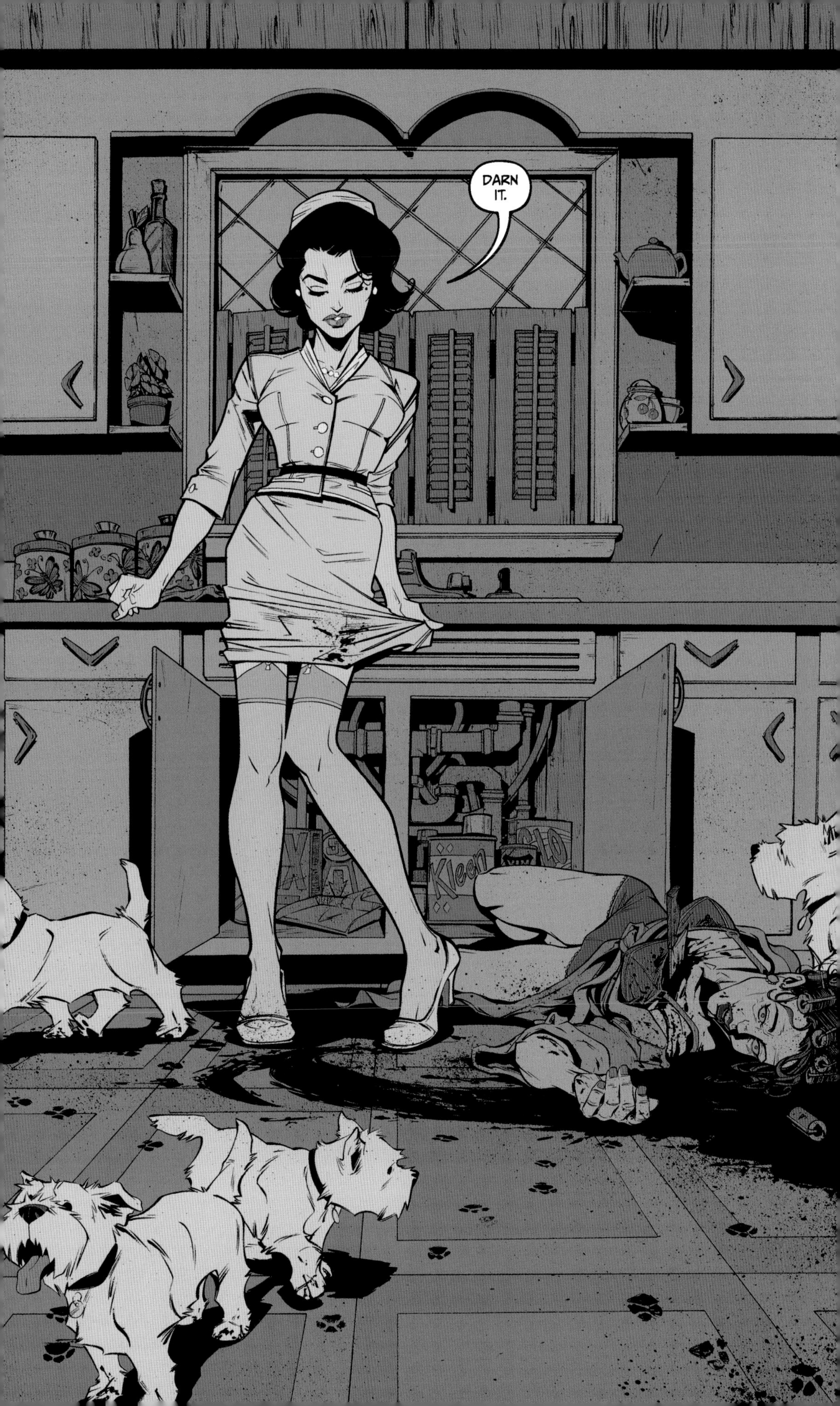
DARN IT.

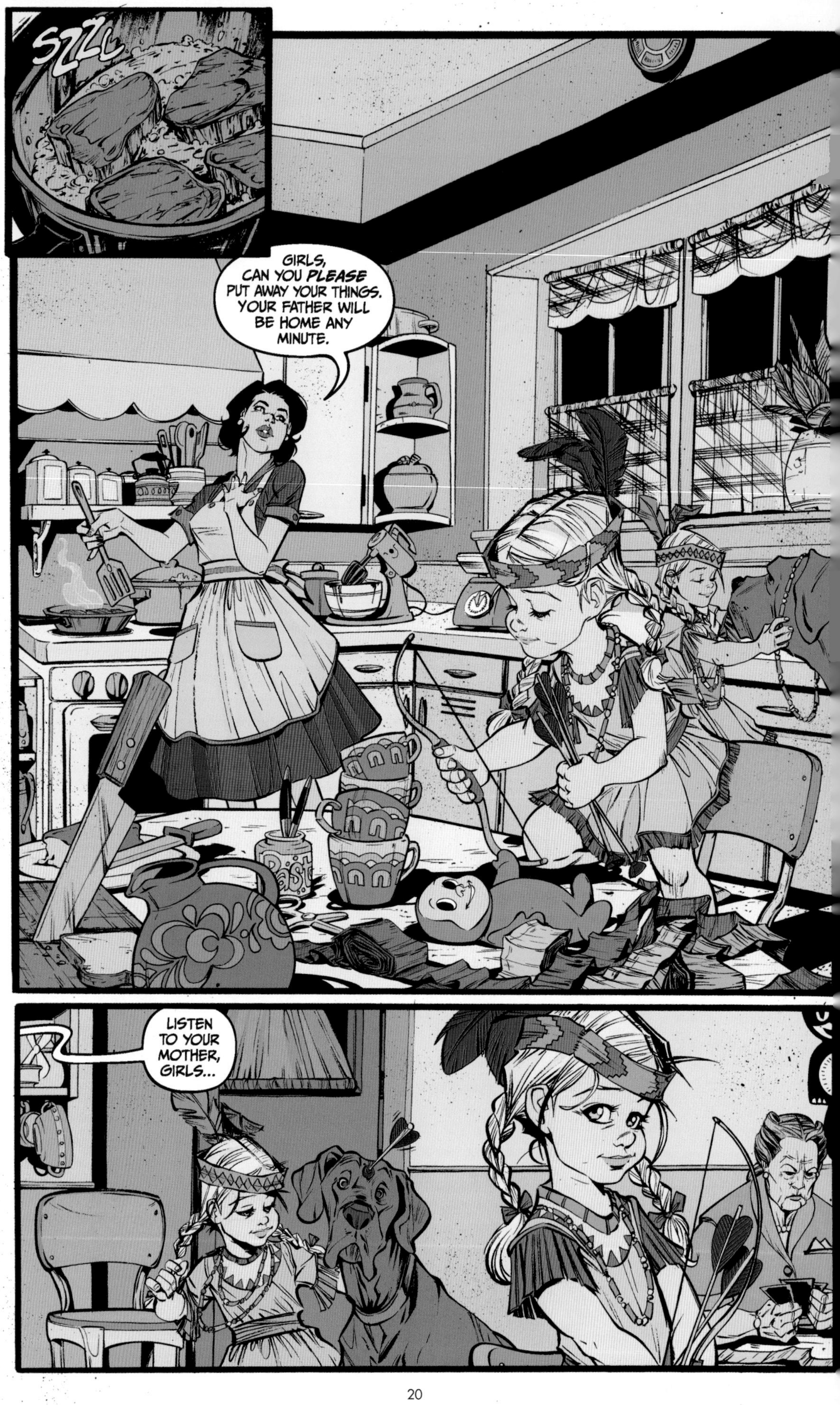
SZZL
GIRLS, CAN YOU *PLEASE* PUT AWAY YOUR THINGS. YOUR FATHER WILL BE HOME ANY MINUTE.
LISTEN TO YOUR MOTHER, GIRLS...

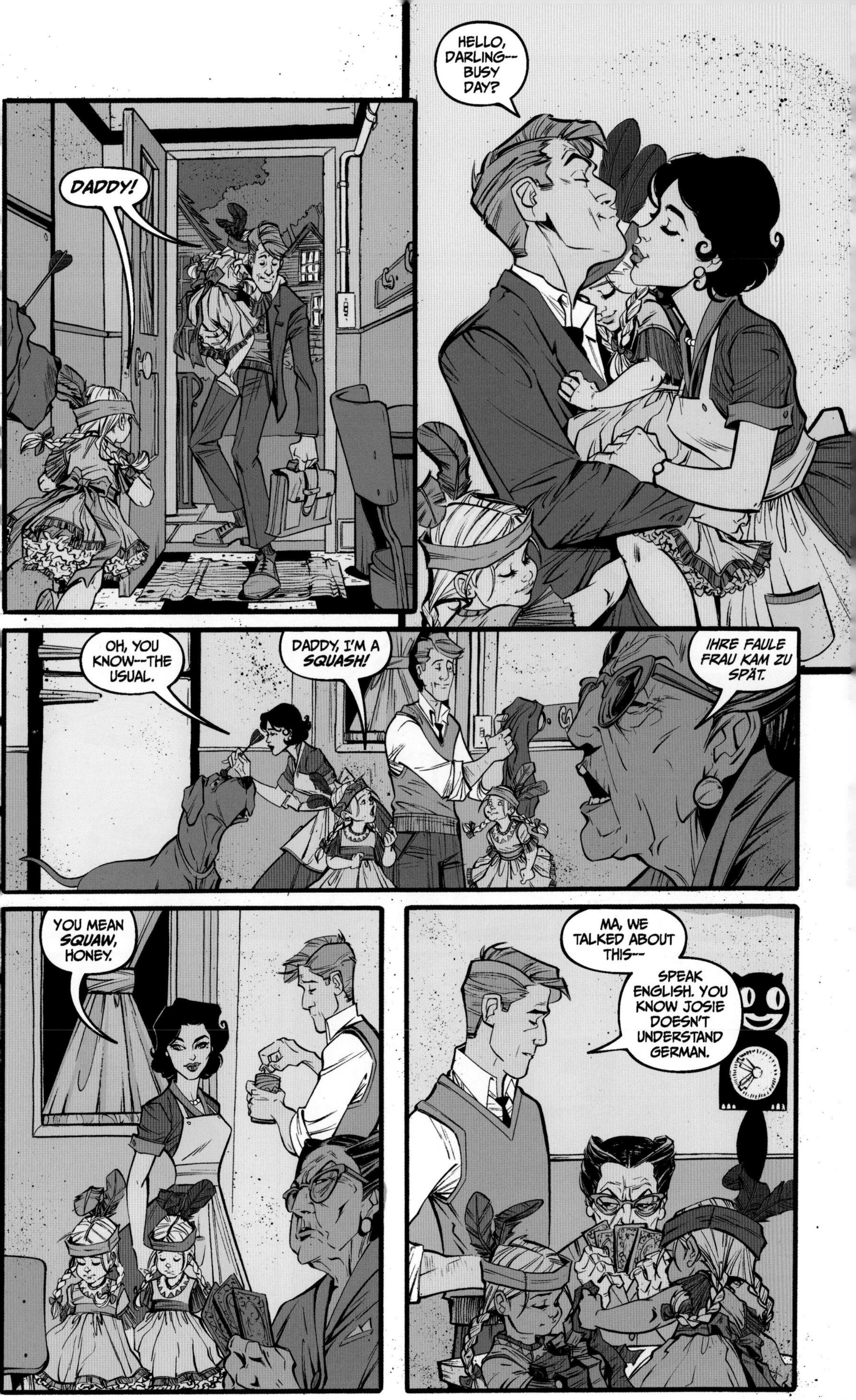
DADDY!
HELLO, DARLING-- BUSY DAY?
OH, YOU KNOW--THE USUAL.
DADDY, I'M A *SQUASH!*
IHRE FAULE FRAU KAM ZU SPÄT.
YOU MEAN *SQUAW,* HONEY.
MA, WE TALKED ABOUT THIS--
SPEAK ENGLISH. YOU KNOW JOSIE DOESN'T UNDERSTAND GERMAN.

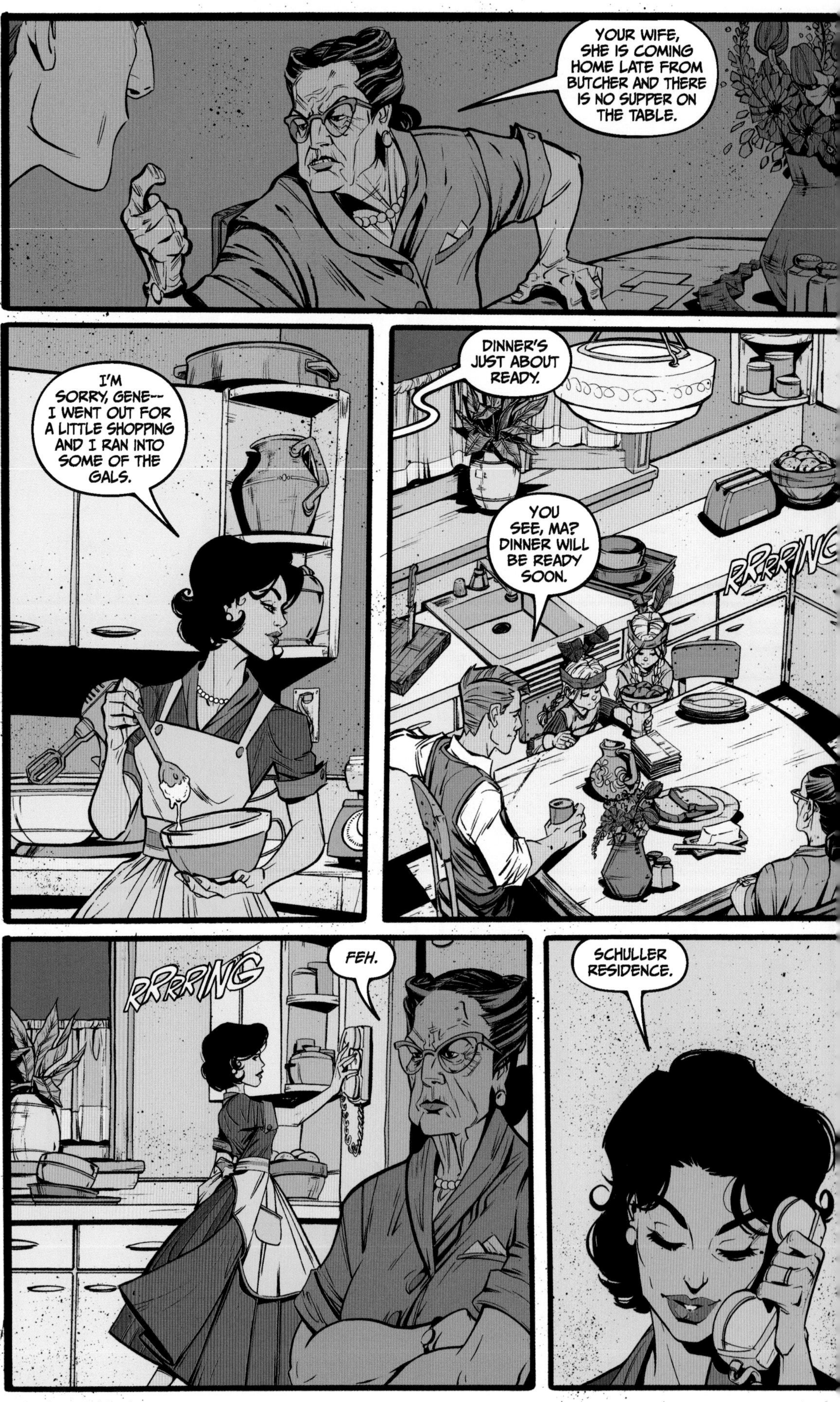
YOUR WIFE, SHE IS COMING HOME LATE FROM BUTCHER AND THERE IS NO SUPPER ON THE TABLE.
I'M SORRY, GENE-- I WENT OUT FOR A LITTLE SHOPPING AND I RAN INTO SOME OF THE GALS.
DINNER'S JUST ABOUT READY.
YOU SEE, MA? DINNER WILL BE READY SOON.
RRRRING
RRRRING
FEH.
SCHULLER RESIDENCE.

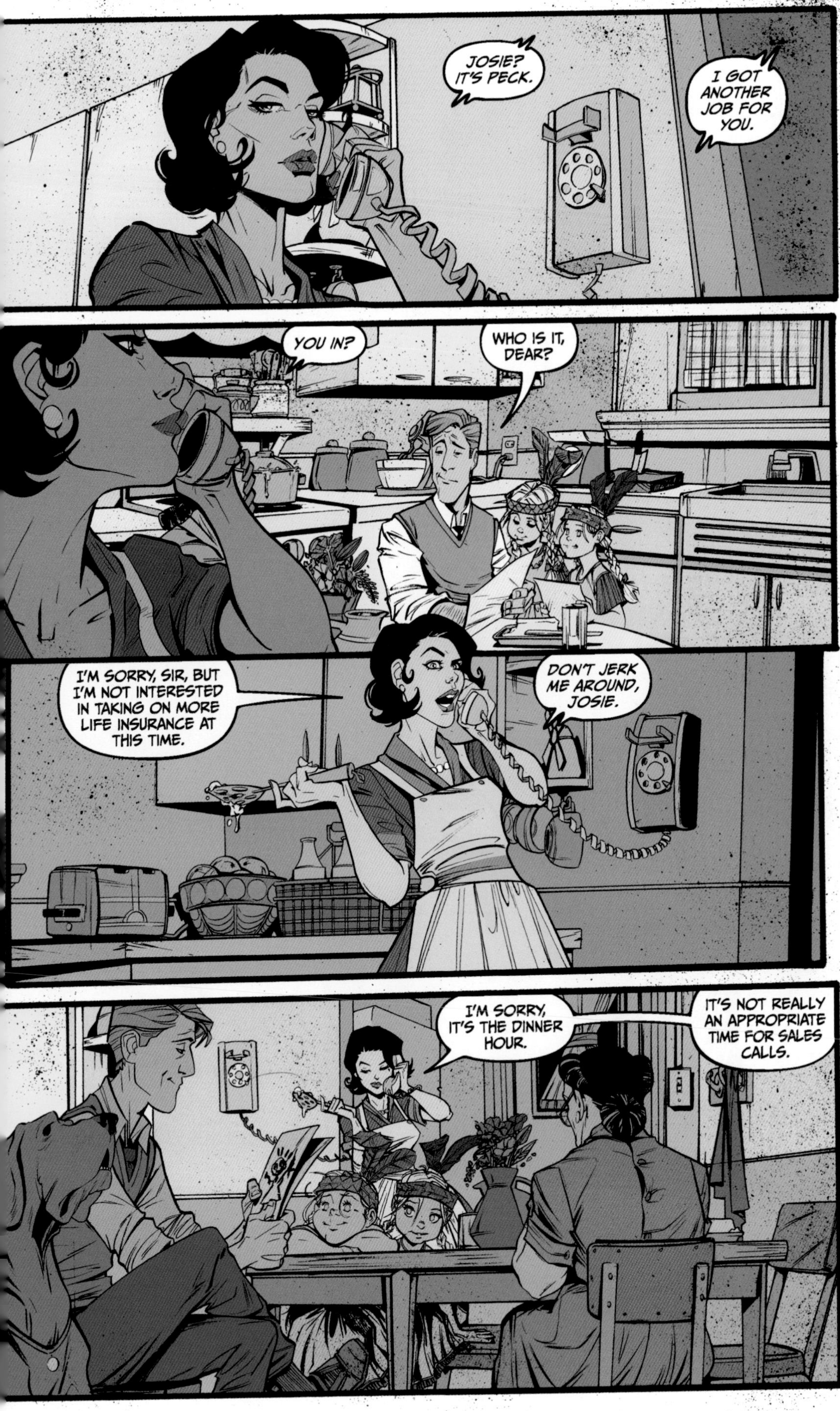

JOSIE? IT'S PECK.
I GOT ANOTHER JOB FOR YOU.
YOU IN?
WHO IS IT, DEAR?
I'M SORRY, SIR, BUT I'M NOT INTERESTED IN TAKING ON MORE LIFE INSURANCE AT THIS TIME.
DON'T JERK ME AROUND, JOSIE.
I'M SORRY, IT'S THE DINNER HOUR.
IT'S NOT REALLY AN APPROPRIATE TIME FOR SALES CALLS.

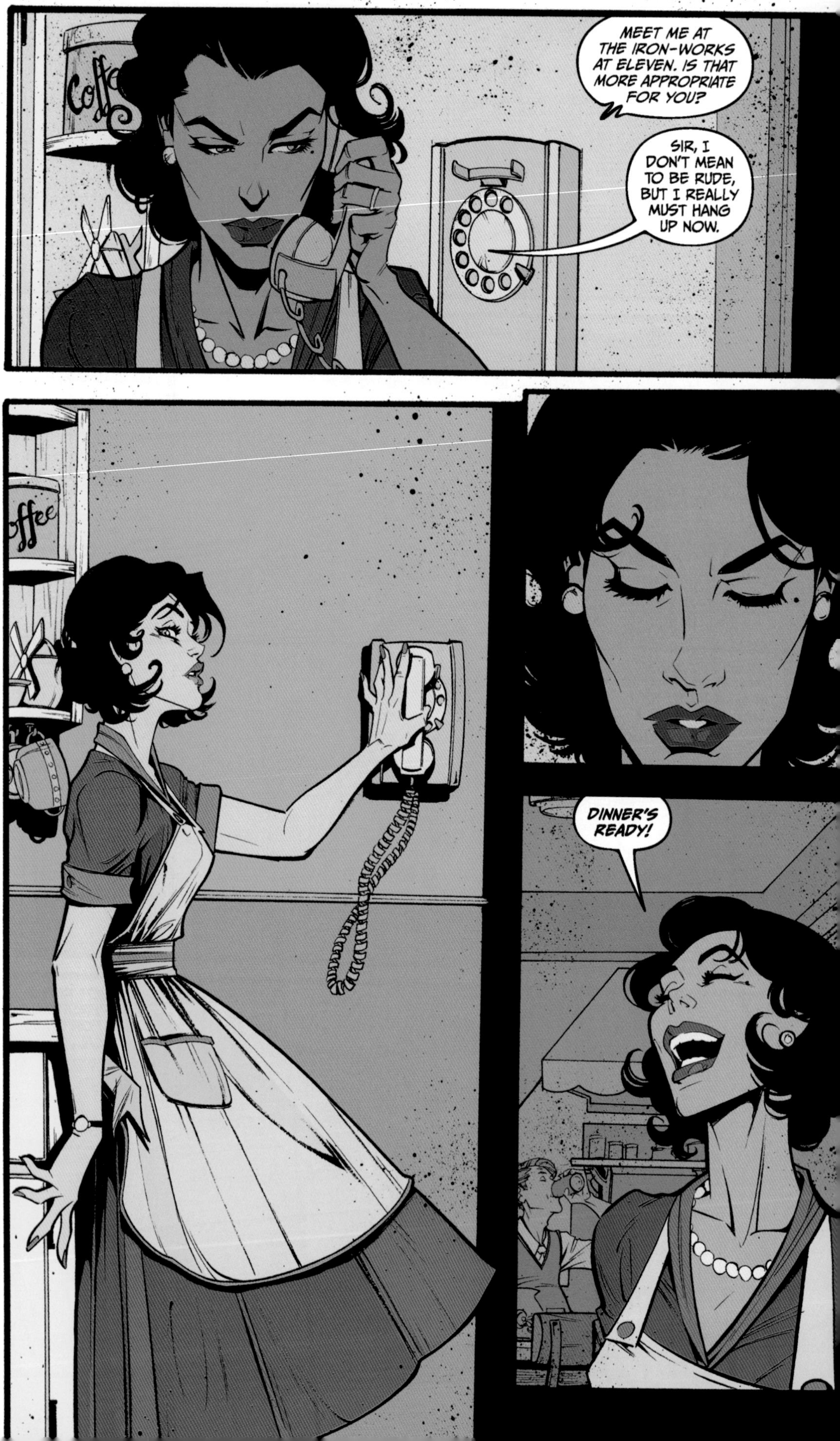
MEET ME AT THE IRON-WORKS AT ELEVEN. IS THAT MORE APPROPRIATE FOR YOU?
SIR, I DON'T MEAN TO BE RUDE, BUT I REALLY MUST HANG UP NOW.
DINNER'S READY!

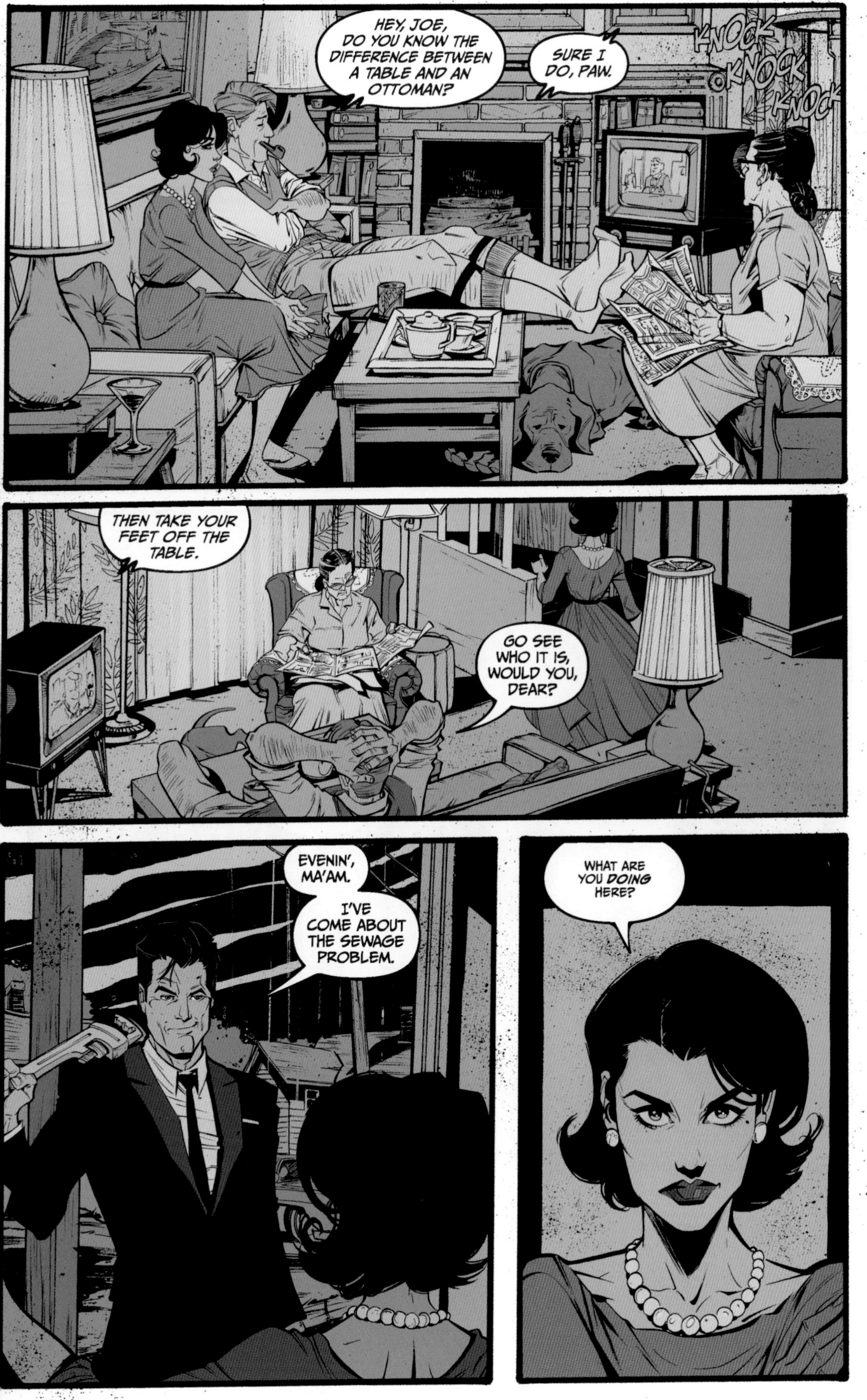
HEY, JOE, DO YOU KNOW THE DIFFERENCE BETWEEN A TABLE AND AN OTTOMAN?
SURE I DO, PAW.
KNOCK KNOCK KNOCK
THEN TAKE YOUR FEET OFF THE TABLE.
GO SEE WHO IT IS, WOULD YOU, DEAR?
EVENIN', MA'AM.
I'VE COME ABOUT THE SEWAGE PROBLEM.
WHAT ARE YOU *DOING* HERE?

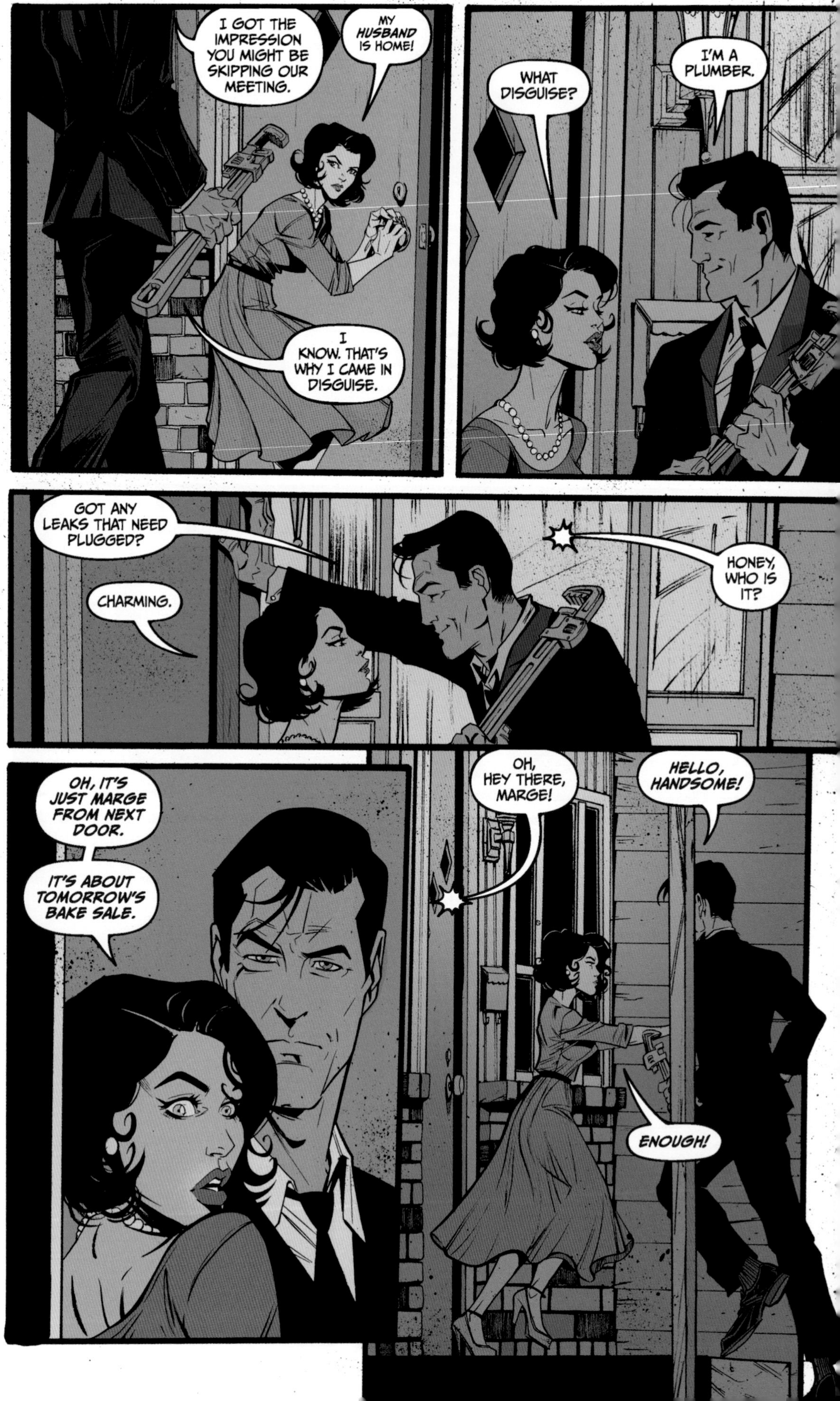
I GOT THE IMPRESSION YOU MIGHT BE SKIPPING OUR MEETING.
MY *HUSBAND* IS HOME!
I KNOW. THAT'S WHY I CAME IN DISGUISE.
WHAT DISGUISE?
I'M A PLUMBER.
GOT ANY LEAKS THAT NEED PLUGGED?
CHARMING.
HONEY, WHO IS IT?
OH, IT'S JUST MARGE FROM NEXT DOOR.
IT'S ABOUT TOMORROW'S BAKE SALE.
OH, HEY THERE, MARGE!
HELLO, HANDSOME!
ENOUGH!

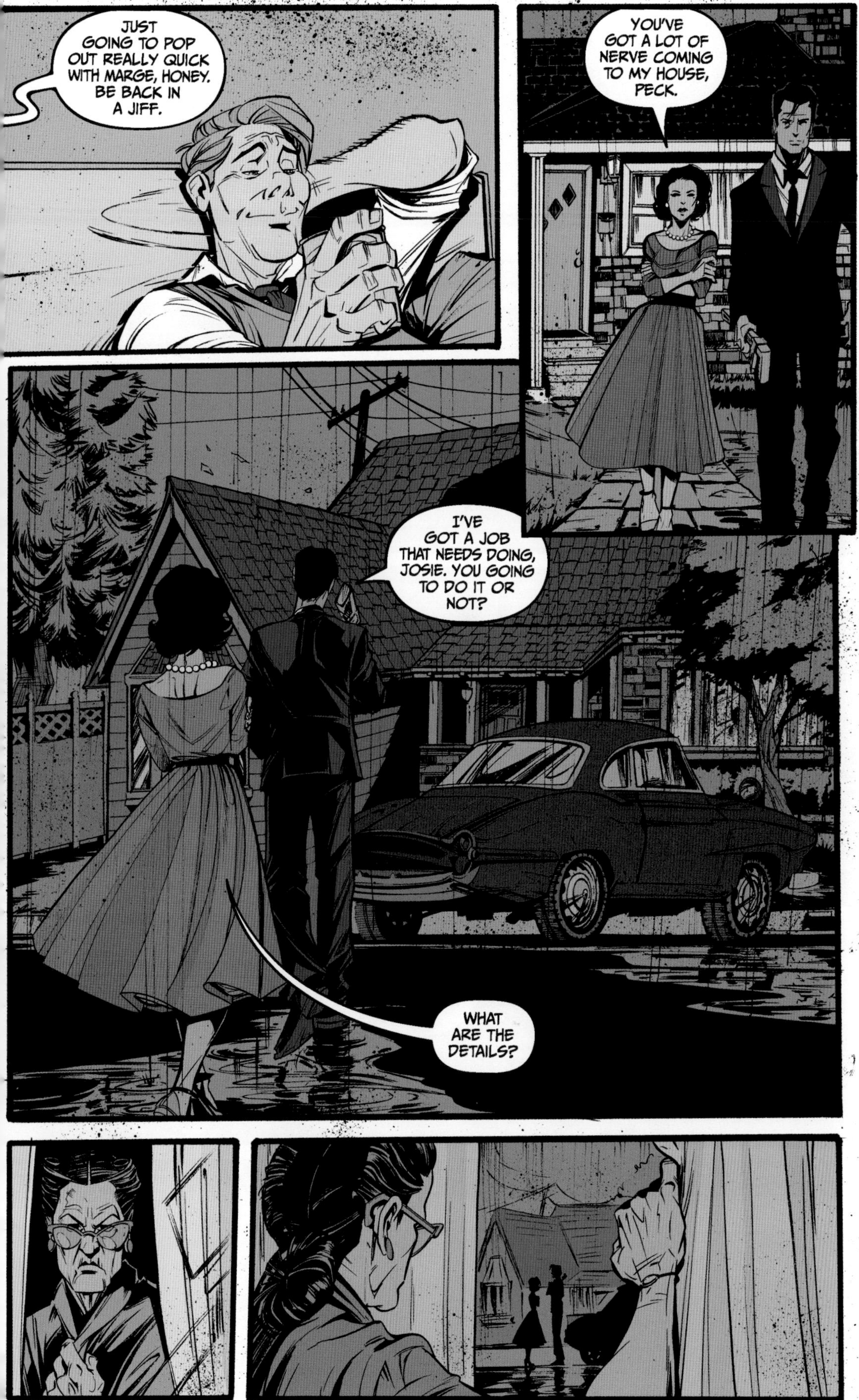
JUST GOING TO POP OUT REALLY QUICK WITH MARGE, HONEY. BE BACK IN A JIFF.
YOU'VE GOT A LOT OF NERVE COMING TO MY HOUSE, PECK.
I'VE GOT A JOB THAT NEEDS DOING, JOSIE. YOU GOING TO DO IT OR NOT?
WHAT ARE THE DETAILS?

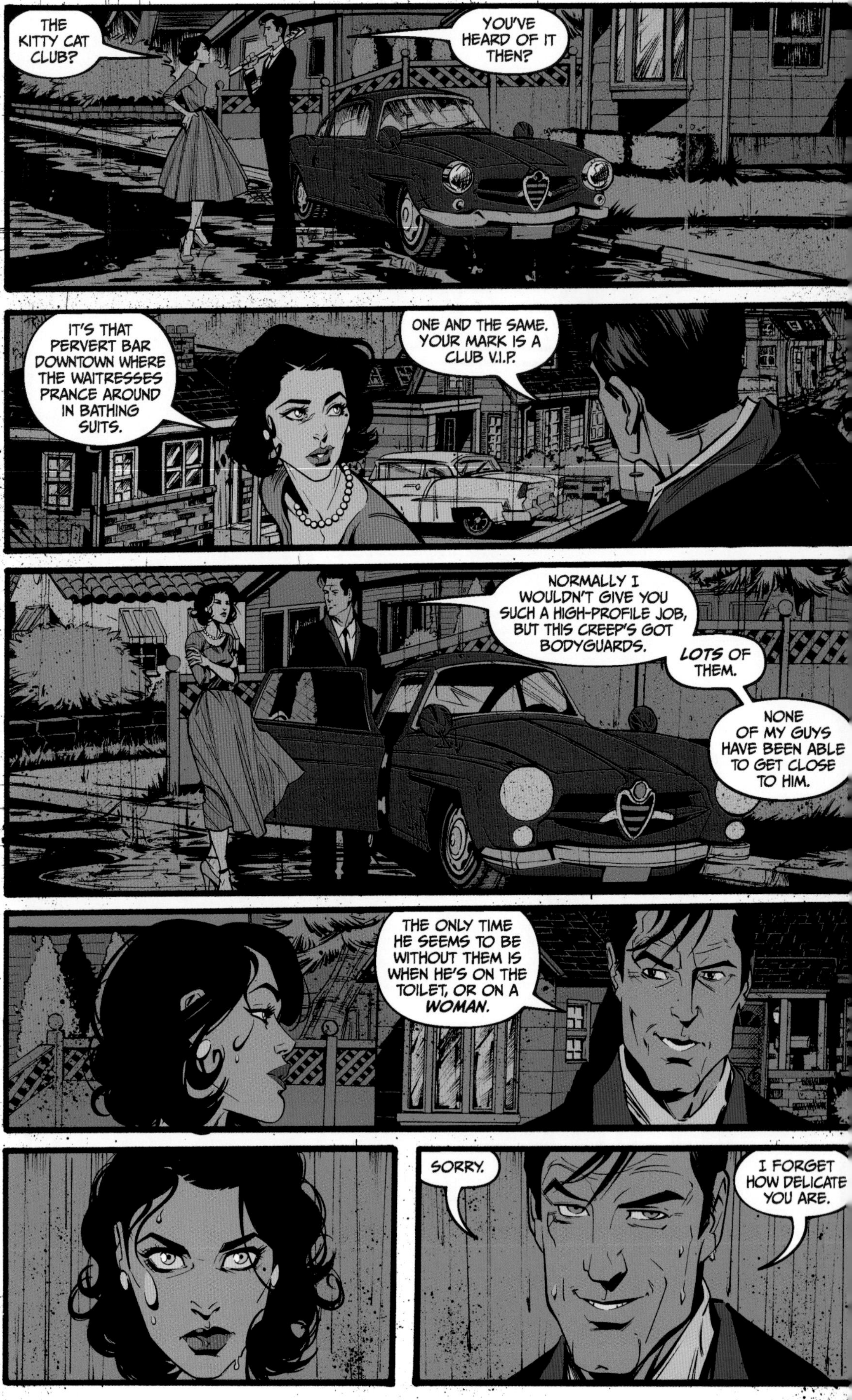
THE KITTY CAT CLUB?
YOU'VE HEARD OF IT THEN?
IT'S THAT PERVERT BAR DOWNTOWN WHERE THE WAITRESSES PRANCE AROUND IN BATHING SUITS.
ONE AND THE SAME. YOUR MARK IS A CLUB V.I.P.
NORMALLY I WOULDN'T GIVE YOU SUCH A HIGH-PROFILE JOB, BUT THIS CREEP'S GOT BODYGUARDS.
LOTS OF THEM.
NONE OF MY GUYS HAVE BEEN ABLE TO GET CLOSE TO HIM.
THE ONLY TIME HE SEEMS TO BE WITHOUT THEM IS WHEN HE'S ON THE TOILET, OR ON A WOMAN.
SORRY.
I FORGET HOW DELICATE YOU ARE.

ANYWAY, POINT IS, YOU HAVE SOMETHING THE OTHER OPERATIVES DON'T.

AND THAT IS?

TITS.

AW, COME ON, I WAS JUST TEASING.

THERE'S NO NEED TO BE VULGAR.

FINE. SORRY.

SIX HAIL MARYS FOR ME.

YOU ARE EXHAUSTING.

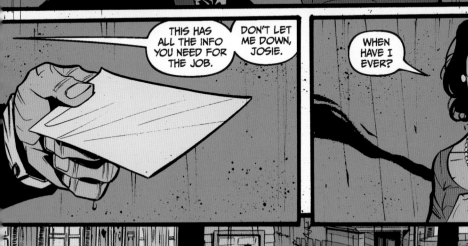

THIS HAS ALL THE INFO YOU NEED FOR THE JOB.

DON'T LET ME DOWN, JOSIE.

WHEN HAVE I EVER?

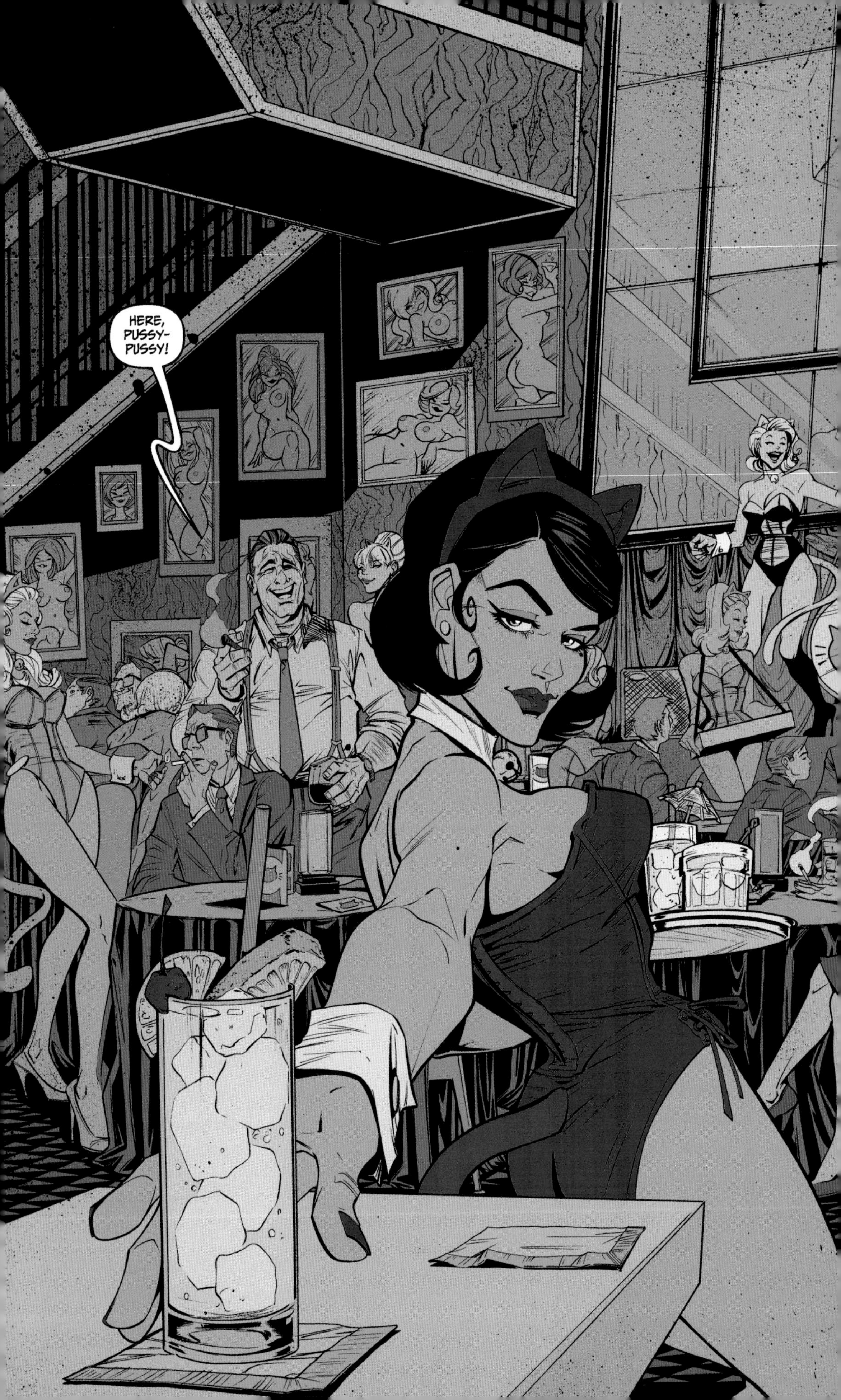
HERE, PUSSY-PUSSY!

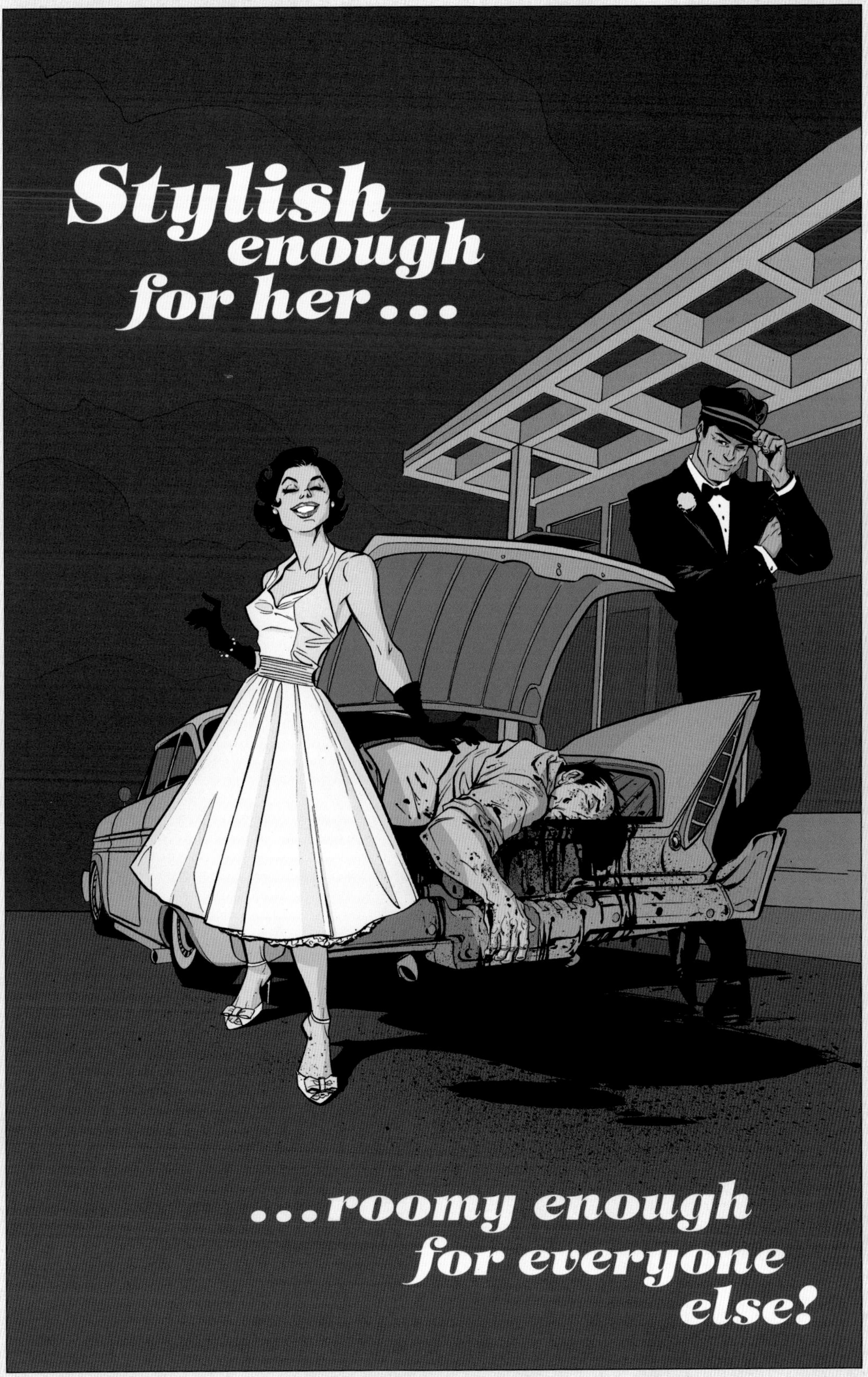
Stylish enough for her...
...roomy enough for everyone else!

CHAPTER TWO

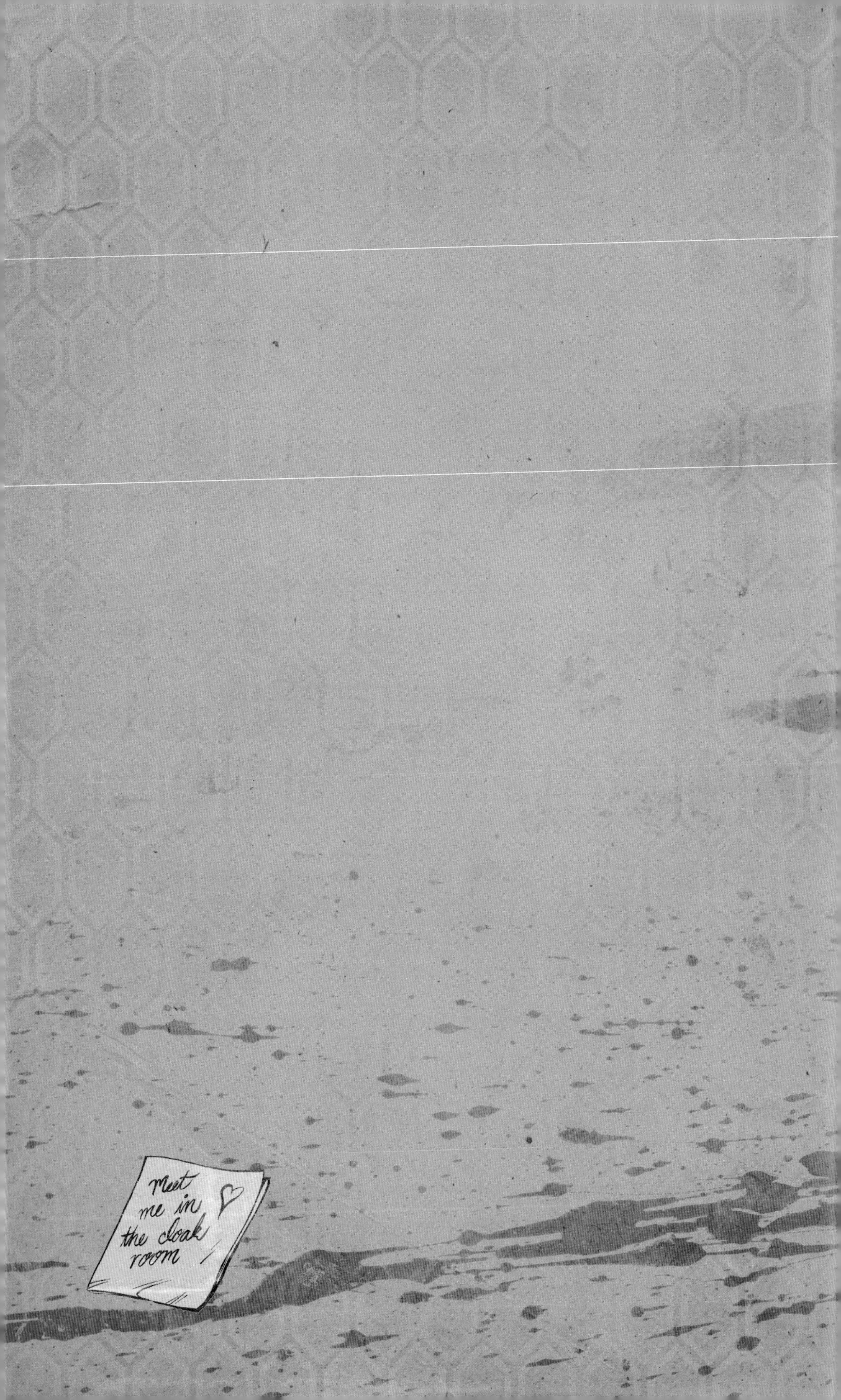
Meet me in the cloak room

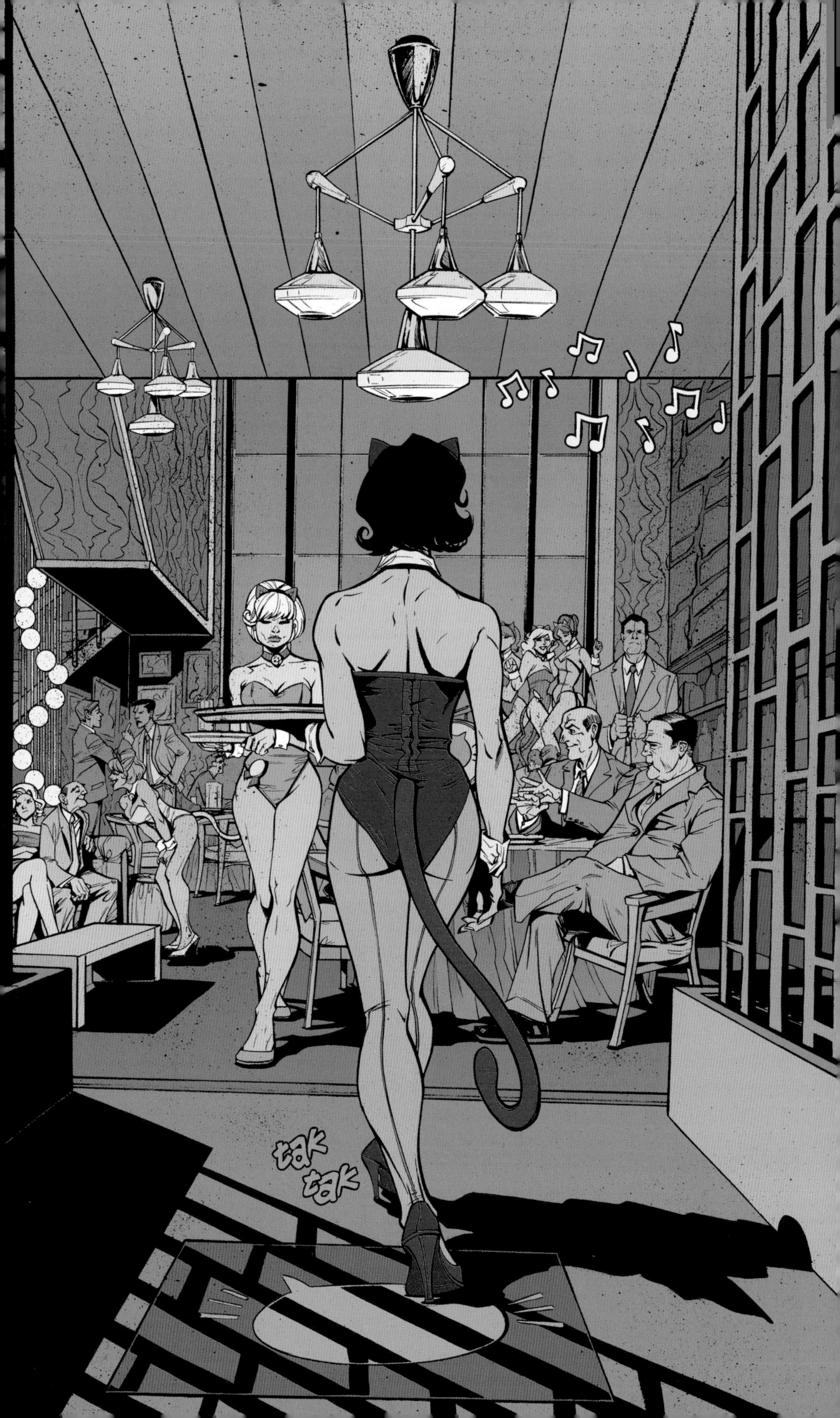
tak
tak

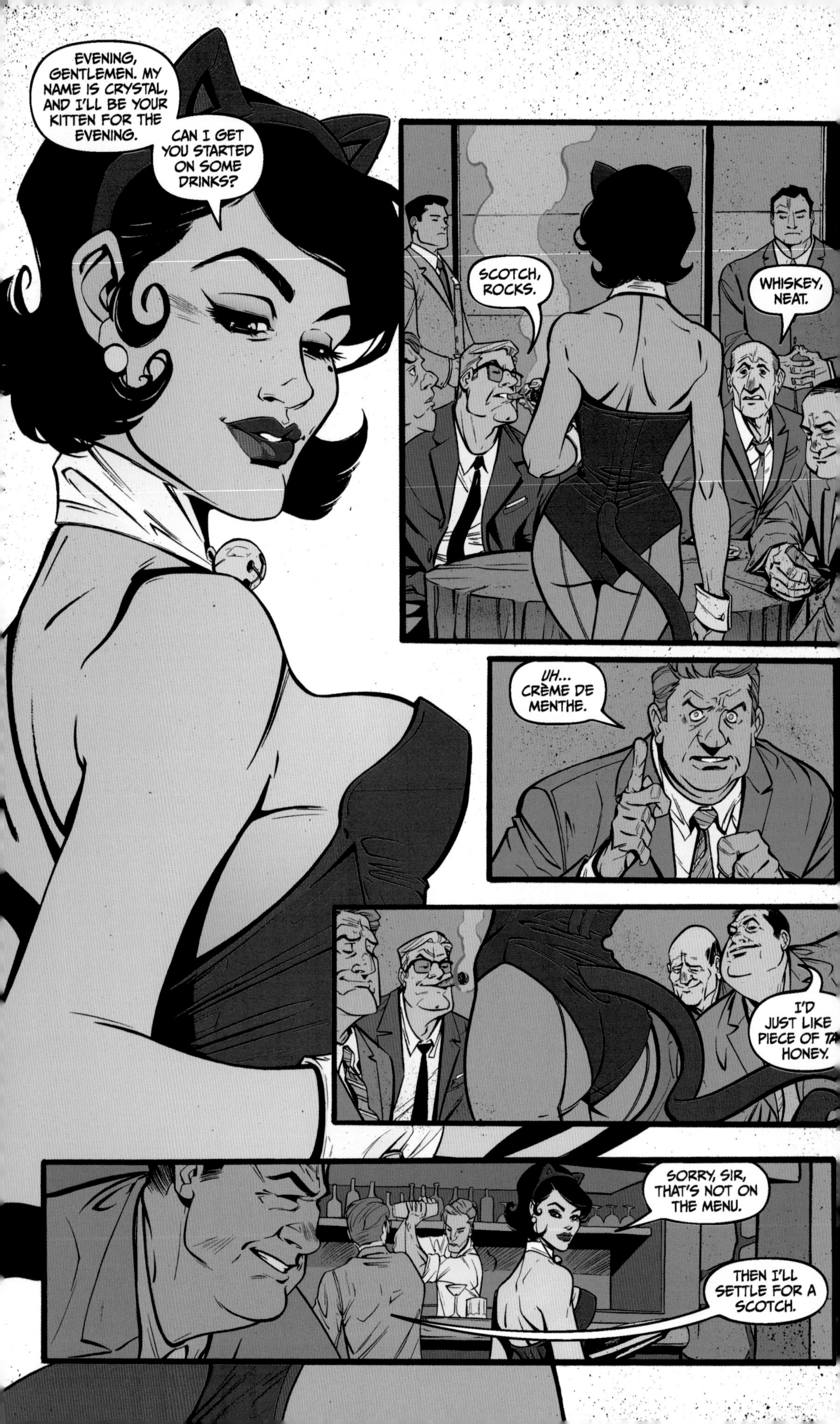
EVENING, GENTLEMEN. MY NAME IS CRYSTAL, AND I'LL BE YOUR KITTEN FOR THE EVENING.
CAN I GET YOU STARTED ON SOME DRINKS?
SCOTCH, ROCKS.
WHISKEY, NEAT.
UH... CRÈME DE MENTHE.
I'D JUST LIKE PIECE OF
HONEY.
SORRY, SIR, THAT'S NOT ON THE MENU.
THEN I'LL SETTLE FOR A SCOTCH.

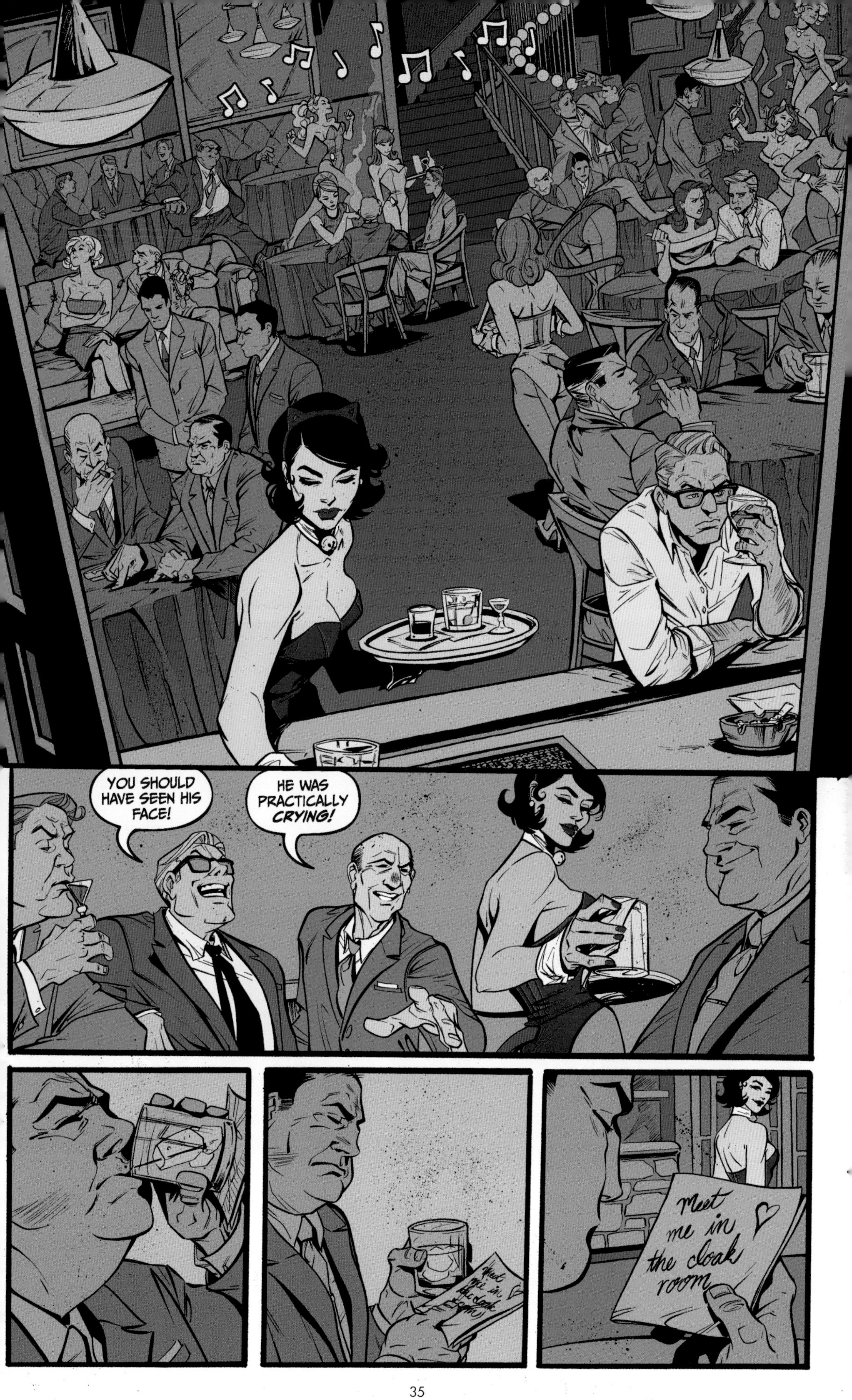
YOU SHOULD HAVE SEEN HIS FACE!
HE WAS PRACTICALLY CRYING!
Meet me in the cloak room

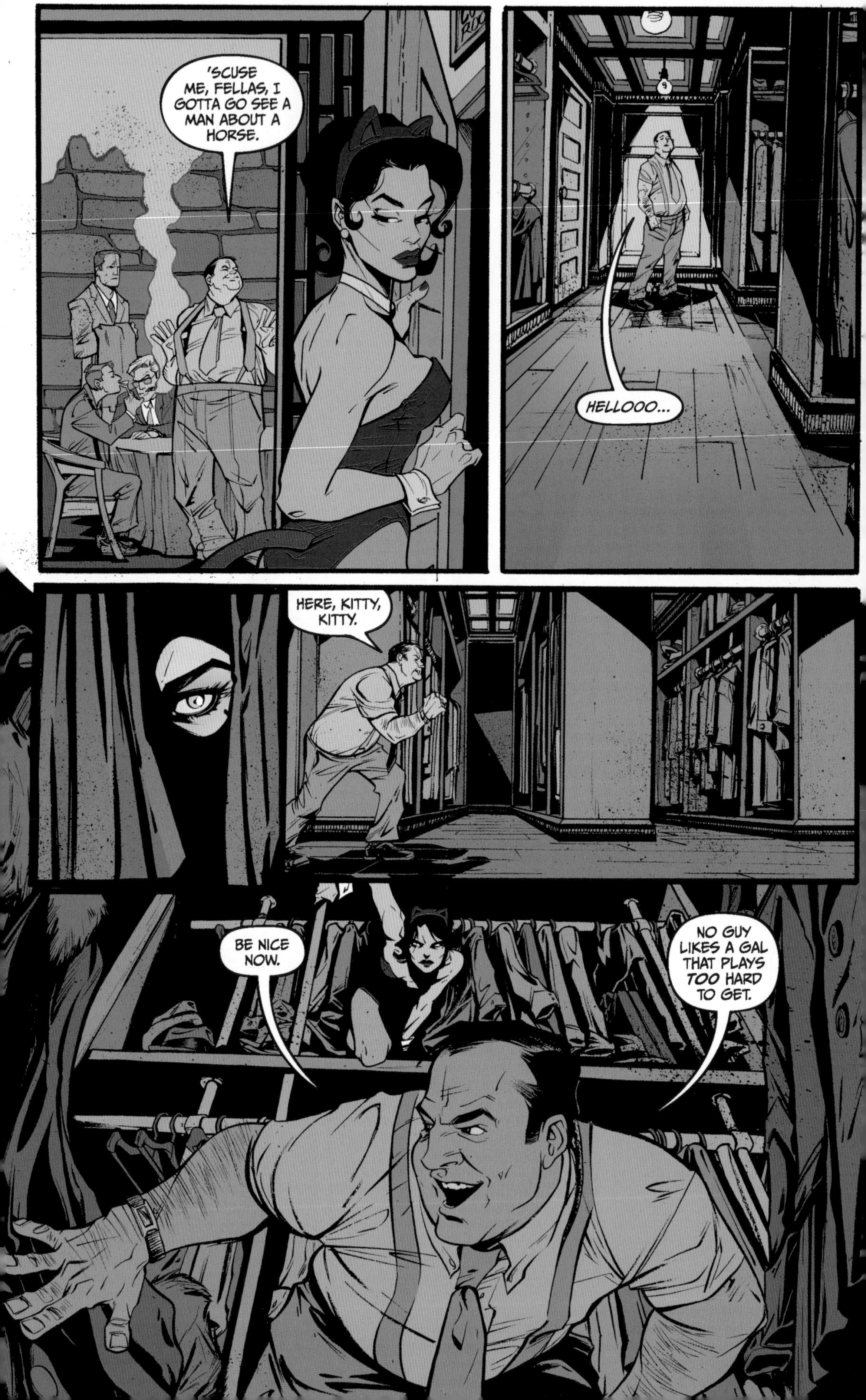
'SCUSE ME, FELLAS, I GOTTA GO SEE A MAN ABOUT A HORSE.
HELLOOO...
HERE, KITTY, KITTY.
BE NICE NOW.
NO GUY LIKES A GAL THAT PLAYS *TOO* HARD TO GET.

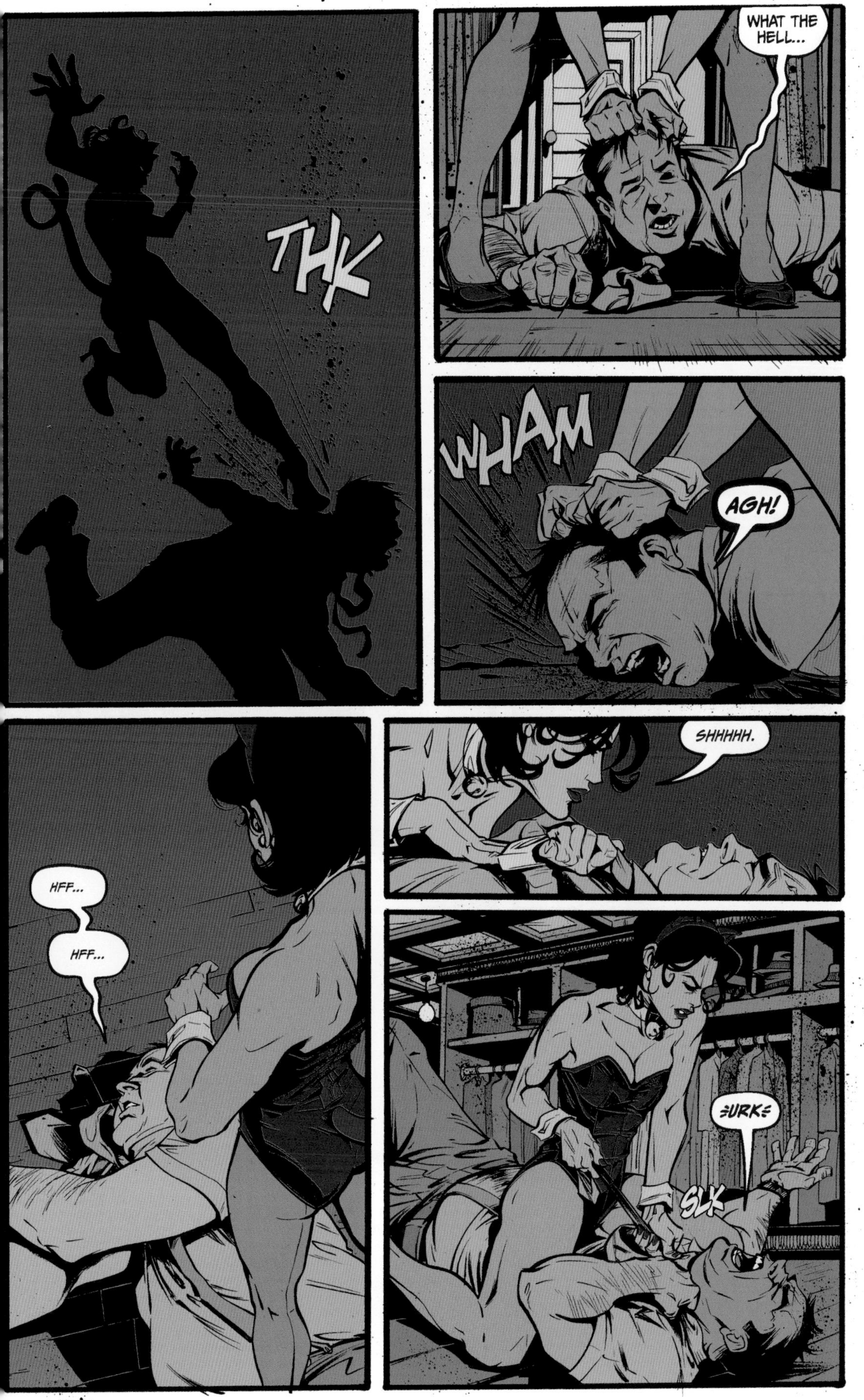
THK
WHAT THE HELL...
WHAM
AGH!
HFF...
HFF...
SHHHHH.
URK
SLK

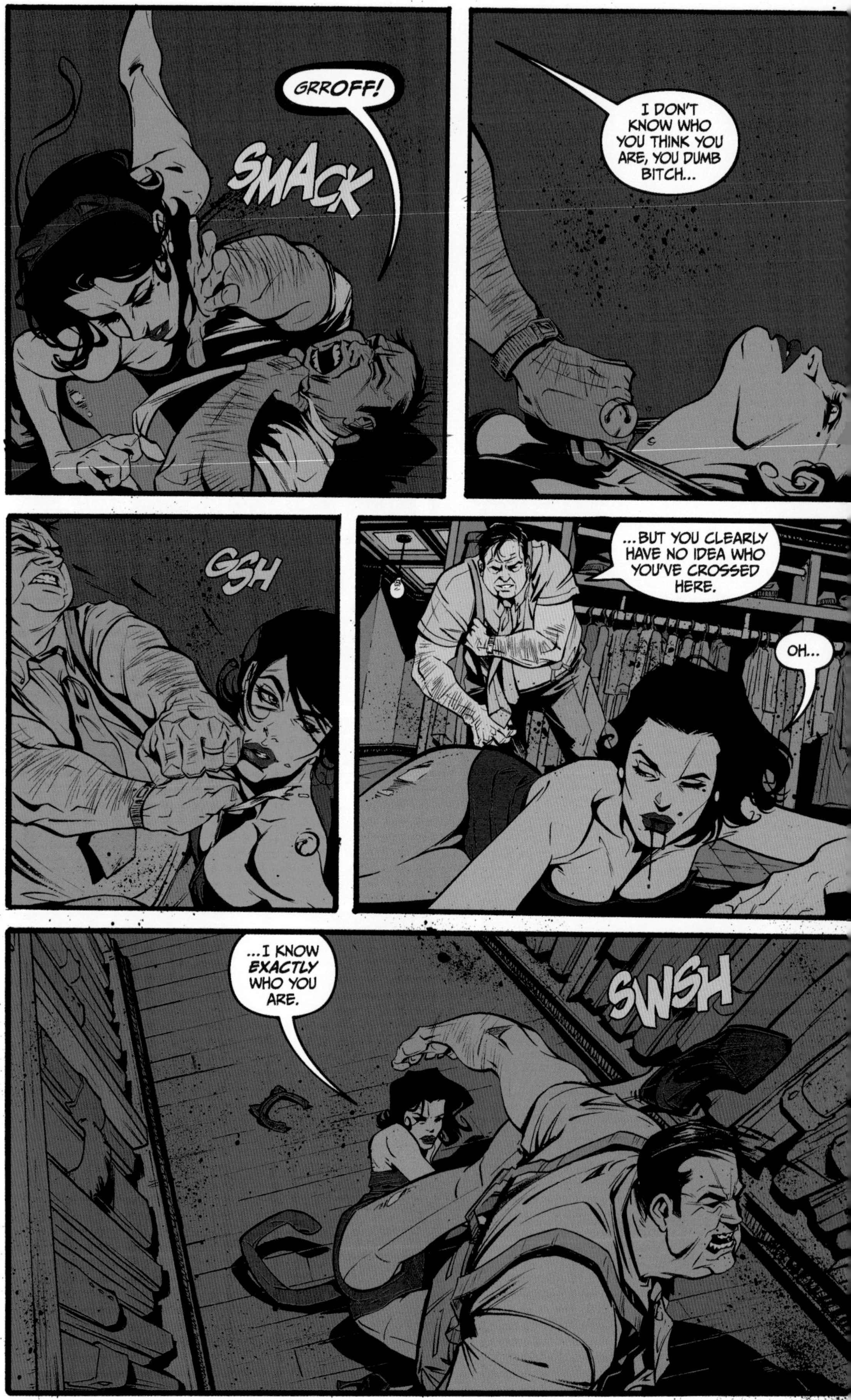
GRROFF!
SMACK
I DON'T KNOW WHO YOU THINK YOU ARE, YOU DUMB BITCH...
GSH
...BUT YOU CLEARLY HAVE NO IDEA WHO YOU'VE CROSSED HERE.
OH...
...I KNOW EXACTLY WHO YOU ARE.
SWSH

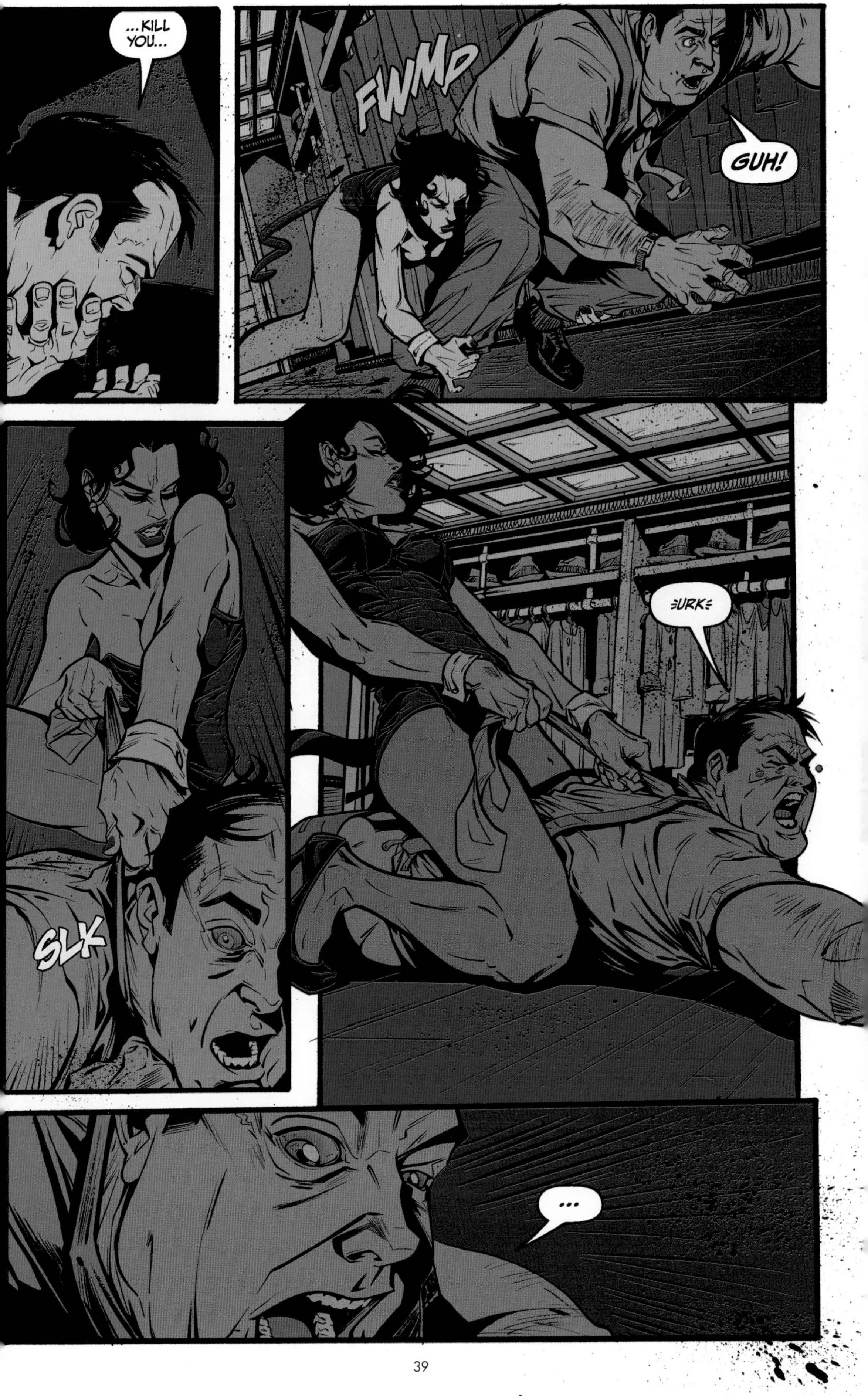
...KILL YOU...
FWMP
GUH!
SLK
URK
...

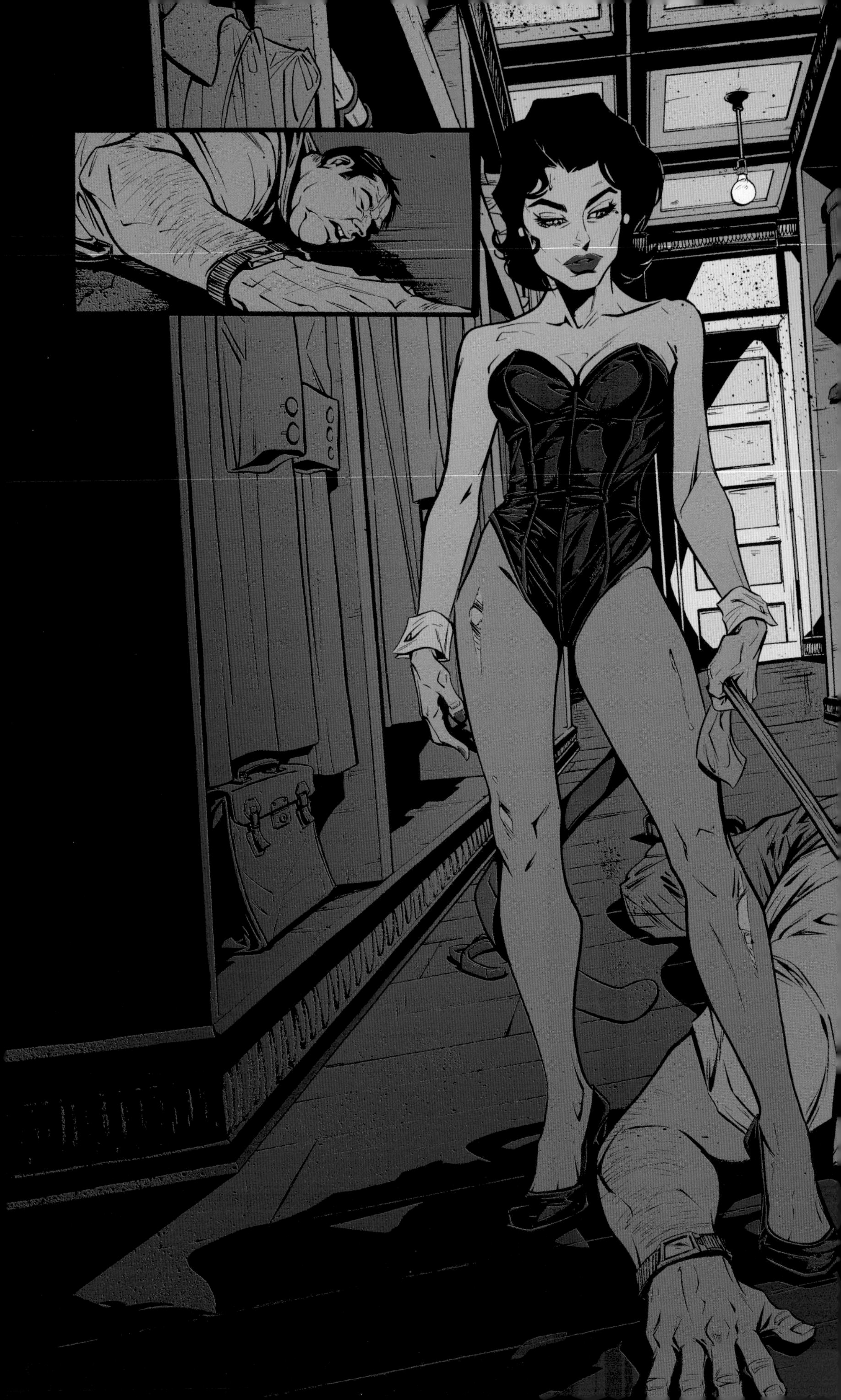

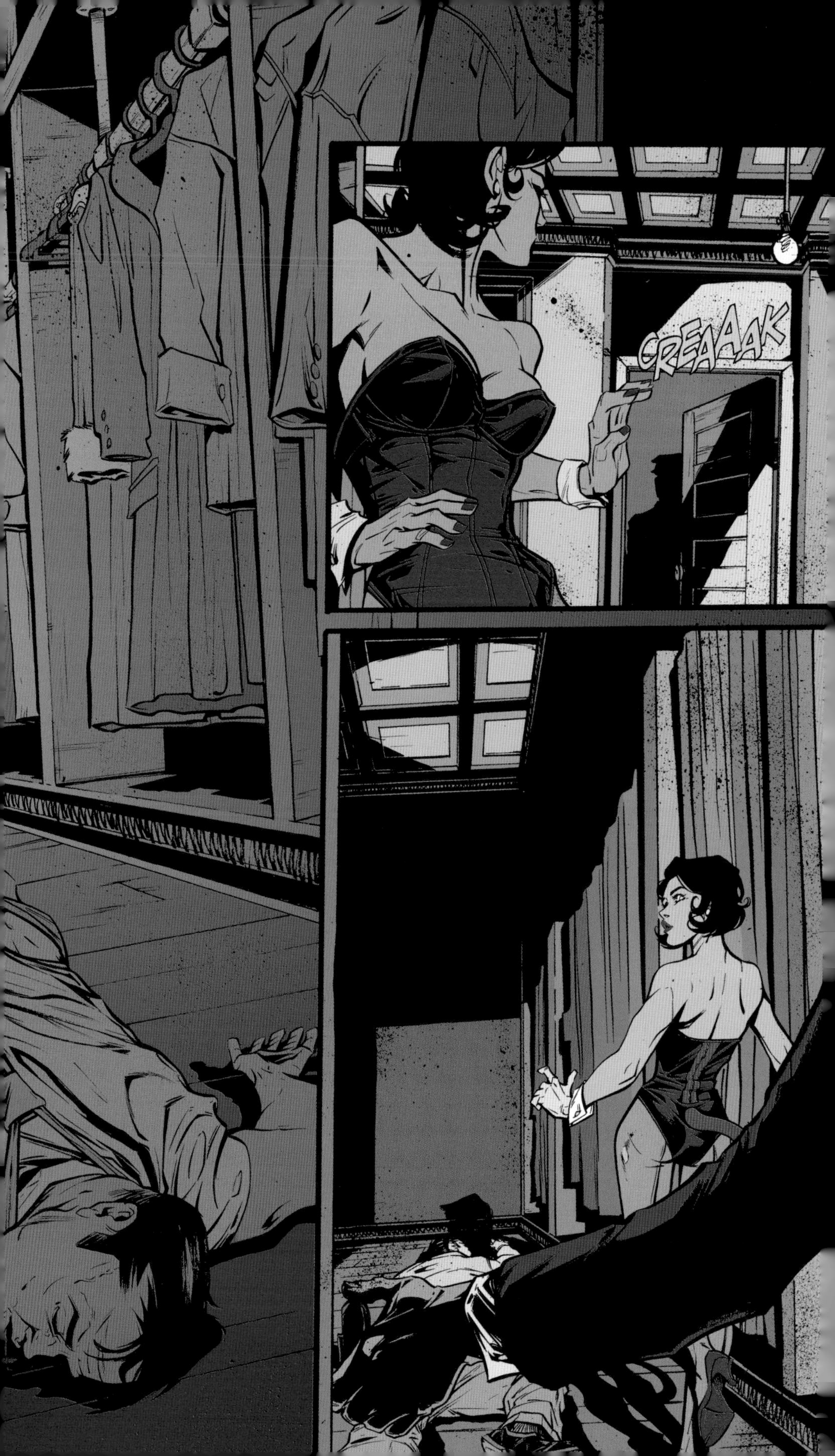
CREAAAK

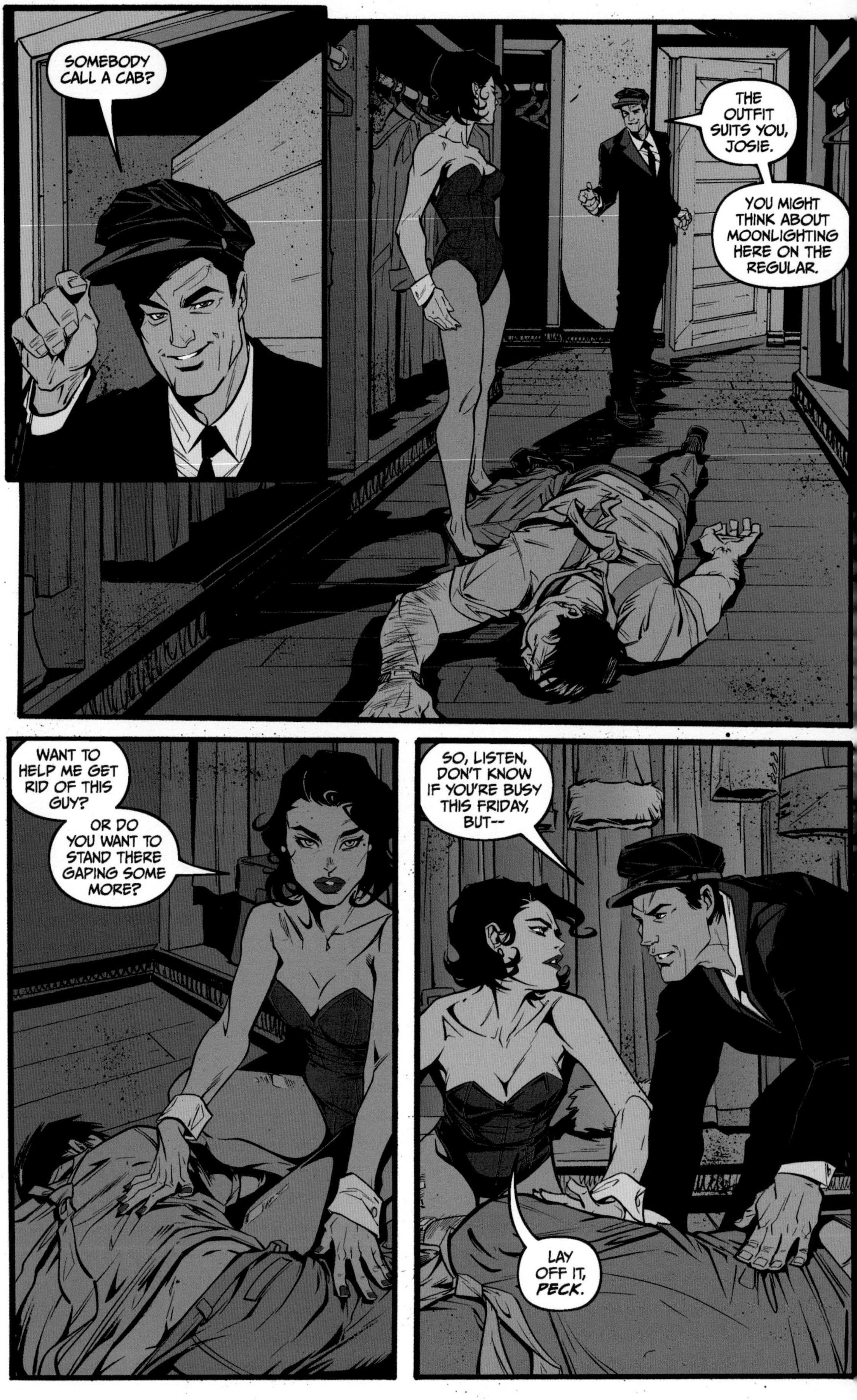
SOMEBODY CALL A CAB?
THE OUTFIT SUITS YOU, JOSIE.
YOU MIGHT THINK ABOUT MOONLIGHTING HERE ON THE REGULAR.
WANT TO HELP ME GET RID OF THIS GUY?
OR DO YOU WANT TO STAND THERE GAPING SOME MORE?
SO, LISTEN, DON'T KNOW IF YOU'RE BUSY THIS FRIDAY, BUT--
LAY OFF IT, PECK.

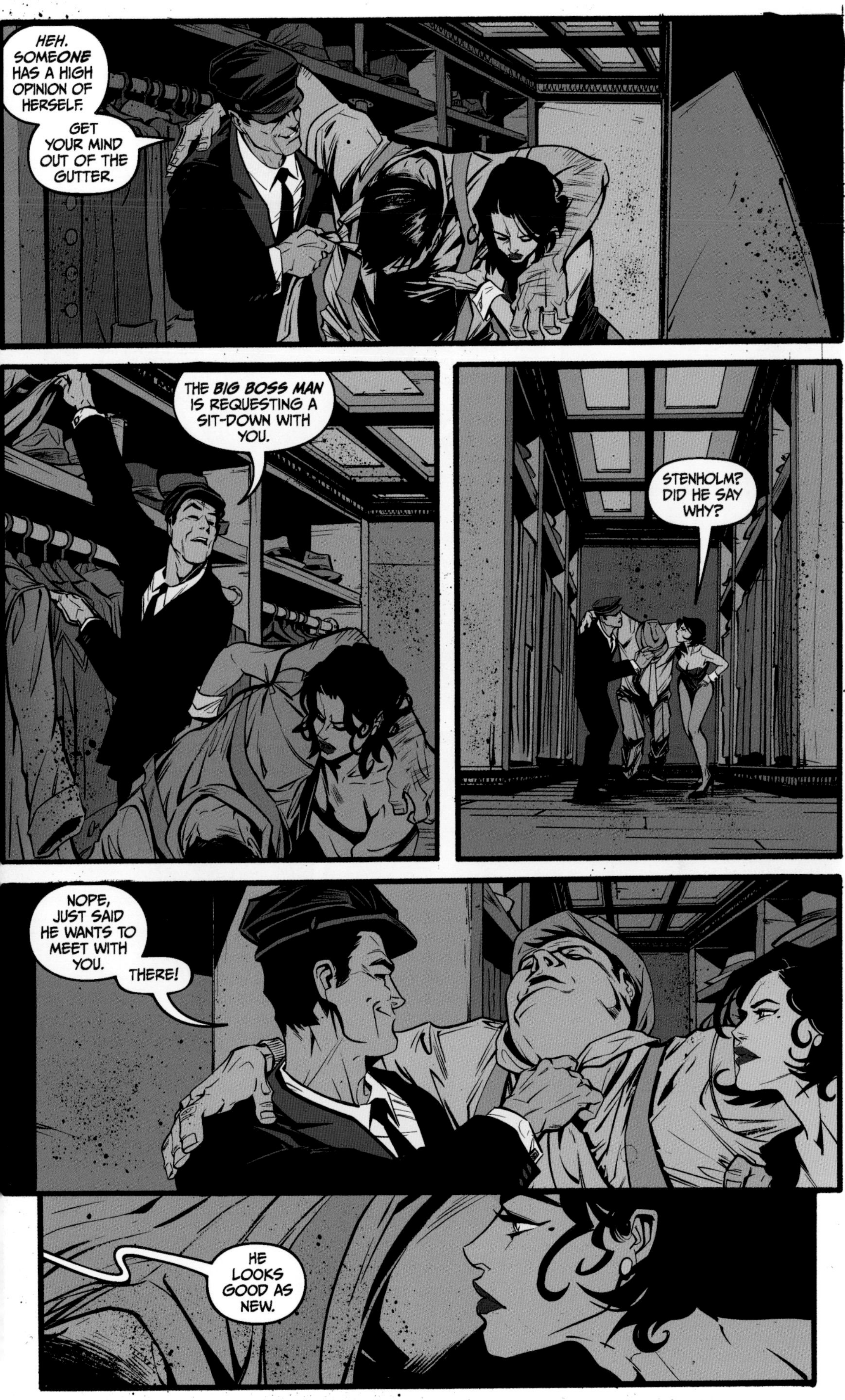
HEH. SOMEONE HAS A HIGH OPINION OF HERSELF.
GET YOUR MIND OUT OF THE GUTTER.
THE BIG BOSS MAN IS REQUESTING A SIT-DOWN WITH YOU.
STENHOLM? DID HE SAY WHY?
NOPE, JUST SAID HE WANTS TO MEET WITH YOU.
THERE!
HE LOOKS GOOD AS NEW.

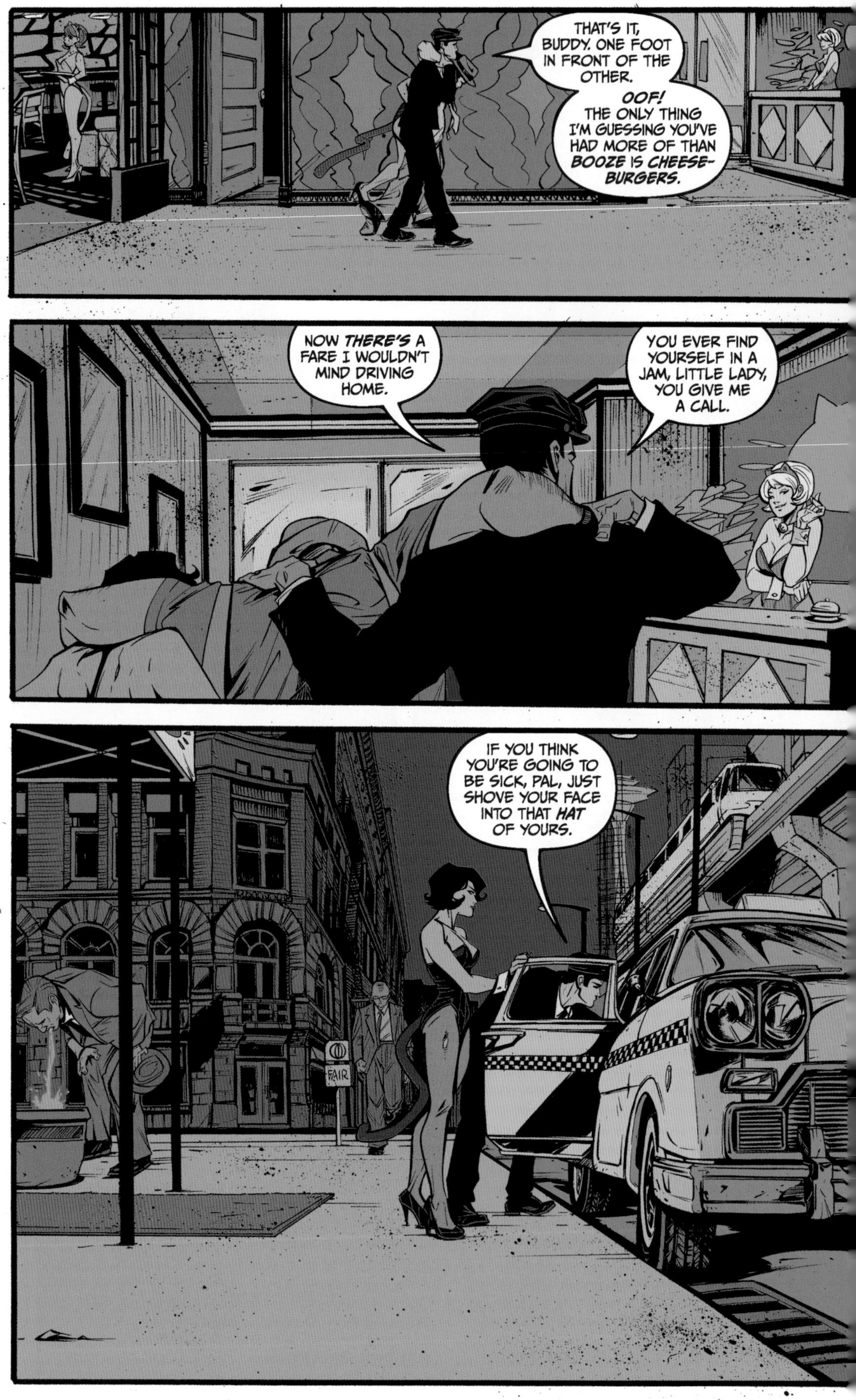
THAT'S IT, BUDDY. ONE FOOT IN FRONT OF THE OTHER.
OOF! THE ONLY THING I'M GUESSING YOU'VE HAD MORE OF THAN BOOZE IS CHEESE-BURGERS.
NOW THERE'S A FARE I WOULDN'T MIND DRIVING HOME.
YOU EVER FIND YOURSELF IN A JAM, LITTLE LADY, YOU GIVE ME A CALL.
IF YOU THINK YOU'RE GOING TO BE SICK, PAL, JUST SHOVE YOUR FACE INTO THAT HAT OF YOURS.
FAIR

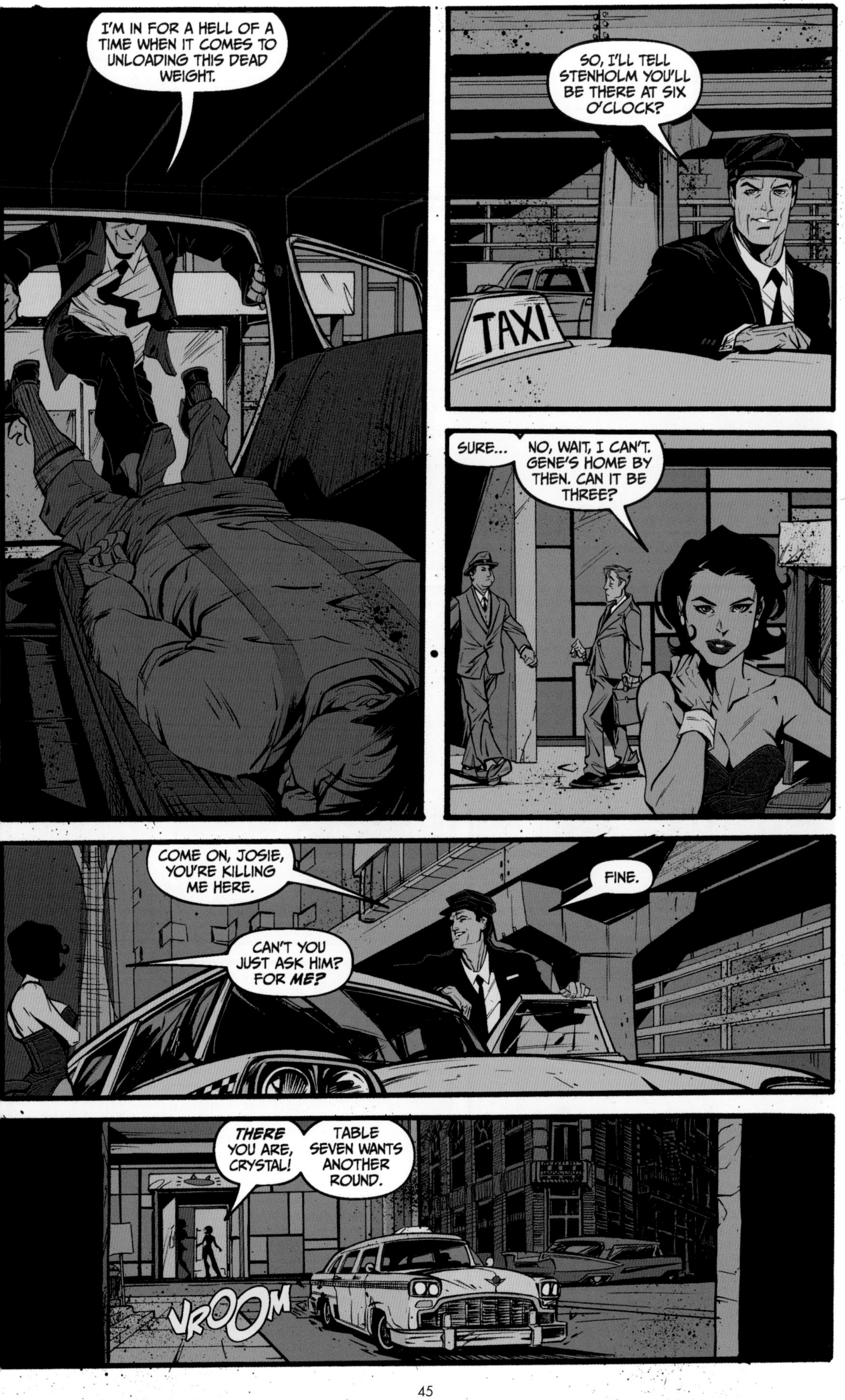

I'M IN FOR A HELL OF A TIME WHEN IT COMES TO UNLOADING THIS DEAD WEIGHT.
SO, I'LL TELL STENHOLM YOU'LL BE THERE AT SIX O'CLOCK?
TAXI
SURE...
NO, WAIT, I CAN'T. GENE'S HOME BY THEN. CAN IT BE THREE?
COME ON, JOSIE, YOU'RE KILLING ME HERE.
FINE.
CAN'T YOU JUST ASK HIM? FOR *ME?*
THERE YOU ARE, CRYSTAL!
TABLE SEVEN WANTS ANOTHER ROUND.
VROOM

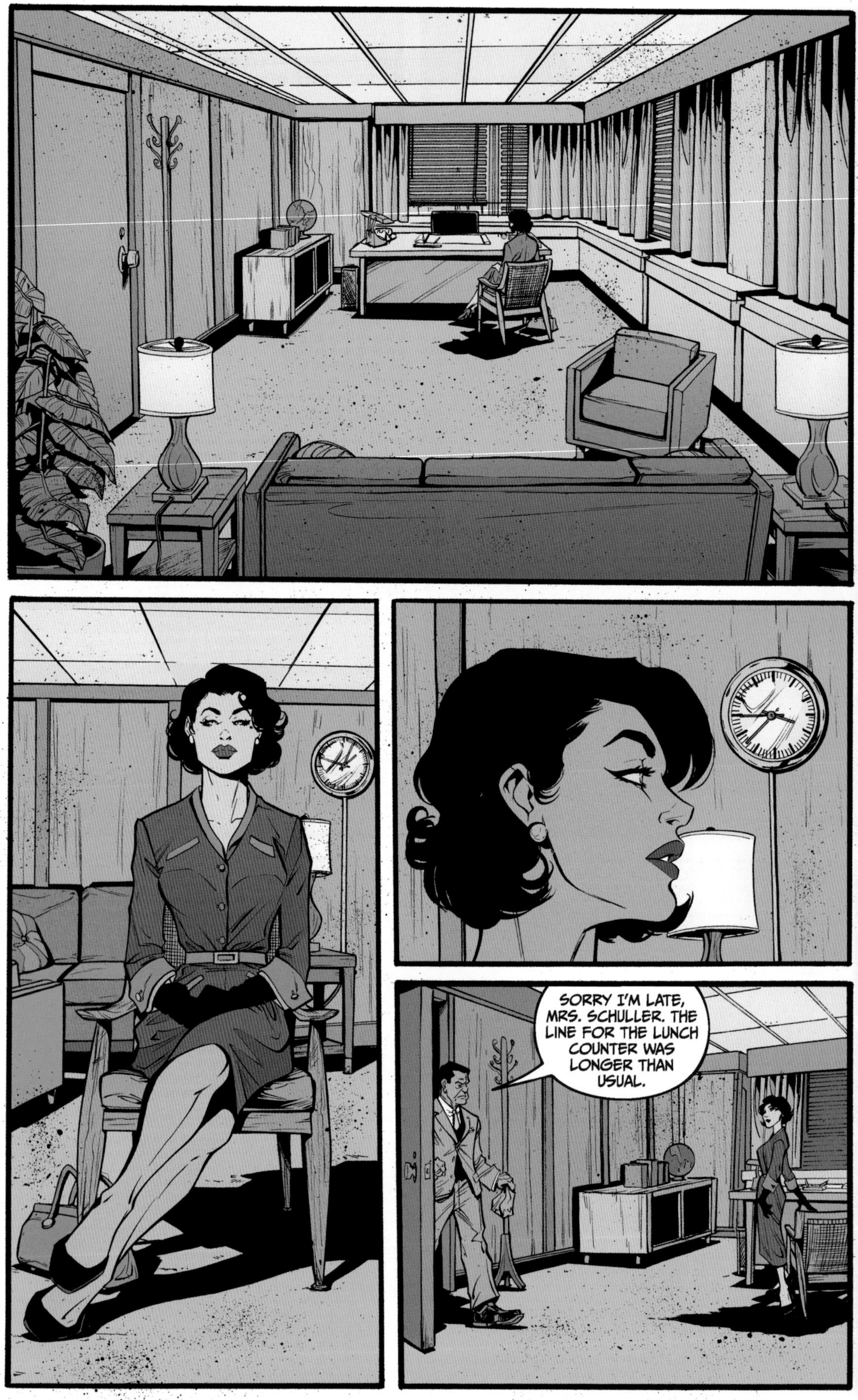
SORRY I'M LATE, MRS. SCHULLER. THE LINE FOR THE LUNCH COUNTER WAS LONGER THAN USUAL.

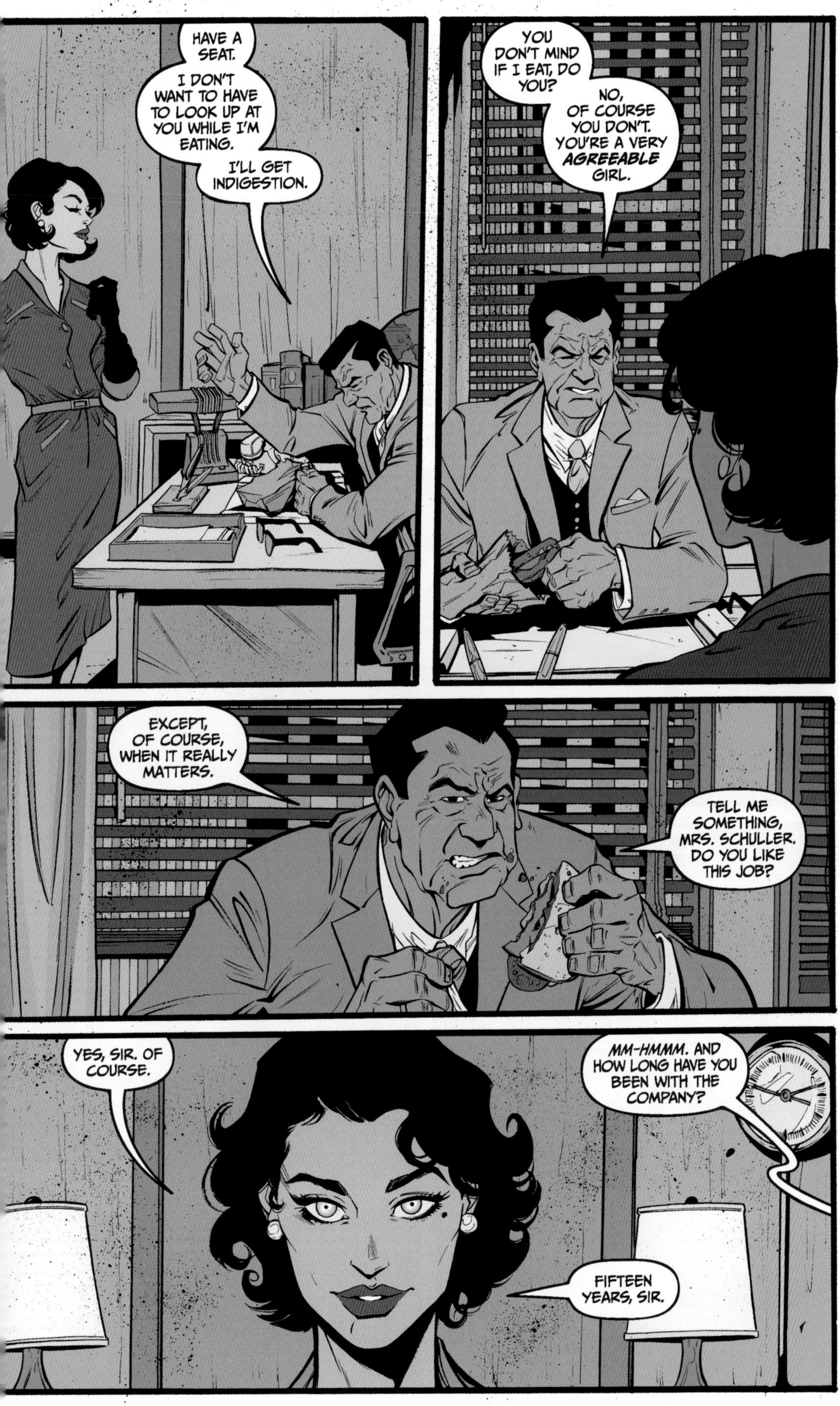
HAVE A SEAT.
I DON'T WANT TO HAVE TO LOOK UP AT YOU WHILE I'M EATING.
I'LL GET INDIGESTION.
YOU DON'T MIND IF I EAT, DO YOU?
NO, OF COURSE YOU DON'T. YOU'RE A VERY AGREEABLE GIRL.
EXCEPT, OF COURSE, WHEN IT REALLY MATTERS.
TELL ME SOMETHING, MRS. SCHULLER. DO YOU LIKE THIS JOB?
YES, SIR. OF COURSE.
MM-HMMM. AND HOW LONG HAVE YOU BEEN WITH THE COMPANY?
FIFTEEN YEARS, SIR.

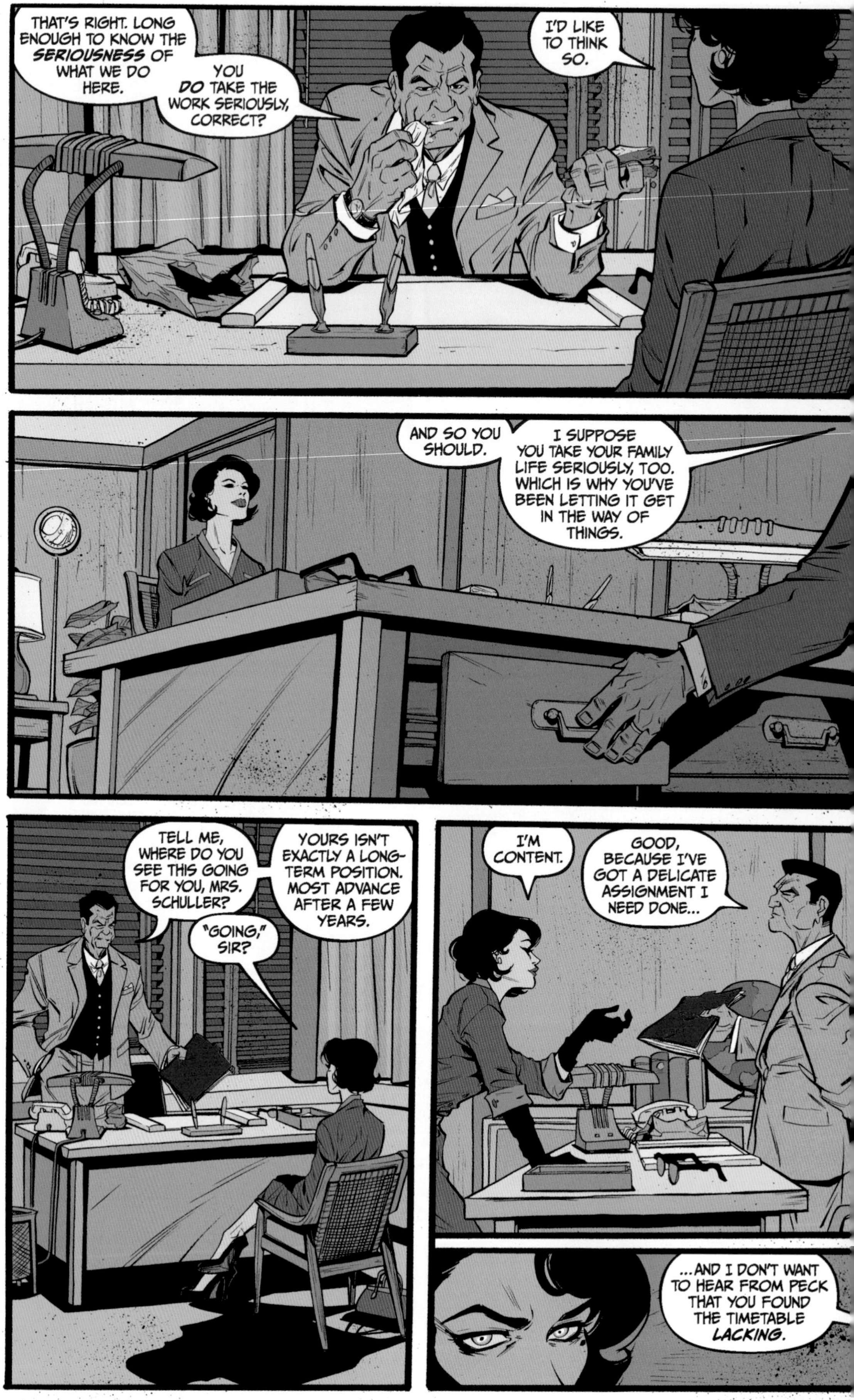

THAT'S RIGHT. LONG ENOUGH TO KNOW THE SERIOUSNESS OF WHAT WE DO HERE.
YOU DO TAKE THE WORK SERIOUSLY, CORRECT?
I'D LIKE TO THINK SO.
AND SO YOU SHOULD.
I SUPPOSE YOU TAKE YOUR FAMILY LIFE SERIOUSLY, TOO. WHICH IS WHY YOU'VE BEEN LETTING IT GET IN THE WAY OF THINGS.
TELL ME, WHERE DO YOU SEE THIS GOING FOR YOU, MRS. SCHULLER?
"GOING," SIR?
YOURS ISN'T EXACTLY A LONG-TERM POSITION. MOST ADVANCE AFTER A FEW YEARS.
I'M CONTENT.
GOOD, BECAUSE I'VE GOT A DELICATE ASSIGNMENT I NEED DONE...
...AND I DON'T WANT TO HEAR FROM PECK THAT YOU FOUND THE TIMETABLE LACKING.

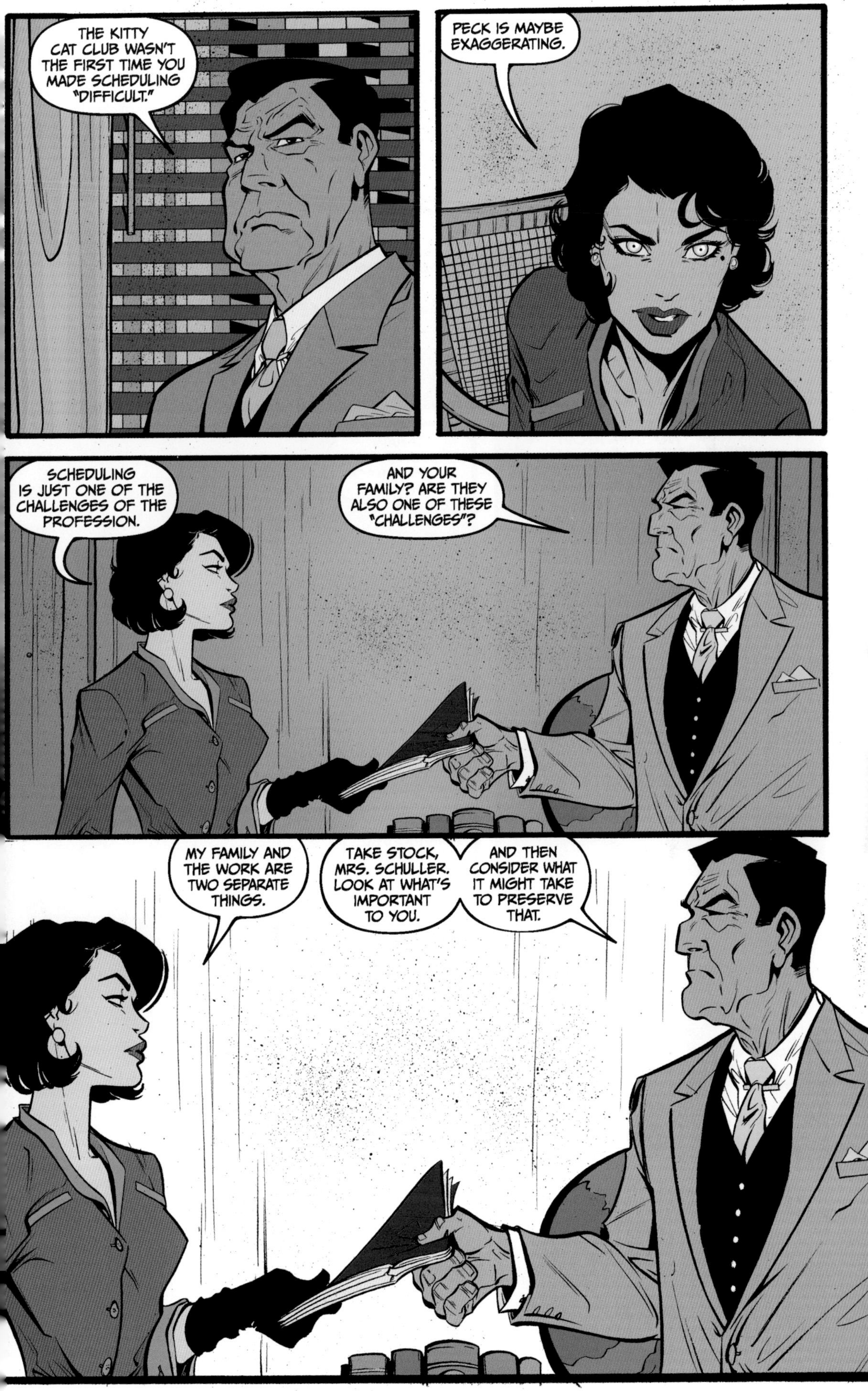
THE KITTY CAT CLUB WASN'T THE FIRST TIME YOU MADE SCHEDULING "DIFFICULT."
PECK IS MAYBE EXAGGERATING.
SCHEDULING IS JUST ONE OF THE CHALLENGES OF THE PROFESSION.
AND YOUR FAMILY? ARE THEY ALSO ONE OF THESE "CHALLENGES"?
MY FAMILY AND THE WORK ARE TWO SEPARATE THINGS.
TAKE STOCK, MRS. SCHULLER. LOOK AT WHAT'S IMPORTANT TO YOU.
AND THEN CONSIDER WHAT IT MIGHT TAKE TO PRESERVE THAT.

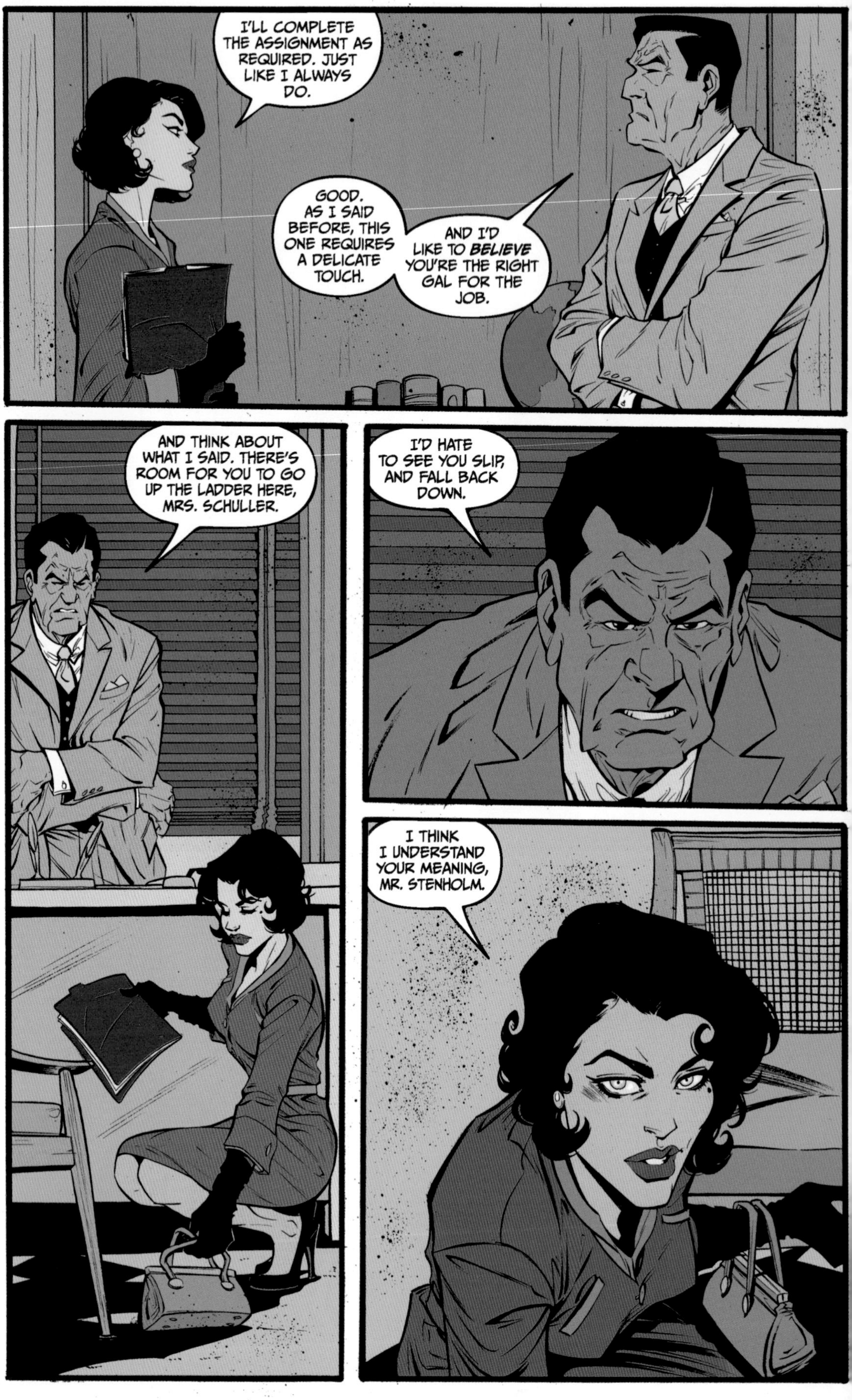
I'LL COMPLETE THE ASSIGNMENT AS REQUIRED. JUST LIKE I ALWAYS DO.
GOOD. AS I SAID BEFORE, THIS ONE REQUIRES A DELICATE TOUCH.
AND I'D LIKE TO *BELIEVE* YOU'RE THE RIGHT GAL FOR THE JOB.
AND THINK ABOUT WHAT I SAID. THERE'S ROOM FOR YOU TO GO UP THE LADDER HERE, MRS. SCHULLER.
I'D HATE TO SEE YOU SLIP, AND FALL BACK DOWN.
I THINK I UNDERSTAND YOUR MEANING, MR. STENHOLM.

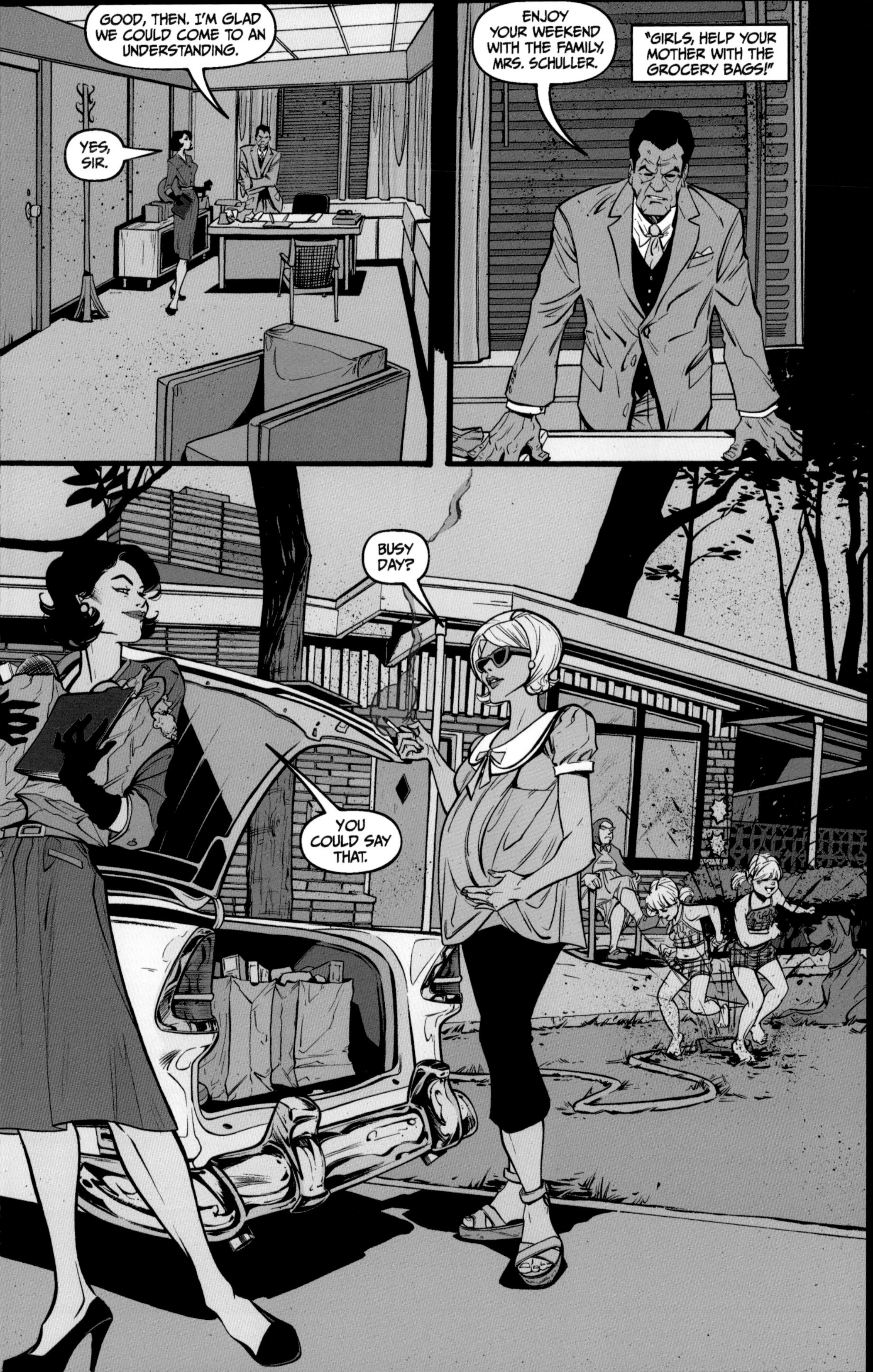
GOOD, THEN. I'M GLAD WE COULD COME TO AN UNDERSTANDING.
YES, SIR.
ENJOY YOUR WEEKEND WITH THE FAMILY, MRS. SCHULLER.
"GIRLS, HELP YOUR MOTHER WITH THE GROCERY BAGS!"
BUSY DAY?
YOU COULD SAY THAT.

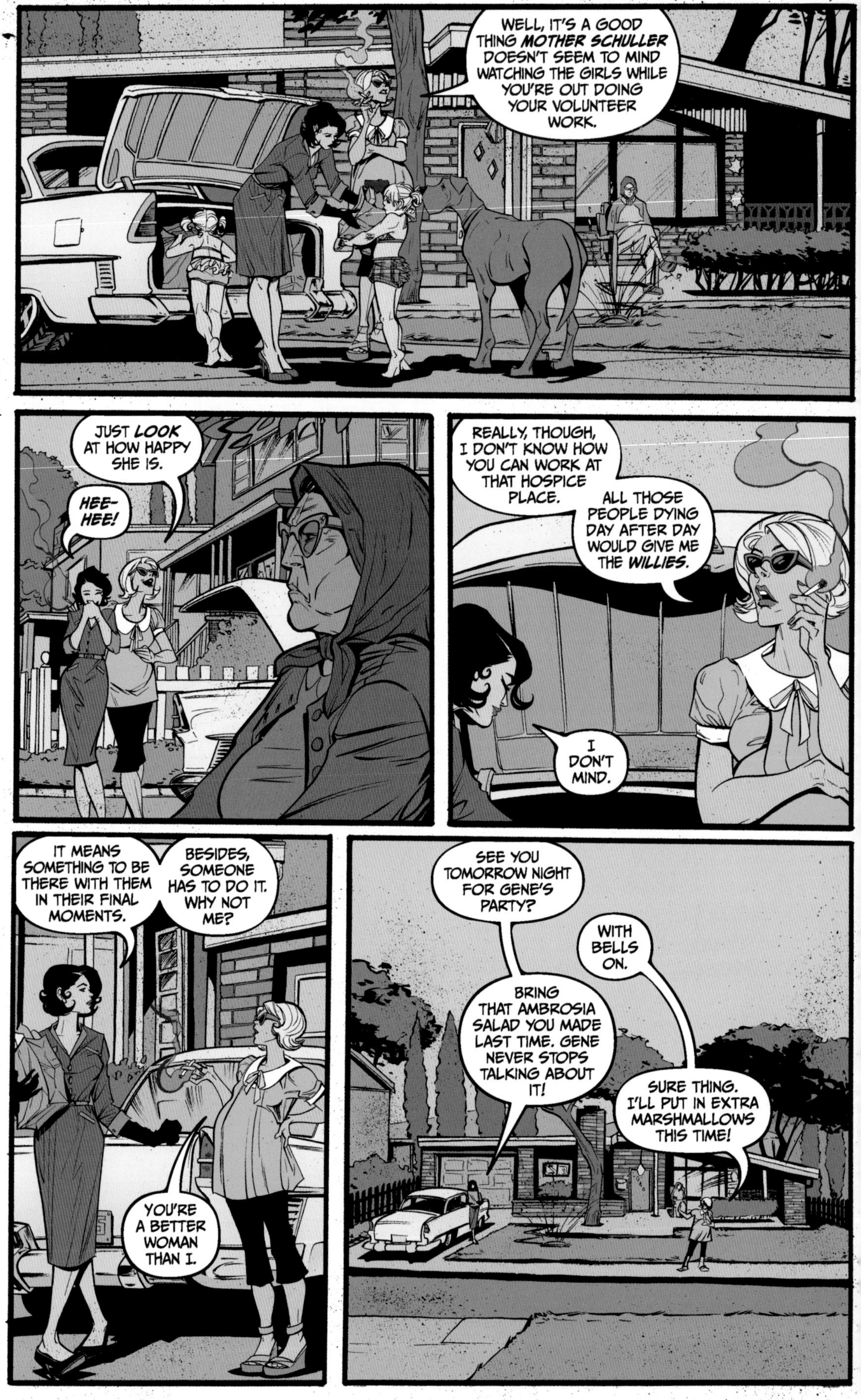

WELL, IT'S A GOOD THING MOTHER SCHULLER DOESN'T SEEM TO MIND WATCHING THE GIRLS WHILE YOU'RE OUT DOING YOUR VOLUNTEER WORK.
JUST LOOK AT HOW HAPPY SHE IS.
HEE-HEE!
REALLY, THOUGH, I DON'T KNOW HOW YOU CAN WORK AT THAT HOSPICE PLACE.
ALL THOSE PEOPLE DYING DAY AFTER DAY WOULD GIVE ME THE WILLIES.
I DON'T MIND.
IT MEANS SOMETHING TO BE THERE WITH THEM IN THEIR FINAL MOMENTS.
BESIDES, SOMEONE HAS TO DO IT. WHY NOT ME?
YOU'RE A BETTER WOMAN THAN I.
SEE YOU TOMORROW NIGHT FOR GENE'S PARTY?
WITH BELLS ON.
BRING THAT AMBROSIA SALAD YOU MADE LAST TIME. GENE NEVER STOPS TALKING ABOUT IT!
SURE THING. I'LL PUT IN EXTRA MARSHMALLOWS THIS TIME!

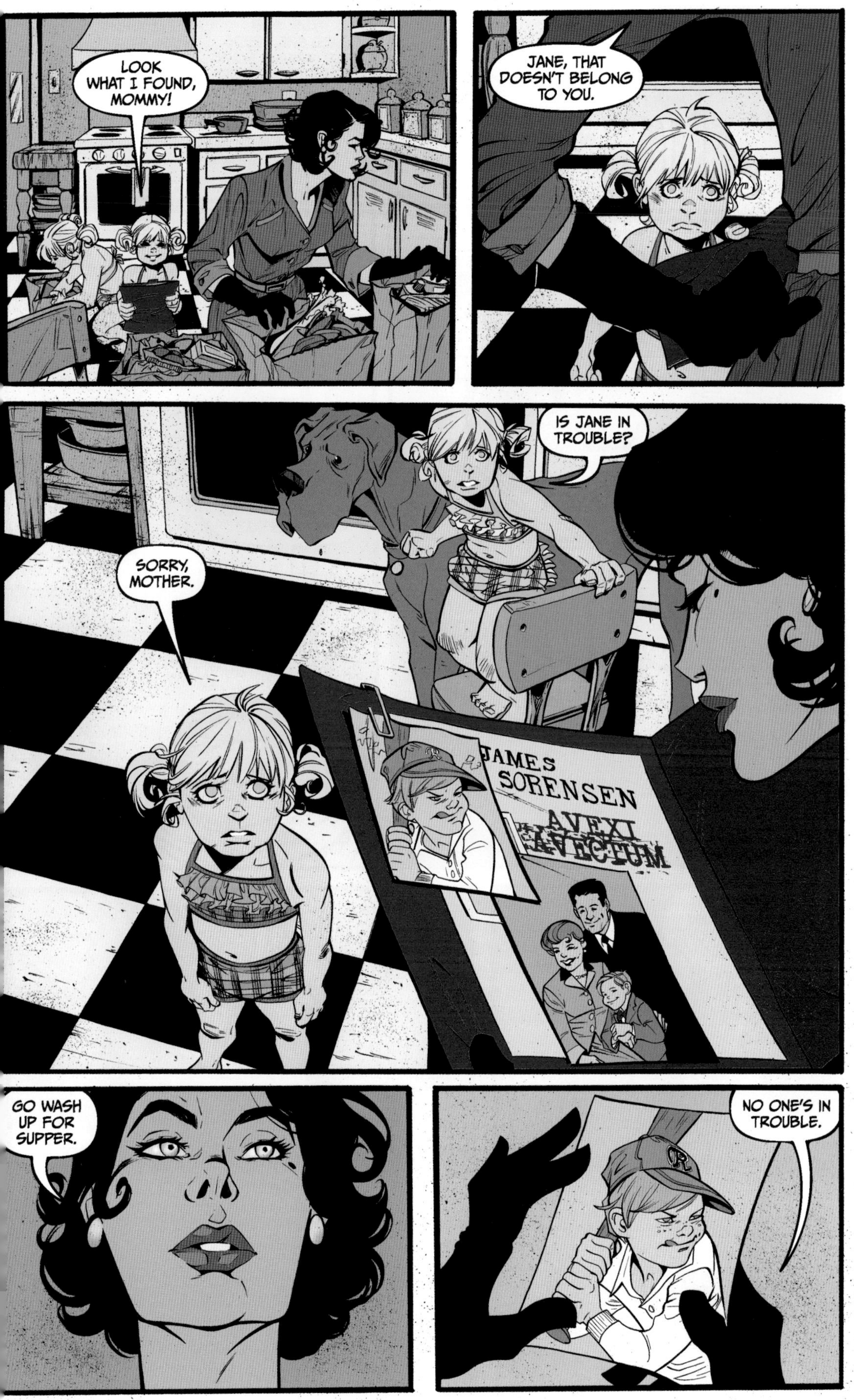
LOOK WHAT I FOUND, MOMMY!
JANE, THAT DOESN'T BELONG TO YOU.
SORRY, MOTHER.
IS JANE IN TROUBLE?
JAMES SORENSEN
AVEXI AVECTUM
GO WASH UP FOR SUPPER.
NO ONE'S IN TROUBLE.

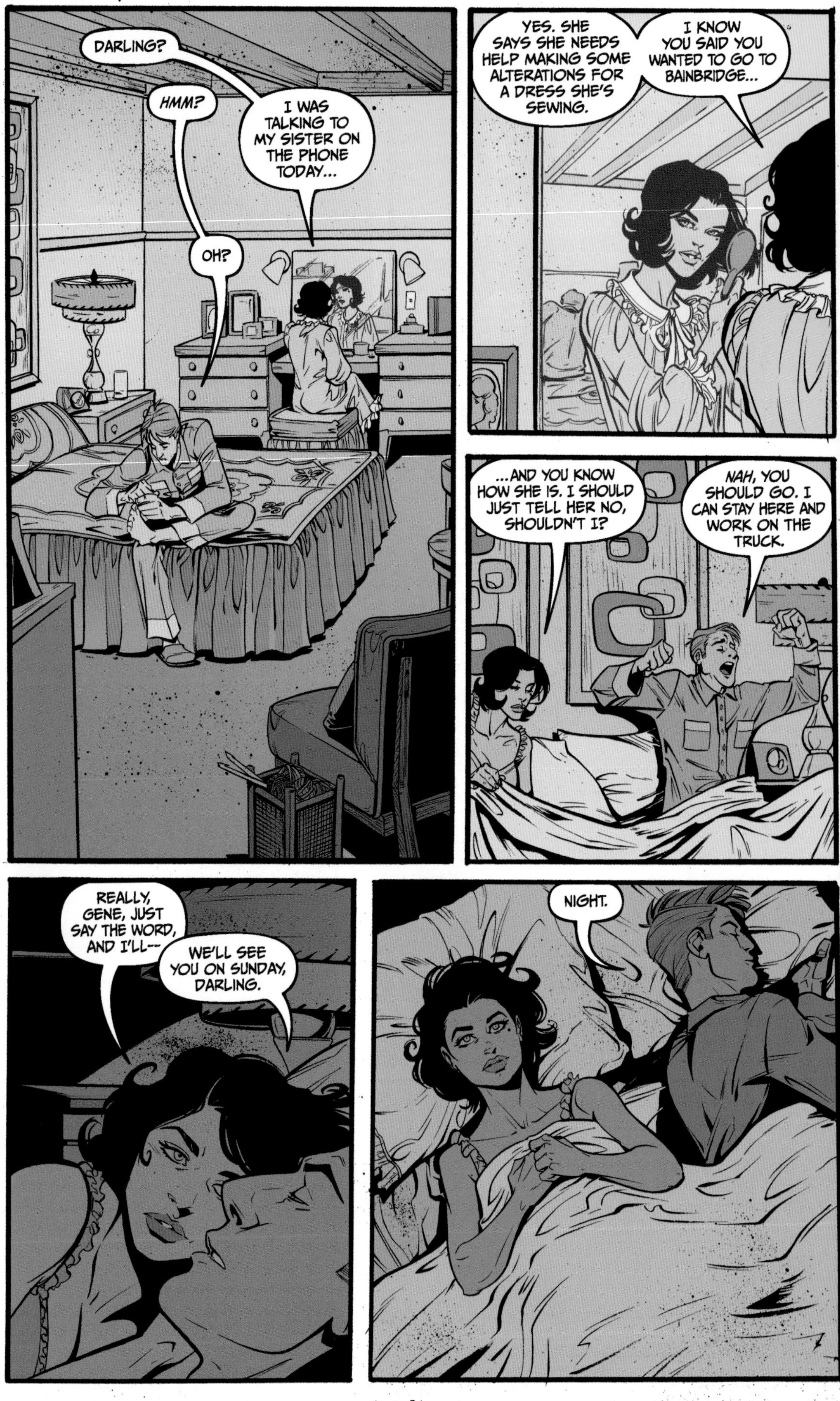
DARLING?
HMM?
I WAS TALKING TO MY SISTER ON THE PHONE TODAY...
OH?
YES. SHE SAYS SHE NEEDS HELP MAKING SOME ALTERATIONS FOR A DRESS SHE'S SEWING.
I KNOW YOU SAID YOU WANTED TO GO TO BAINBRIDGE...
...AND YOU KNOW HOW SHE IS. I SHOULD JUST TELL HER NO, SHOULDN'T I?
NAH, YOU SHOULD GO. I CAN STAY HERE AND WORK ON THE TRUCK.
REALLY, GENE, JUST SAY THE WORD, AND I'LL--
WE'LL SEE YOU ON SUNDAY, DARLING.
NIGHT.

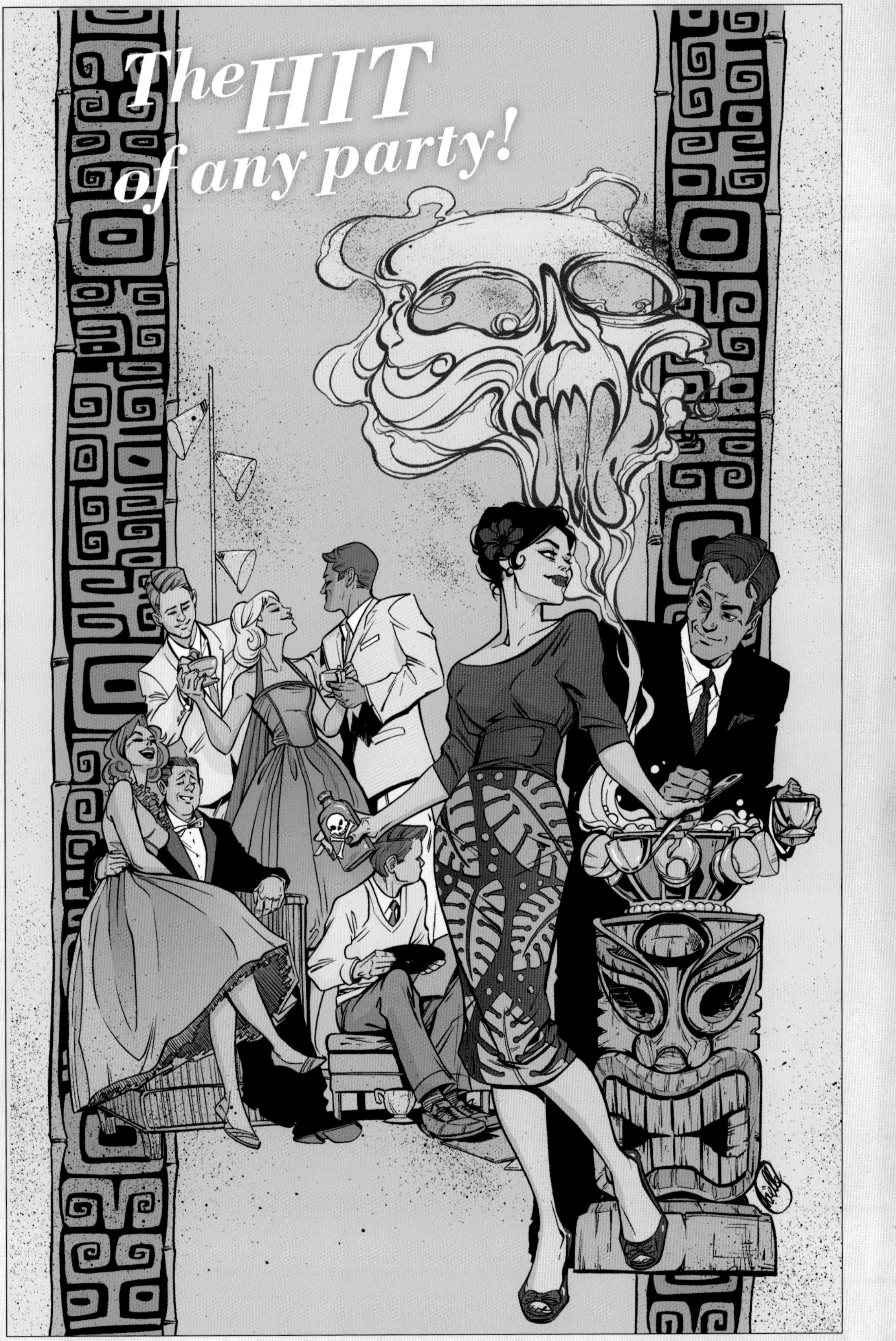
The HIT of any party!

CHAPTER THREE

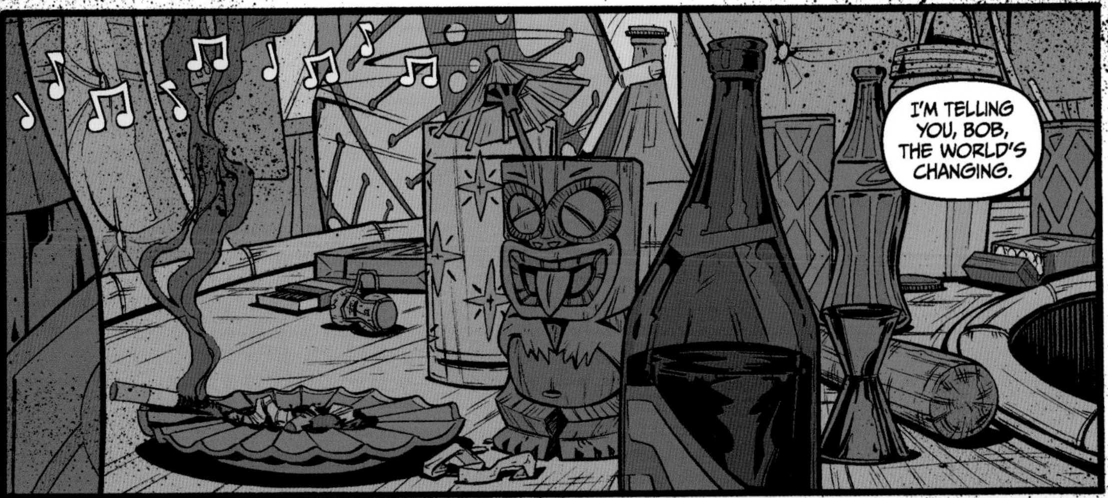
I'M TELLING YOU, BOB, THE WORLD'S CHANGING.

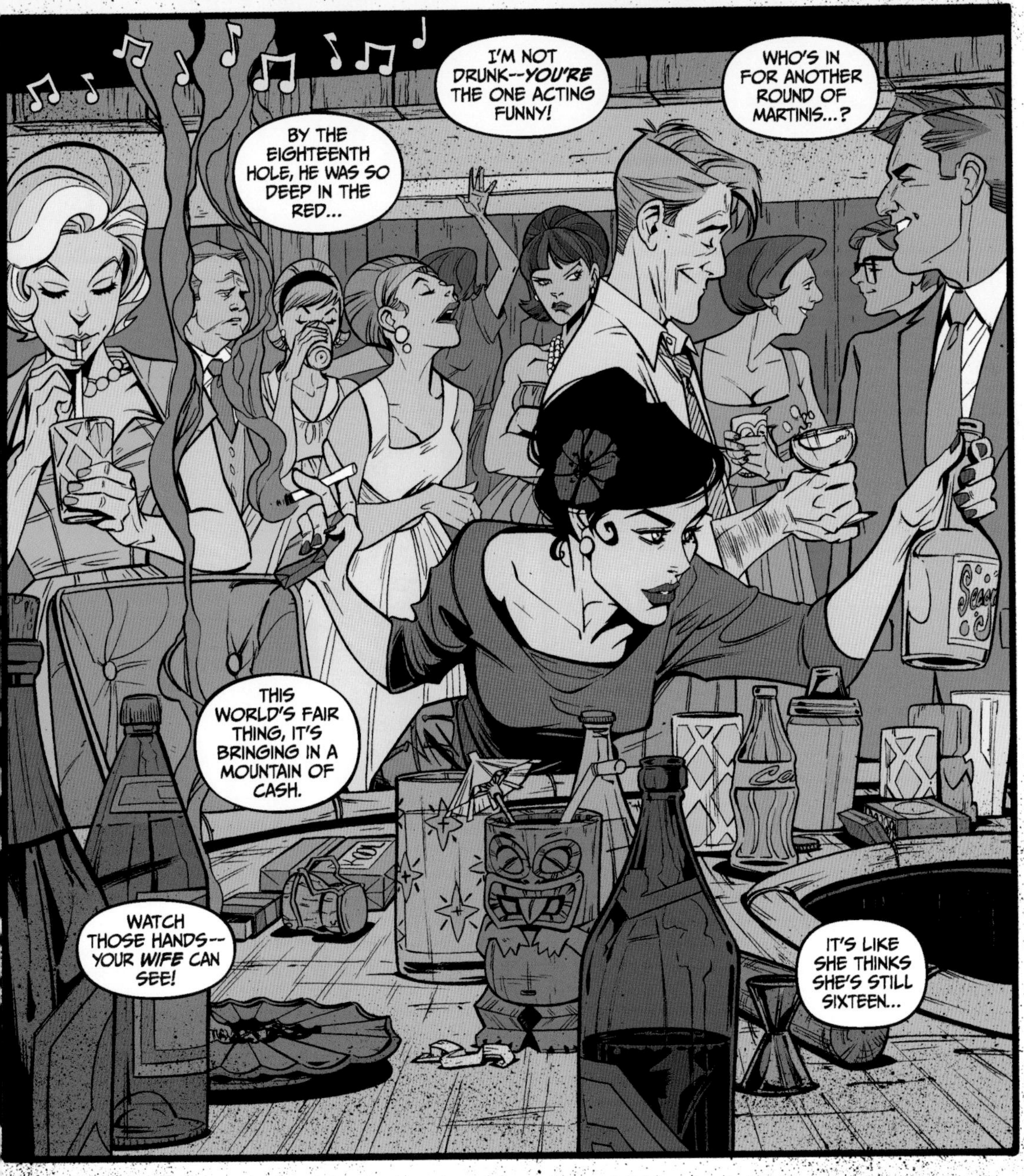
BY THE EIGHTEENTH HOLE, HE WAS SO DEEP IN THE RED...
I'M NOT DRUNK--*YOU'RE* THE ONE ACTING FUNNY!
WHO'S IN FOR ANOTHER ROUND OF MARTINIS...?
THIS WORLD'S FAIR THING, IT'S BRINGING IN A MOUNTAIN OF CASH.
WATCH THOSE HANDS--YOUR *WIFE* CAN SEE!
IT'S LIKE SHE THINKS SHE'S STILL SIXTEEN...

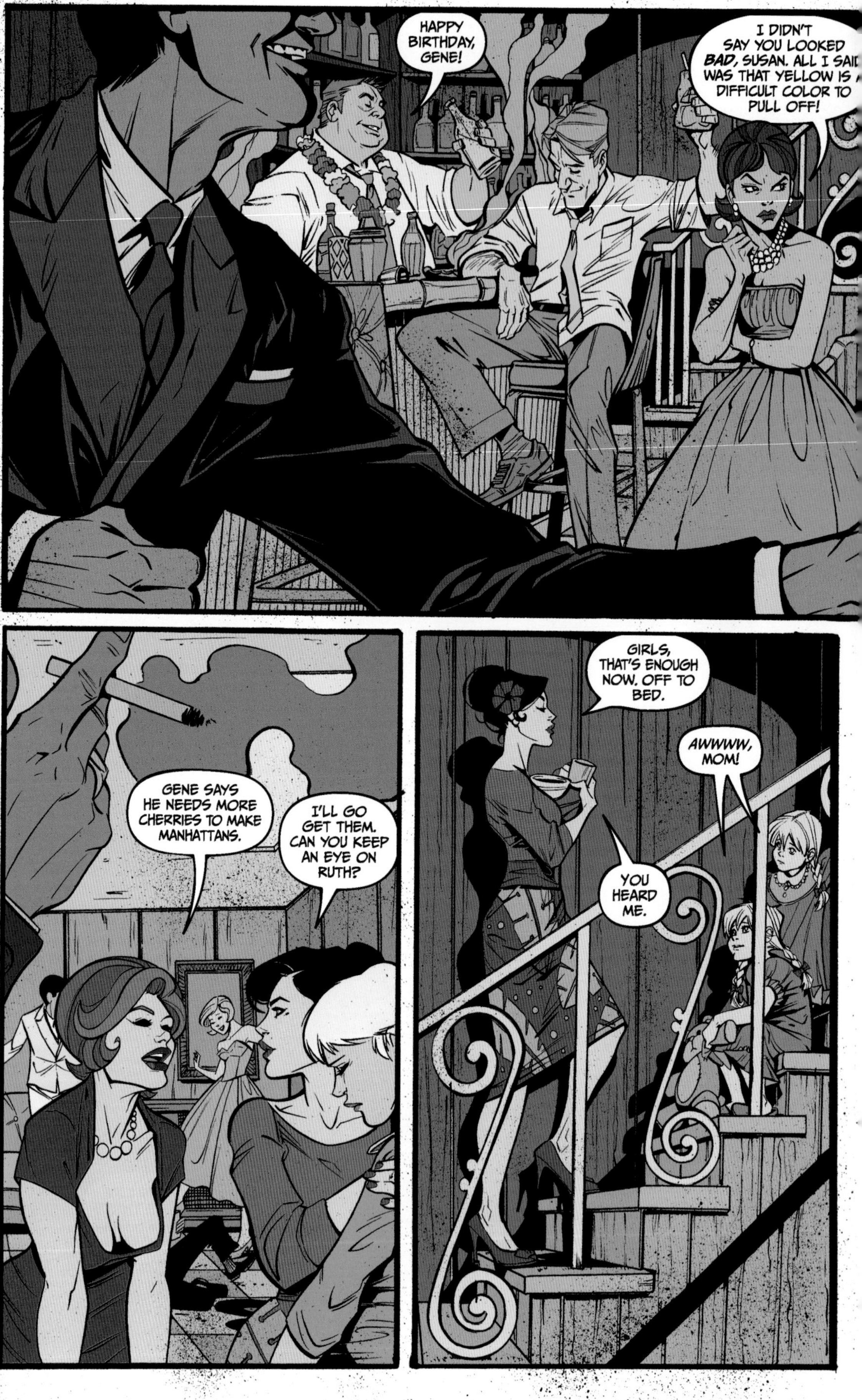
HAPPY BIRTHDAY, GENE!
I DIDN'T SAY YOU LOOKED BAD, SUSAN. ALL I SAID WAS THAT YELLOW IS A DIFFICULT COLOR TO PULL OFF!
GENE SAYS HE NEEDS MORE CHERRIES TO MAKE MANHATTANS.
I'LL GO GET THEM. CAN YOU KEEP AN EYE ON RUTH?
GIRLS, THAT'S ENOUGH NOW. OFF TO BED.
AWWWW, MOM!
YOU HEARD ME.

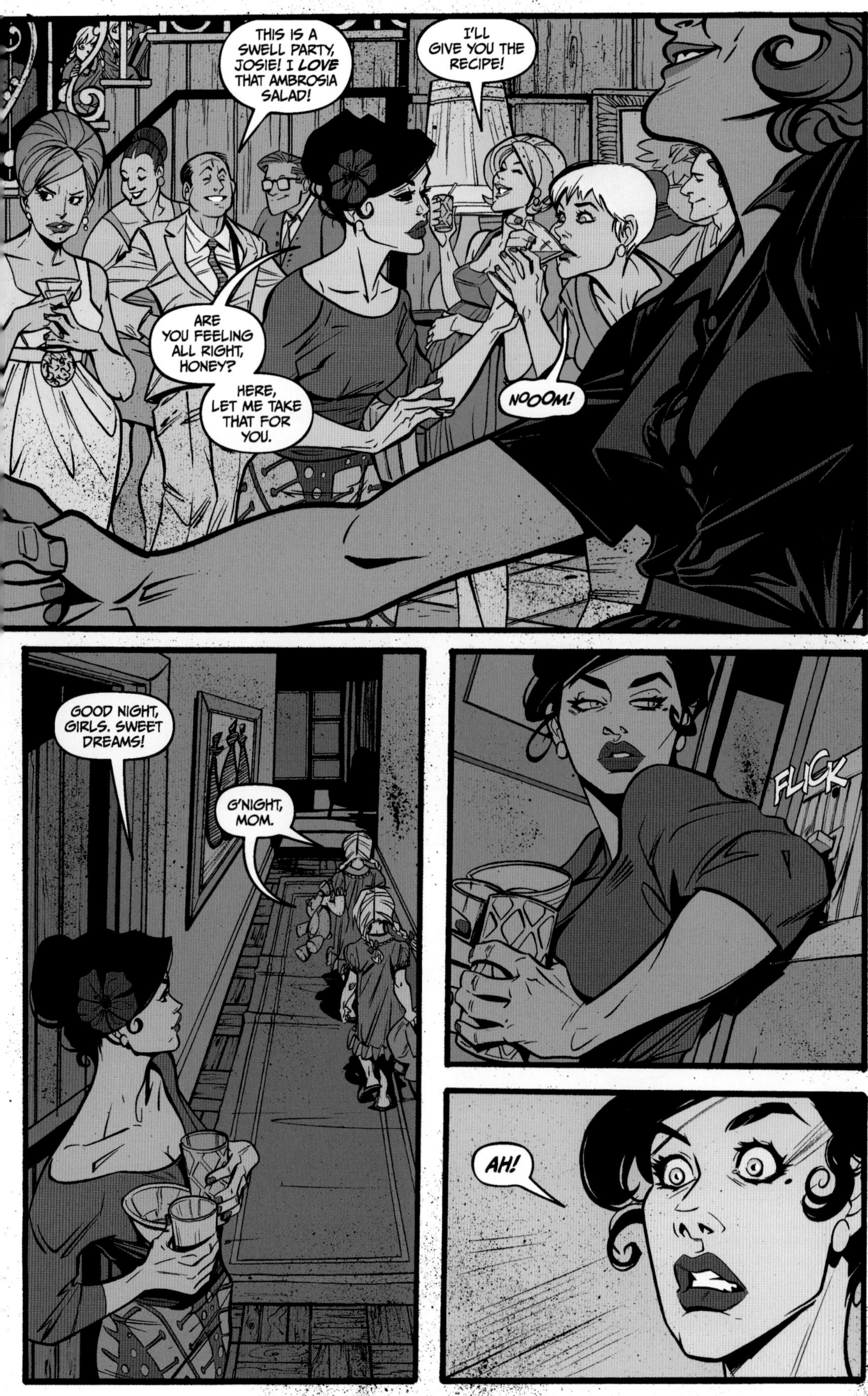

THIS IS A SWELL PARTY, JOSIE! I LOVE THAT AMBROSIA SALAD!
I'LL GIVE YOU THE RECIPE!
ARE YOU FEELING ALL RIGHT, HONEY?
HERE, LET ME TAKE THAT FOR YOU.
NOOOM!
GOOD NIGHT, GIRLS. SWEET DREAMS!
G'NIGHT, MOM.
FLICK
AH!

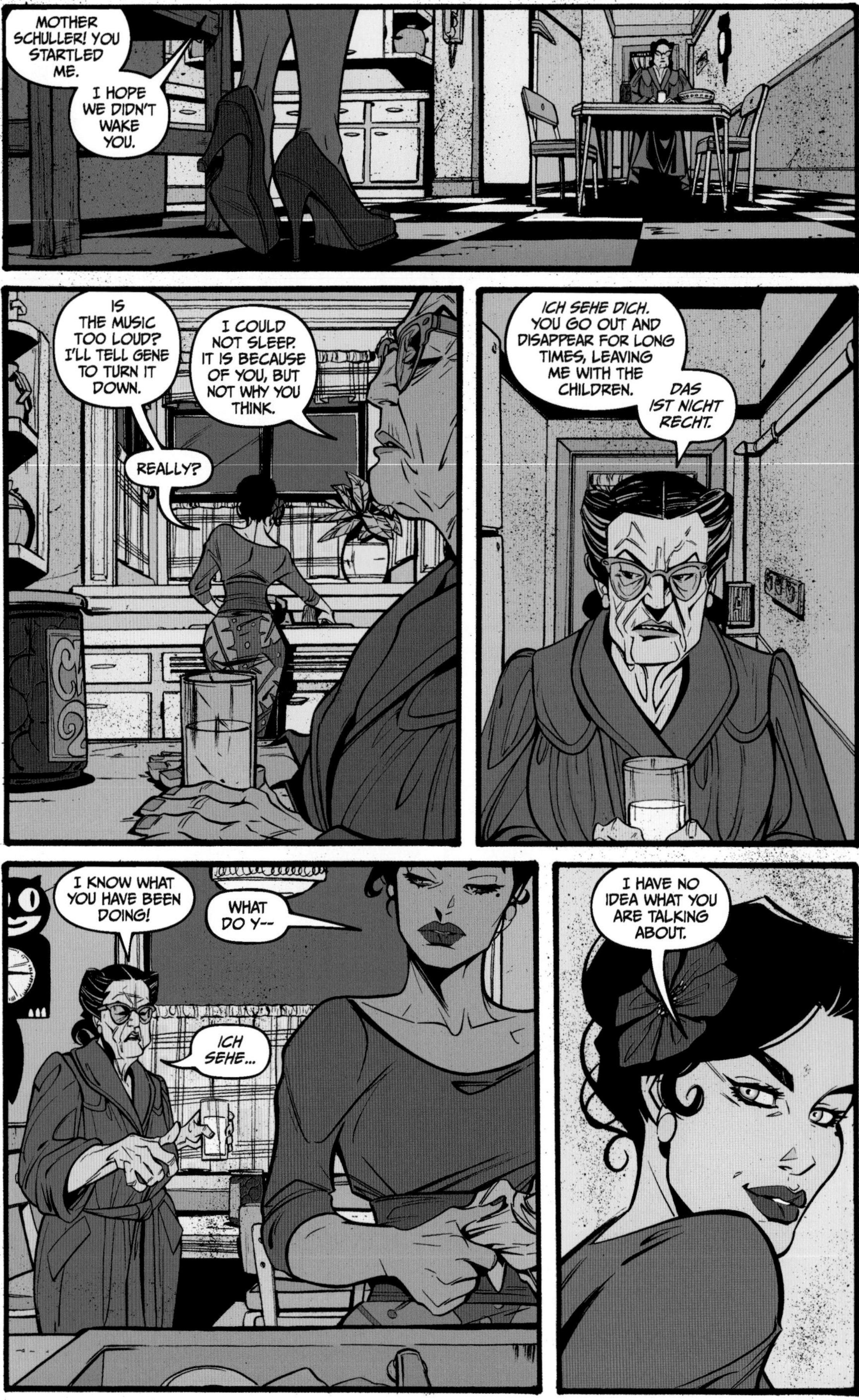
MOTHER SCHULLER! YOU STARTLED ME.
I HOPE WE DIDN'T WAKE YOU.
IS THE MUSIC TOO LOUD? I'LL TELL GENE TO TURN IT DOWN.
I COULD NOT SLEEP. IT IS BECAUSE OF YOU, BUT NOT WHY YOU THINK.
REALLY?
ICH SEHE DICH. YOU GO OUT AND DISAPPEAR FOR LONG TIMES, LEAVING ME WITH THE CHILDREN.
DAS IST NICHT RECHT.
I KNOW WHAT YOU HAVE BEEN DOING!
WHAT DO Y--
ICH SEHE...
I HAVE NO IDEA WHAT YOU ARE TALKING ABOUT.

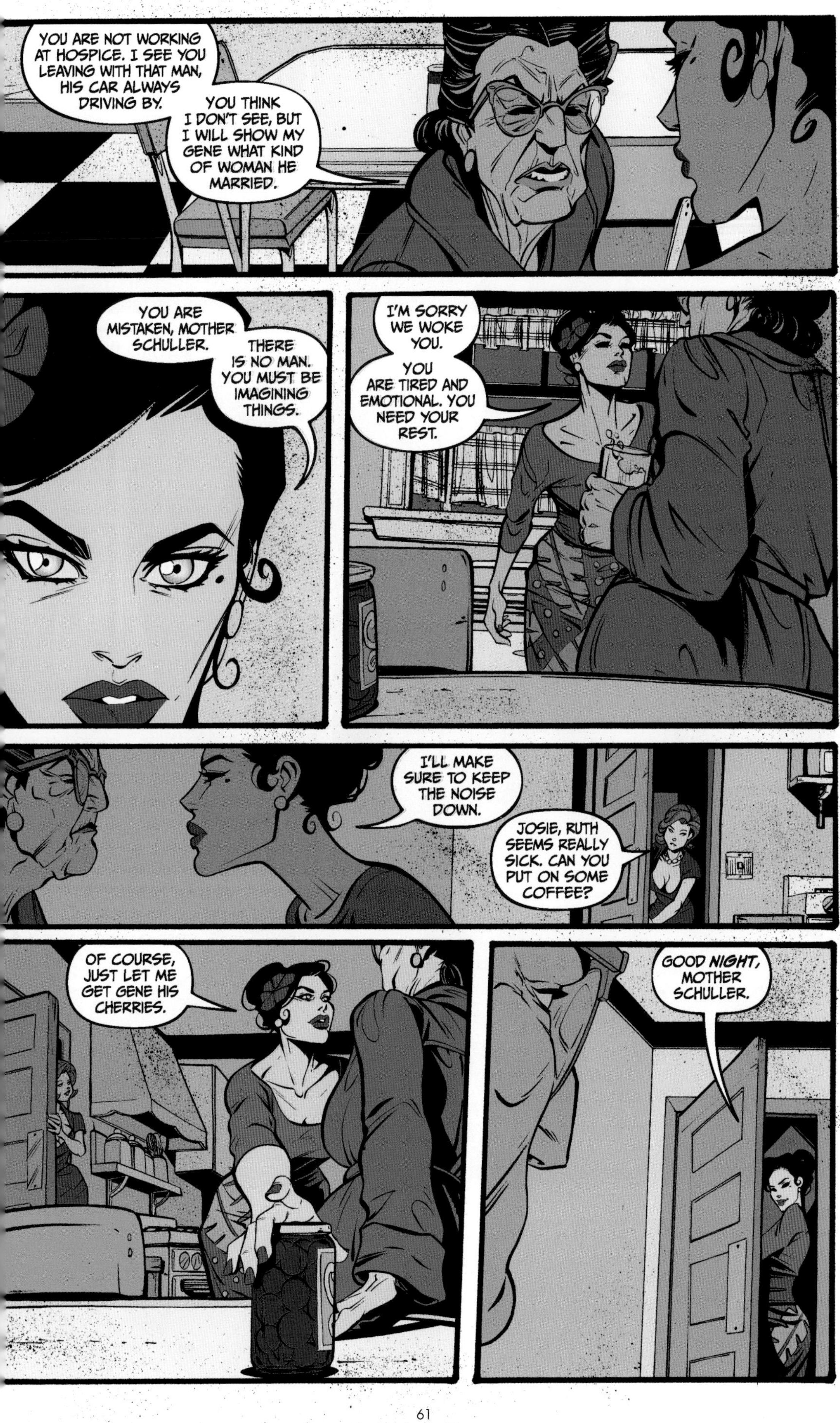
YOU ARE NOT WORKING AT HOSPICE. I SEE YOU LEAVING WITH THAT MAN, HIS CAR ALWAYS DRIVING BY.
YOU THINK I DON'T SEE, BUT I WILL SHOW MY GENE WHAT KIND OF WOMAN HE MARRIED.
YOU ARE MISTAKEN, MOTHER SCHULLER.
THERE IS NO MAN. YOU MUST BE IMAGINING THINGS.
I'M SORRY WE WOKE YOU.
YOU ARE TIRED AND EMOTIONAL. YOU NEED YOUR REST.
I'LL MAKE SURE TO KEEP THE NOISE DOWN.
JOSIE, RUTH SEEMS REALLY SICK. CAN YOU PUT ON SOME COFFEE?
OF COURSE, JUST LET ME GET GENE HIS CHERRIES.
GOOD NIGHT, MOTHER SCHULLER.

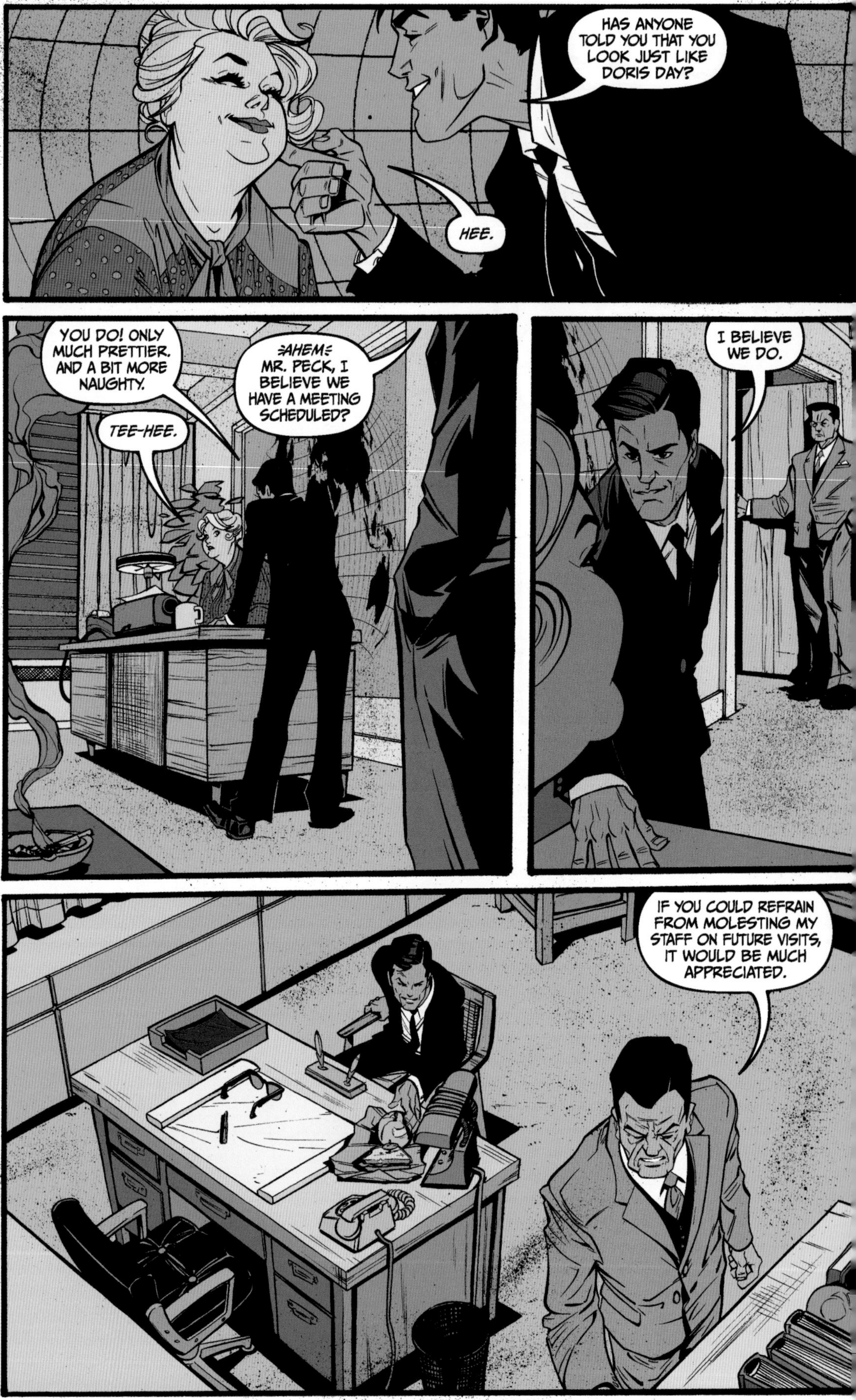
HAS ANYONE TOLD YOU THAT YOU LOOK JUST LIKE DORIS DAY?
HEE.
YOU DO! ONLY MUCH PRETTIER. AND A BIT MORE NAUGHTY.
TEE-HEE.
=AHEM= MR. PECK, I BELIEVE WE HAVE A MEETING SCHEDULED?
I BELIEVE WE DO.
IF YOU COULD REFRAIN FROM MOLESTING MY STAFF ON FUTURE VISITS, IT WOULD BE MUCH APPRECIATED.

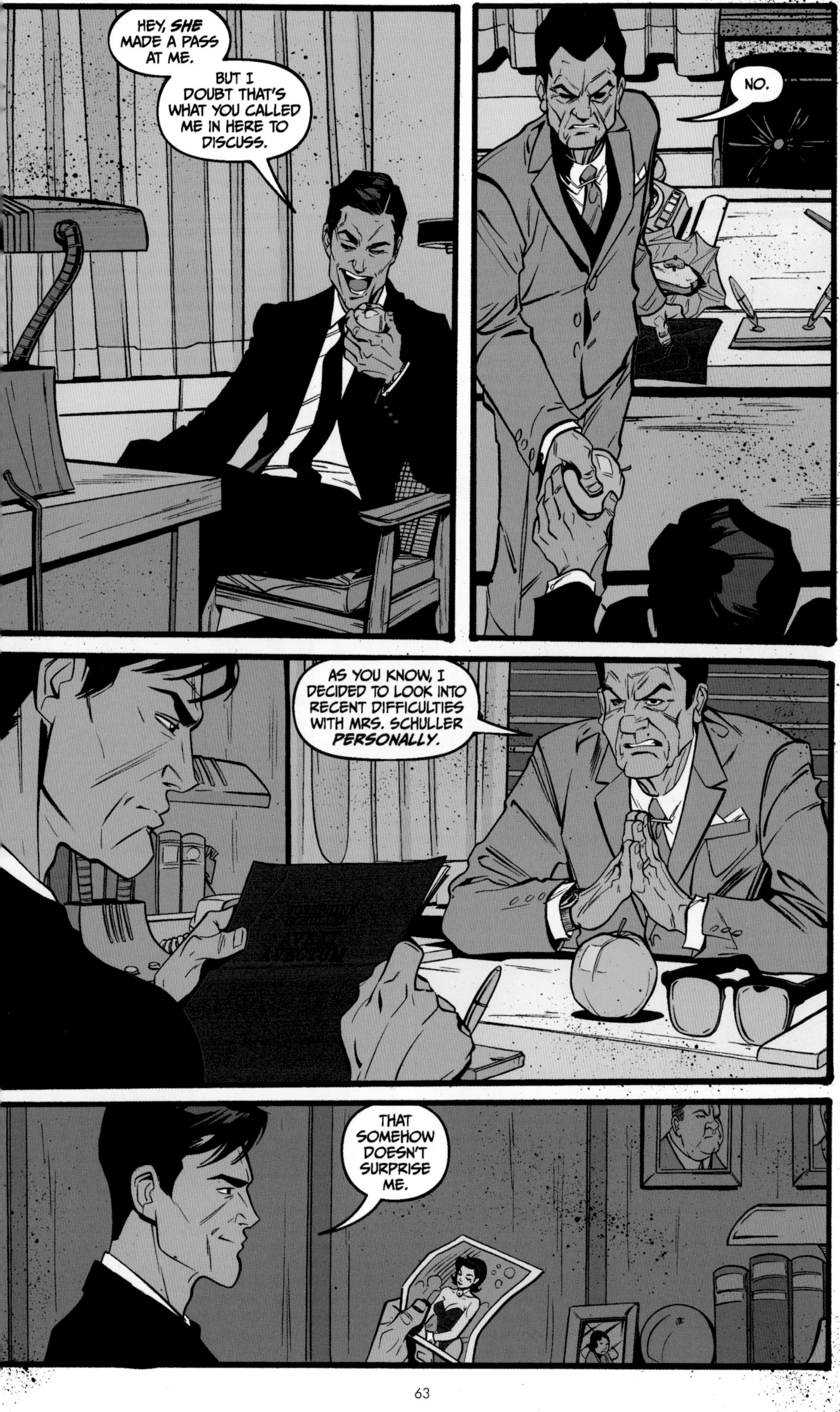
HEY, SHE MADE A PASS AT ME.
BUT I DOUBT THAT'S WHAT YOU CALLED ME IN HERE TO DISCUSS.
NO.
AS YOU KNOW, I DECIDED TO LOOK INTO RECENT DIFFICULTIES WITH MRS. SCHULLER PERSONALLY.
THAT SOMEHOW DOESN'T SURPRISE ME.

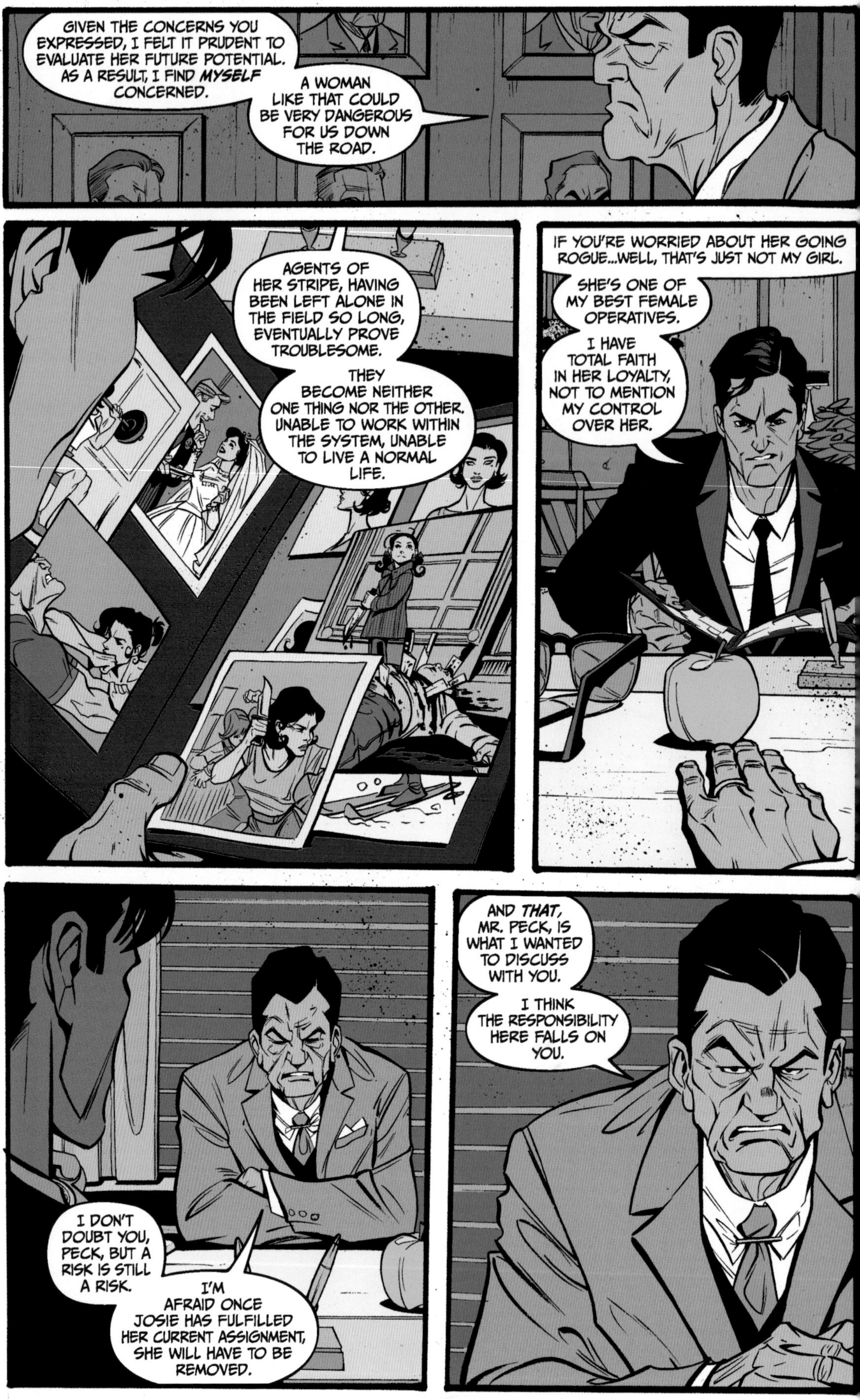
GIVEN THE CONCERNS YOU EXPRESSED, I FELT IT PRUDENT TO EVALUATE HER FUTURE POTENTIAL. AS A RESULT, I FIND *MYSELF* CONCERNED.
A WOMAN LIKE THAT COULD BE VERY DANGEROUS FOR US DOWN THE ROAD.
AGENTS OF HER STRIPE, HAVING BEEN LEFT ALONE IN THE FIELD SO LONG, EVENTUALLY PROVE TROUBLESOME.
THEY BECOME NEITHER ONE THING NOR THE OTHER. UNABLE TO WORK WITHIN THE SYSTEM, UNABLE TO LIVE A NORMAL LIFE.
IF YOU'RE WORRIED ABOUT HER GOING ROGUE...WELL, THAT'S JUST NOT MY GIRL.
SHE'S ONE OF MY BEST FEMALE OPERATIVES.
I HAVE TOTAL FAITH IN HER LOYALTY, NOT TO MENTION MY CONTROL OVER HER.
I DON'T DOUBT YOU, PECK, BUT A RISK IS STILL A RISK.
I'M AFRAID ONCE JOSIE HAS FULFILLED HER CURRENT ASSIGNMENT, SHE WILL HAVE TO BE REMOVED.
AND *THAT*, MR. PECK, IS WHAT I WANTED TO DISCUSS WITH YOU.
I THINK THE RESPONSIBILITY HERE FALLS ON YOU.

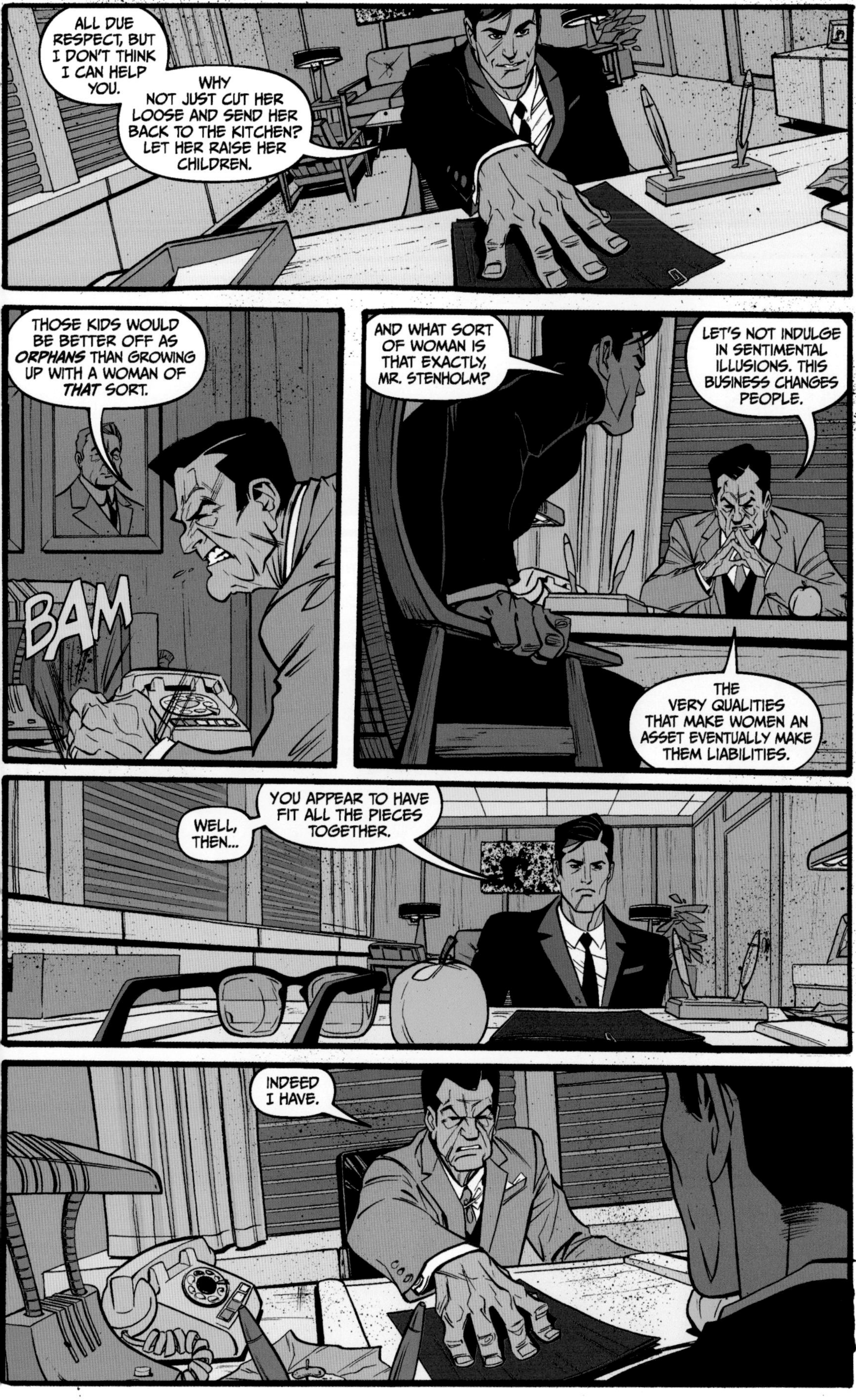
ALL DUE RESPECT, BUT I DON'T THINK I CAN HELP YOU.
WHY NOT JUST CUT HER LOOSE AND SEND HER BACK TO THE KITCHEN? LET HER RAISE HER CHILDREN.
THOSE KIDS WOULD BE BETTER OFF AS *ORPHANS* THAN GROWING UP WITH A WOMAN OF *THAT* SORT.
BAM
AND WHAT SORT OF WOMAN IS THAT EXACTLY, MR. STENHOLM?
LET'S NOT INDULGE IN SENTIMENTAL ILLUSIONS. THIS BUSINESS CHANGES PEOPLE.
THE VERY QUALITIES THAT MAKE WOMEN AN ASSET EVENTUALLY MAKE THEM LIABILITIES.
WELL, THEN...
YOU APPEAR TO HAVE FIT ALL THE PIECES TOGETHER.
INDEED I HAVE.

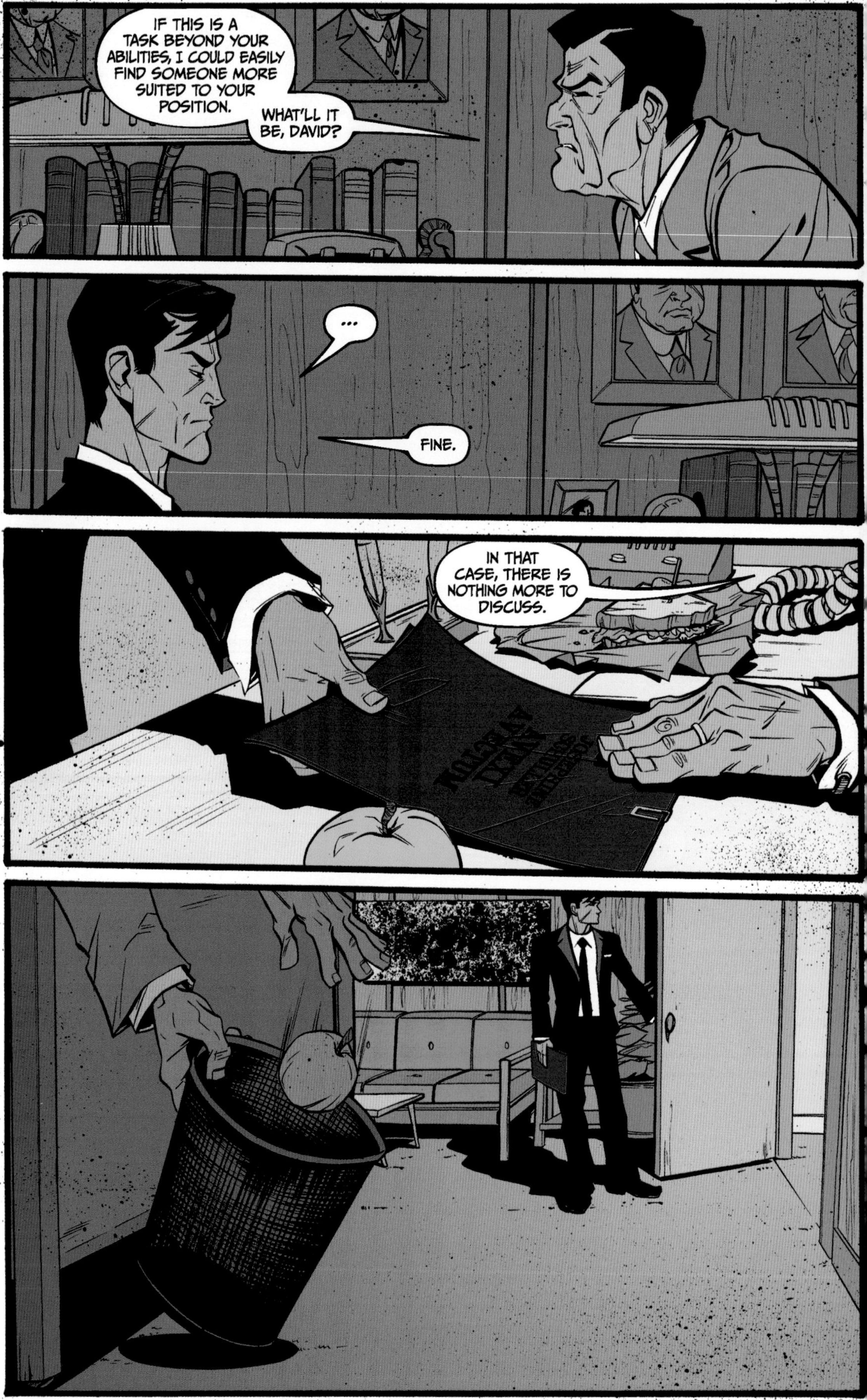
IF THIS IS A TASK BEYOND YOUR ABILITIES, I COULD EASILY FIND SOMEONE MORE SUITED TO YOUR POSITION.
WHAT'LL IT BE, DAVID?
...
FINE.
IN THAT CASE, THERE IS NOTHING MORE TO DISCUSS.

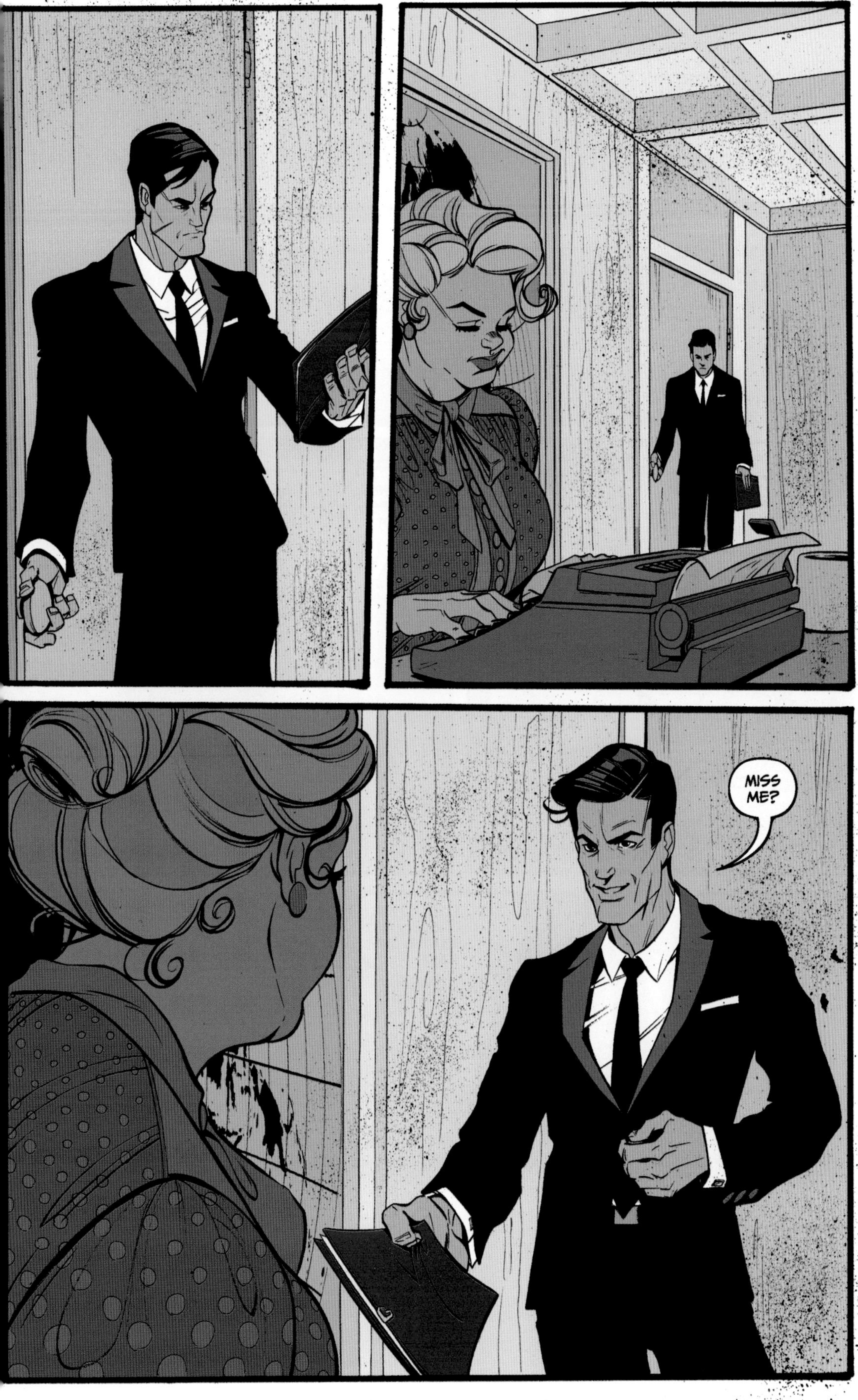
MISS ME?

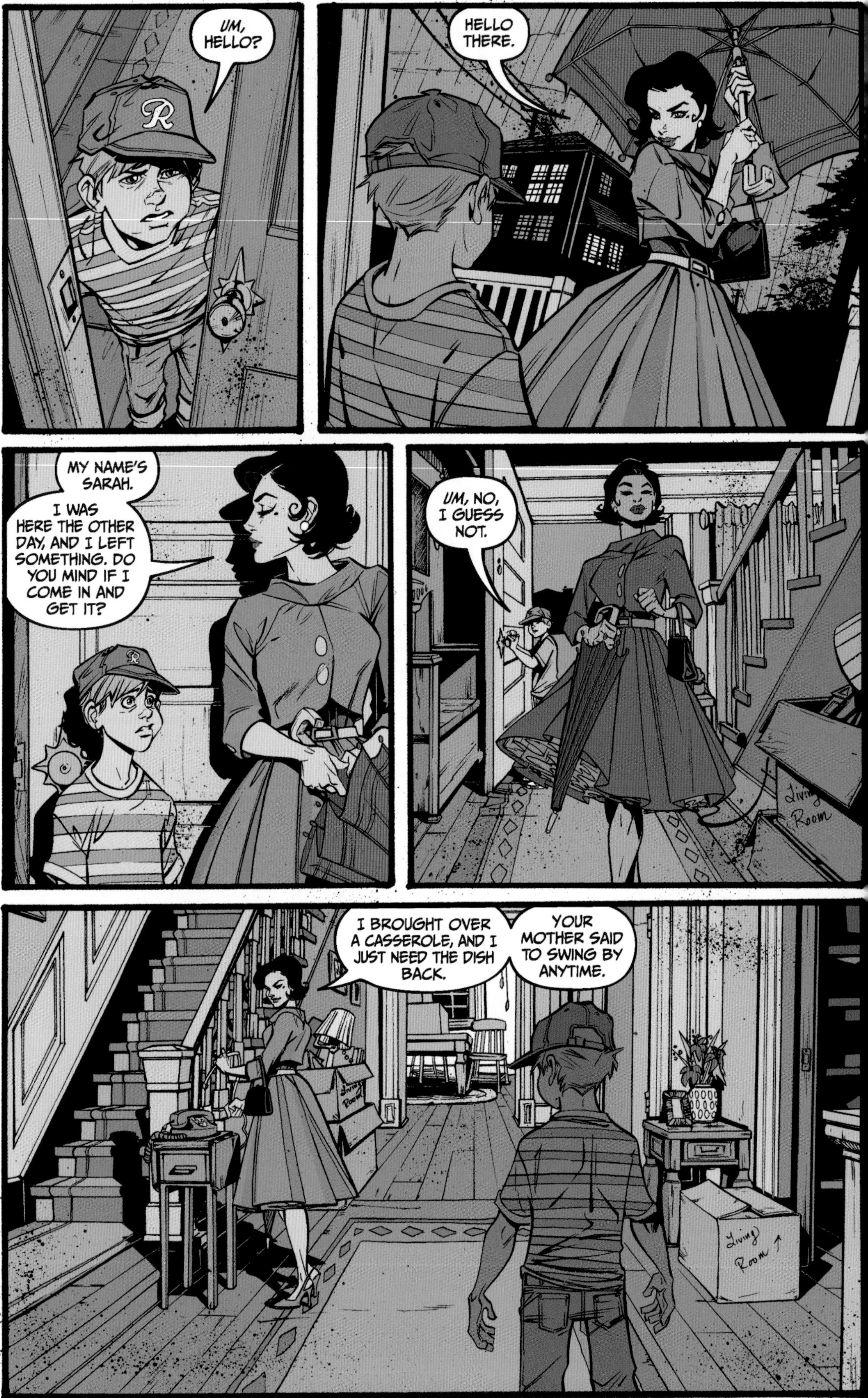
UM, HELLO?
HELLO THERE.
MY NAME'S SARAH.
I WAS HERE THE OTHER DAY, AND I LEFT SOMETHING. DO YOU MIND IF I COME IN AND GET IT?
UM, NO, I GUESS NOT.
Living Room
I BROUGHT OVER A CASSEROLE, AND I JUST NEED THE DISH BACK.
YOUR MOTHER SAID TO SWING BY ANYTIME.
Living Room ↑

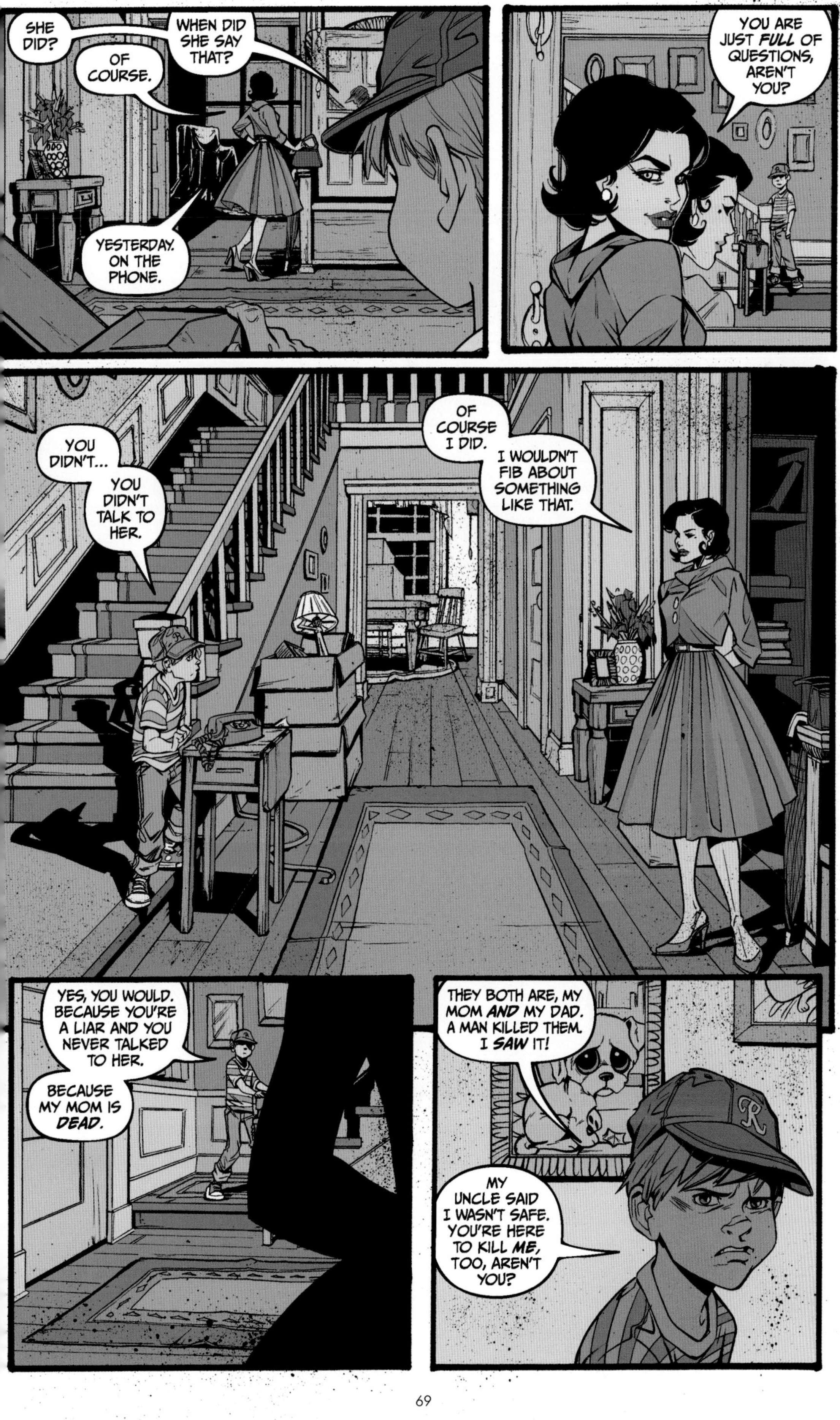
SHE DID?
WHEN DID SHE SAY THAT?
OF COURSE.
YESTERDAY. ON THE PHONE.
YOU ARE JUST FULL OF QUESTIONS, AREN'T YOU?
YOU DIDN'T...
YOU DIDN'T TALK TO HER.
OF COURSE I DID.
I WOULDN'T FIB ABOUT SOMETHING LIKE THAT.
YES, YOU WOULD. BECAUSE YOU'RE A LIAR AND YOU NEVER TALKED TO HER.
BECAUSE MY MOM IS DEAD.
THEY BOTH ARE, MY MOM AND MY DAD. A MAN KILLED THEM. I SAW IT!
MY UNCLE SAID I WASN'T SAFE. YOU'RE HERE TO KILL ME, TOO, AREN'T YOU?

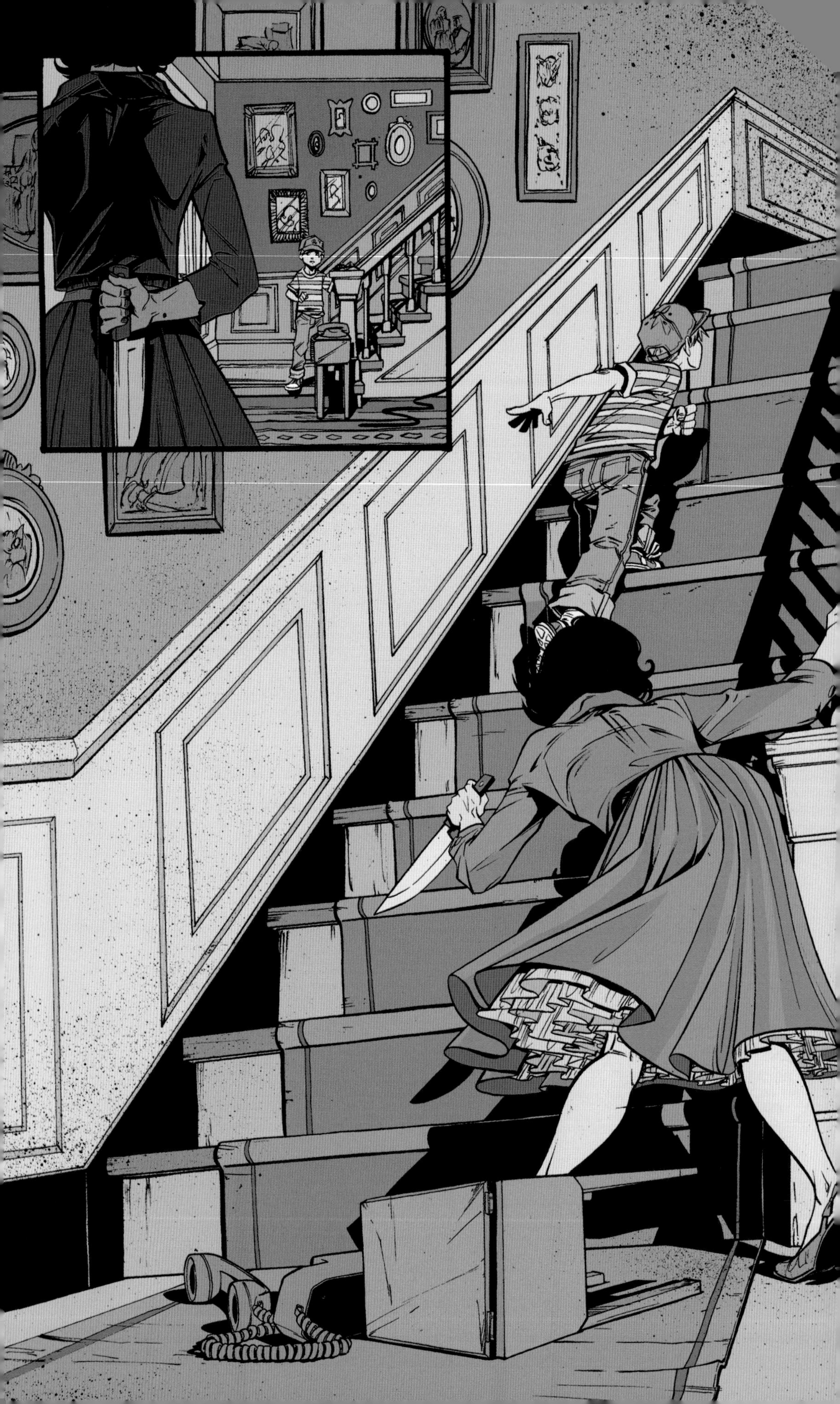

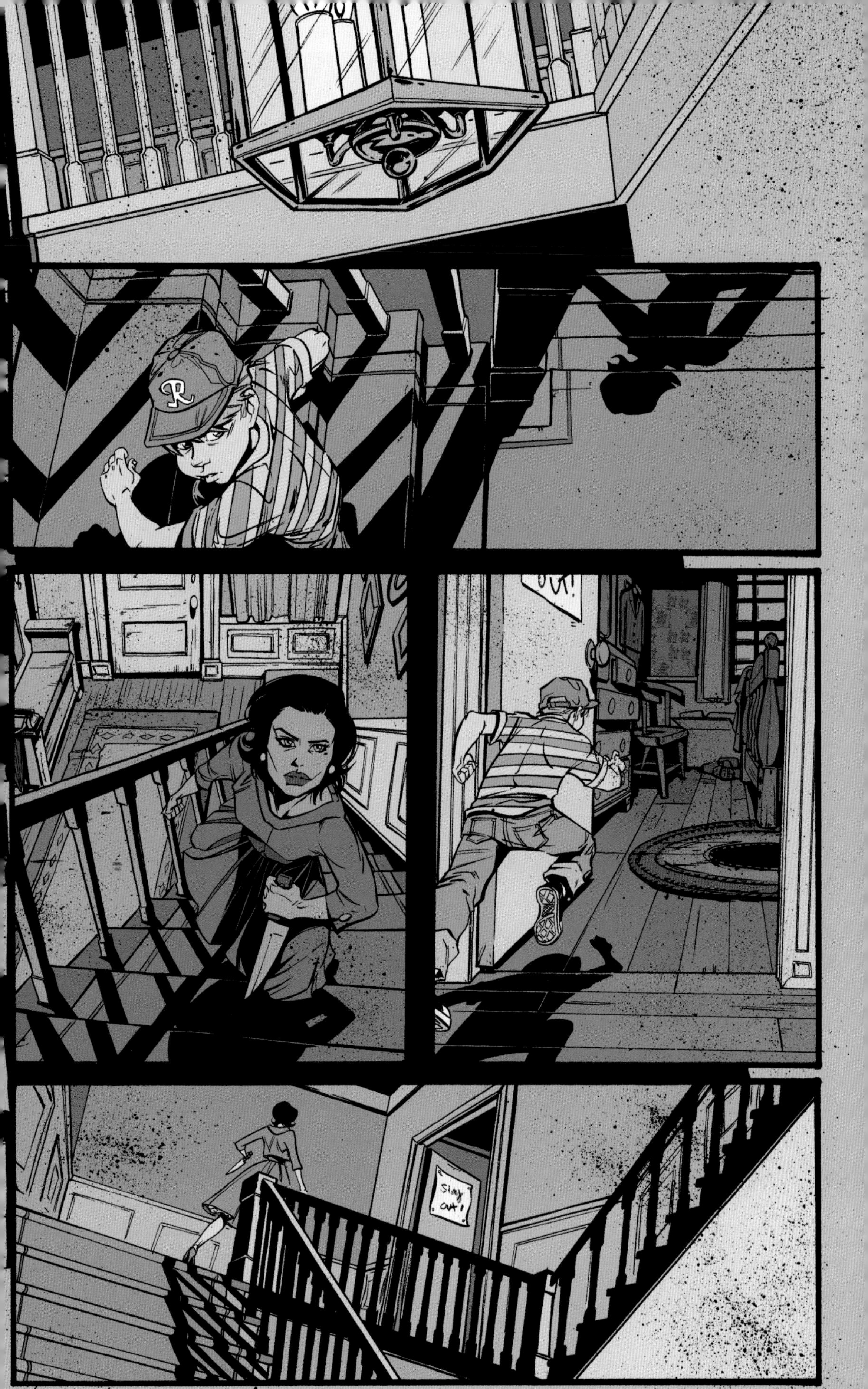
Stay out!

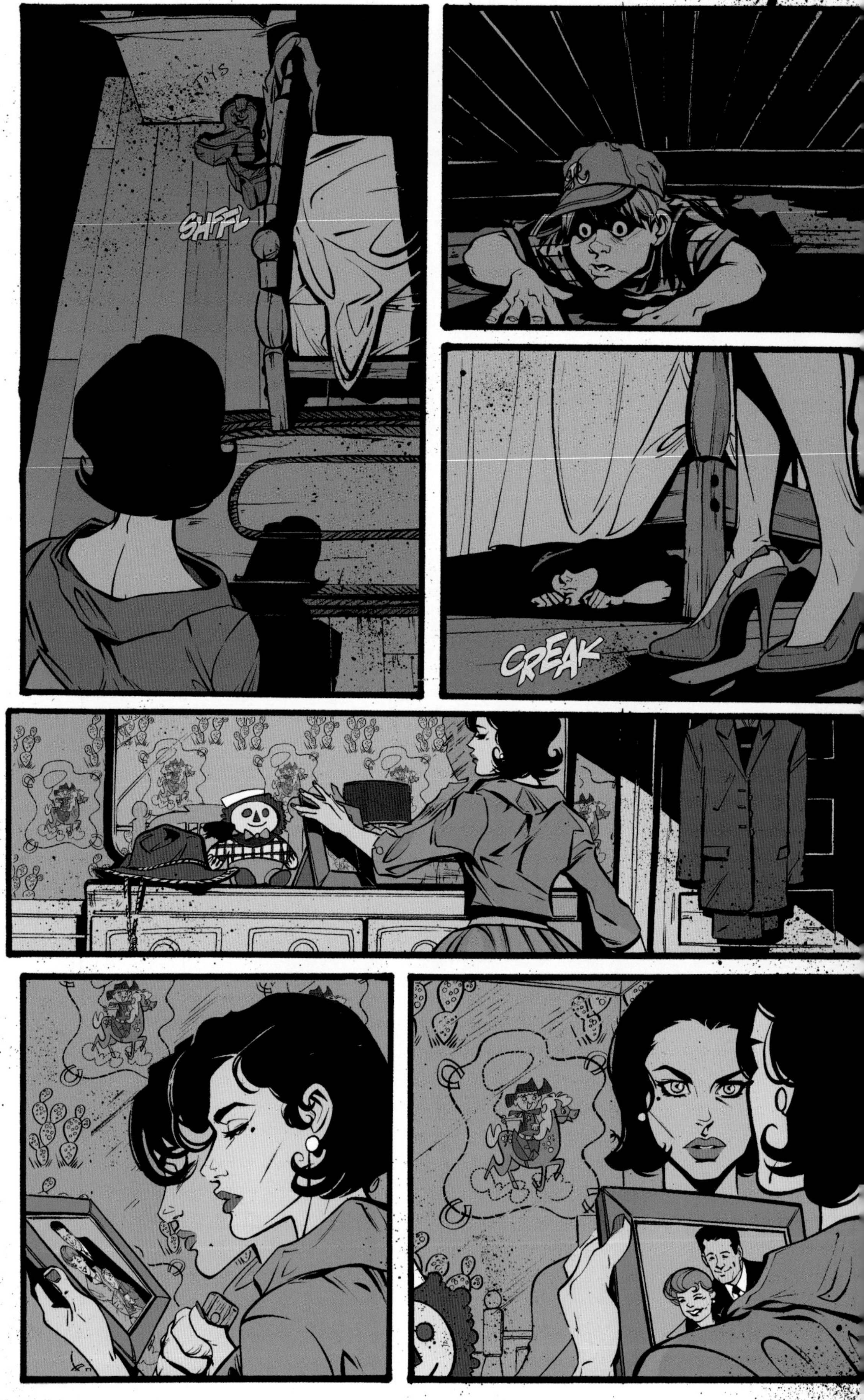
TOYS
SHFFL
CREAK

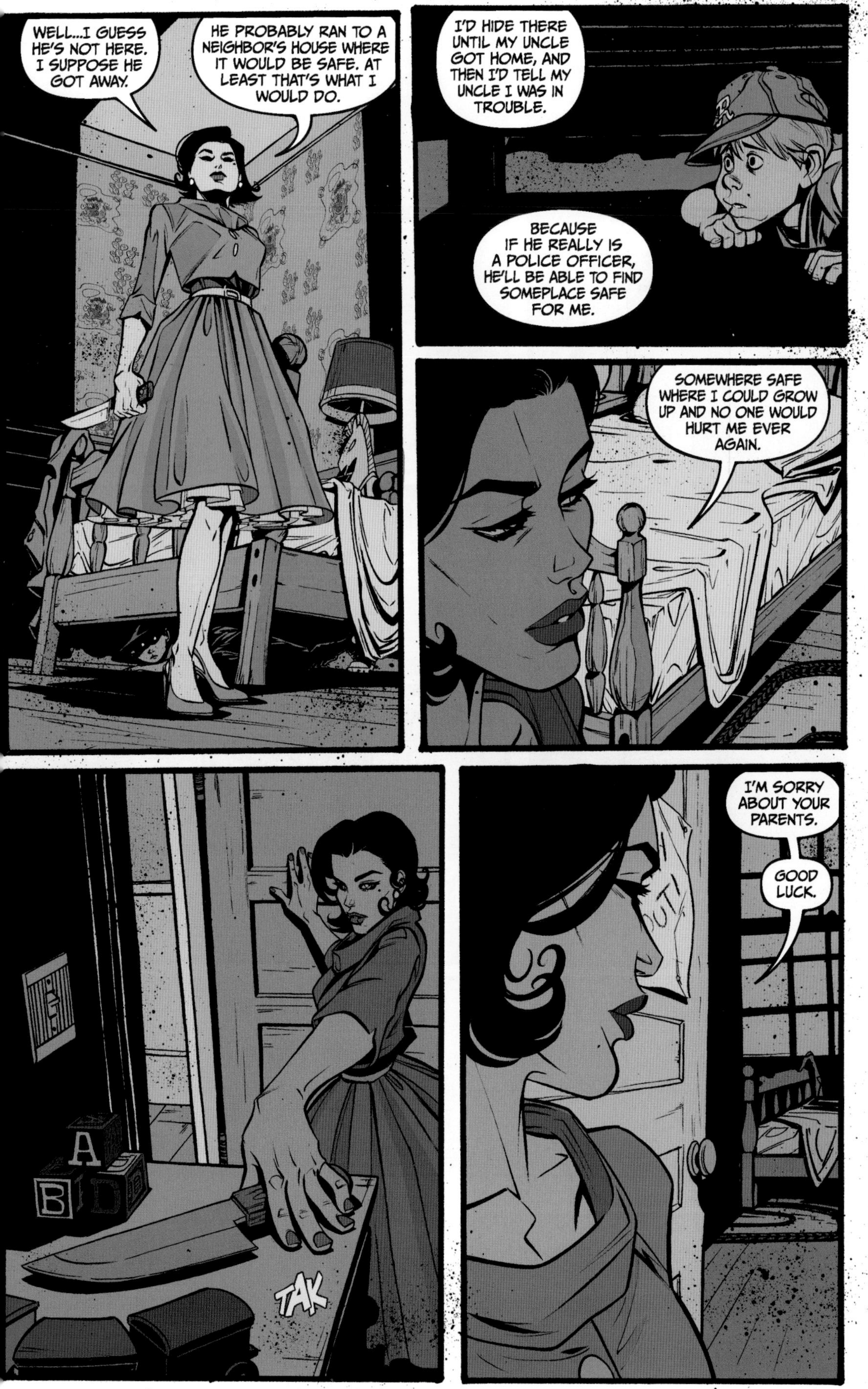
WELL...I GUESS HE'S NOT HERE. I SUPPOSE HE GOT AWAY.
HE PROBABLY RAN TO A NEIGHBOR'S HOUSE WHERE IT WOULD BE SAFE. AT LEAST THAT'S WHAT I WOULD DO.
I'D HIDE THERE UNTIL MY UNCLE GOT HOME, AND THEN I'D TELL MY UNCLE I WAS IN TROUBLE.
BECAUSE IF HE REALLY IS A POLICE OFFICER, HE'LL BE ABLE TO FIND SOMEPLACE SAFE FOR ME.
SOMEWHERE SAFE WHERE I COULD GROW UP AND NO ONE WOULD HURT ME EVER AGAIN.
TAK
I'M SORRY ABOUT YOUR PARENTS.
GOOD LUCK.

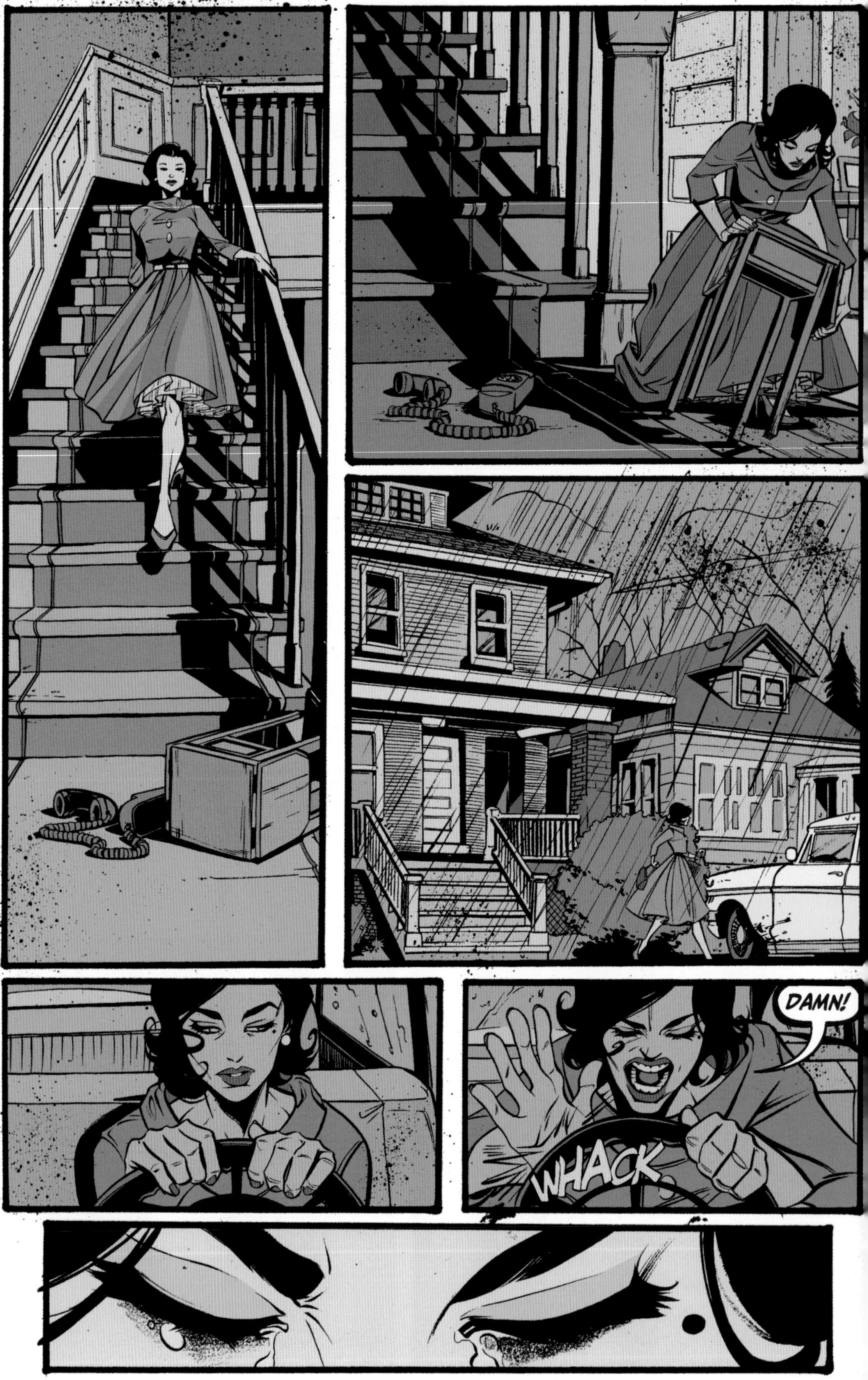
DAMN!
WHACK

SKREEEE

VROOOM

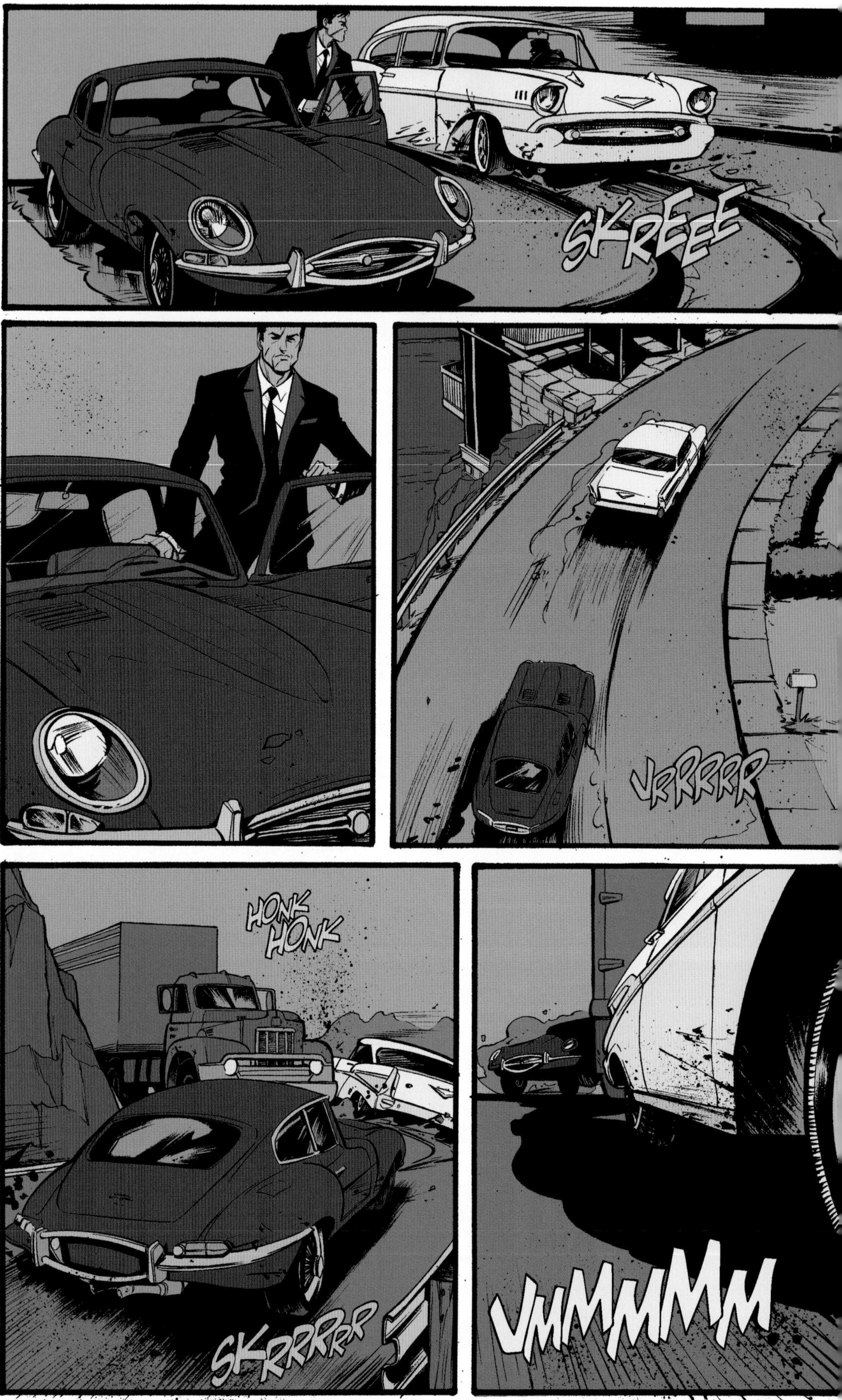
SKREEE
VRRRRR
HONK HONK
SKRRRRP
VMMMMM

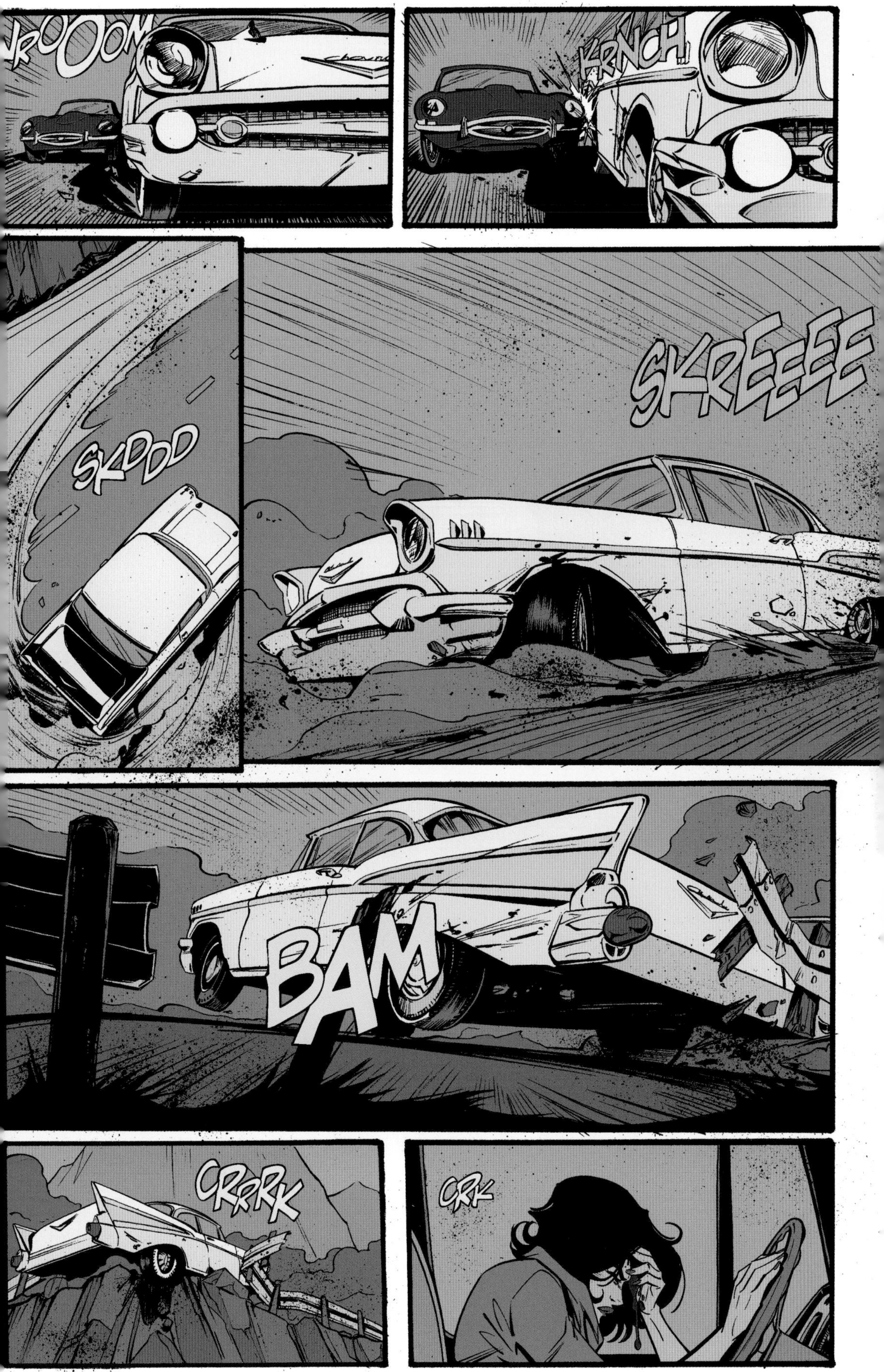
VROOOOM
KRNCH
SKDDD
SKREEEEE
BAM
CRRRK
CRK

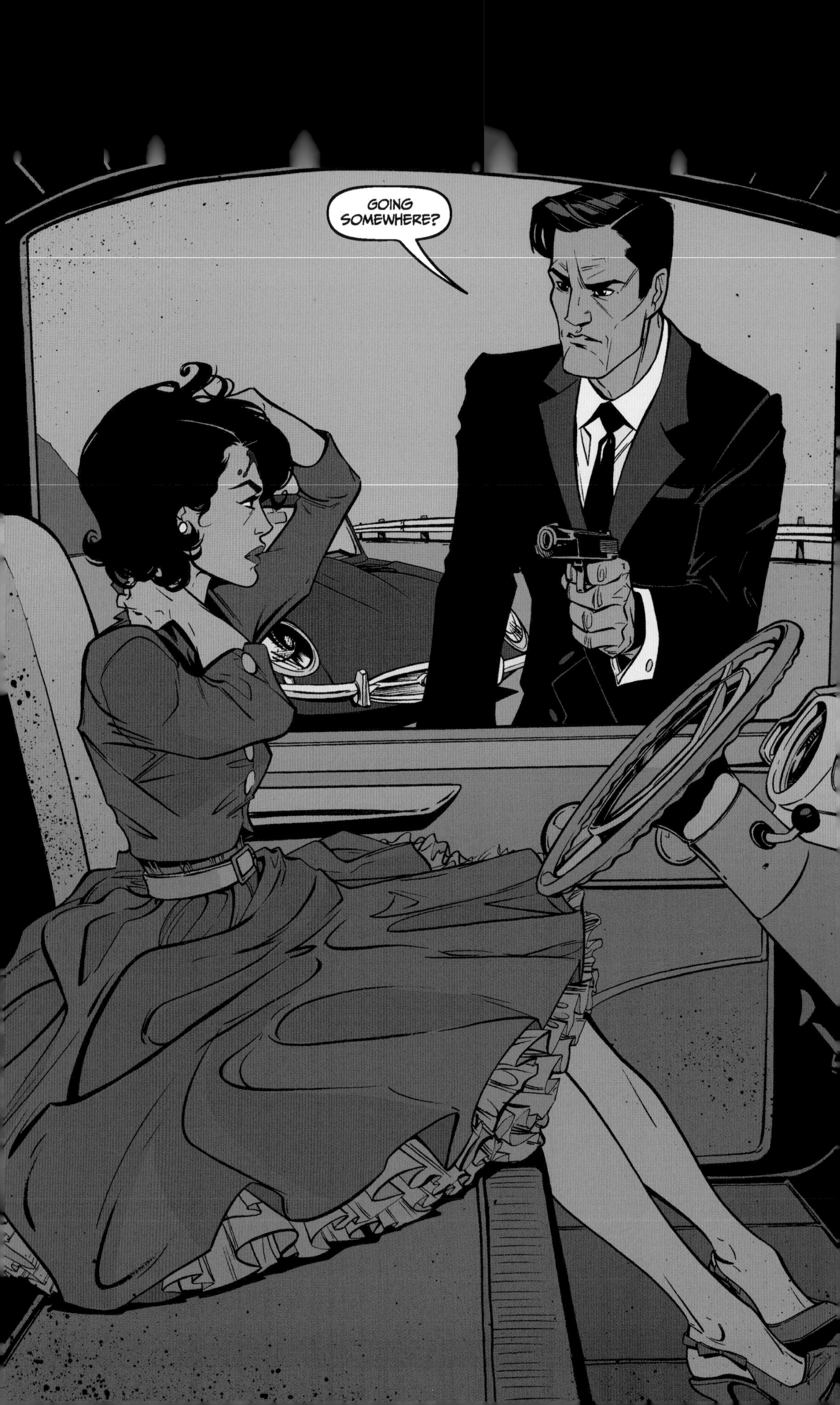
GOING SOMEWHERE?

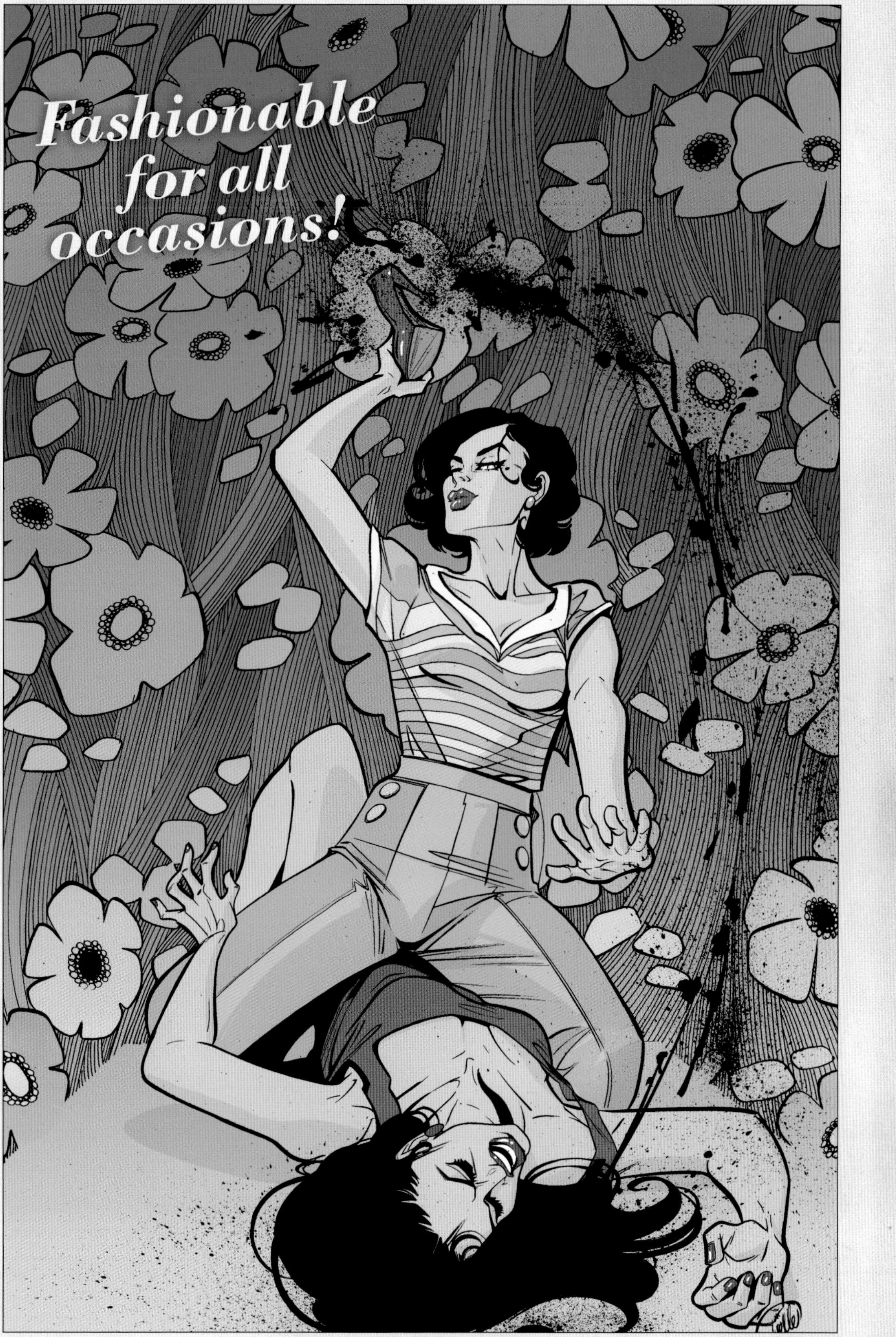
Fashionable for all occasions!

CHAPTER FOUR

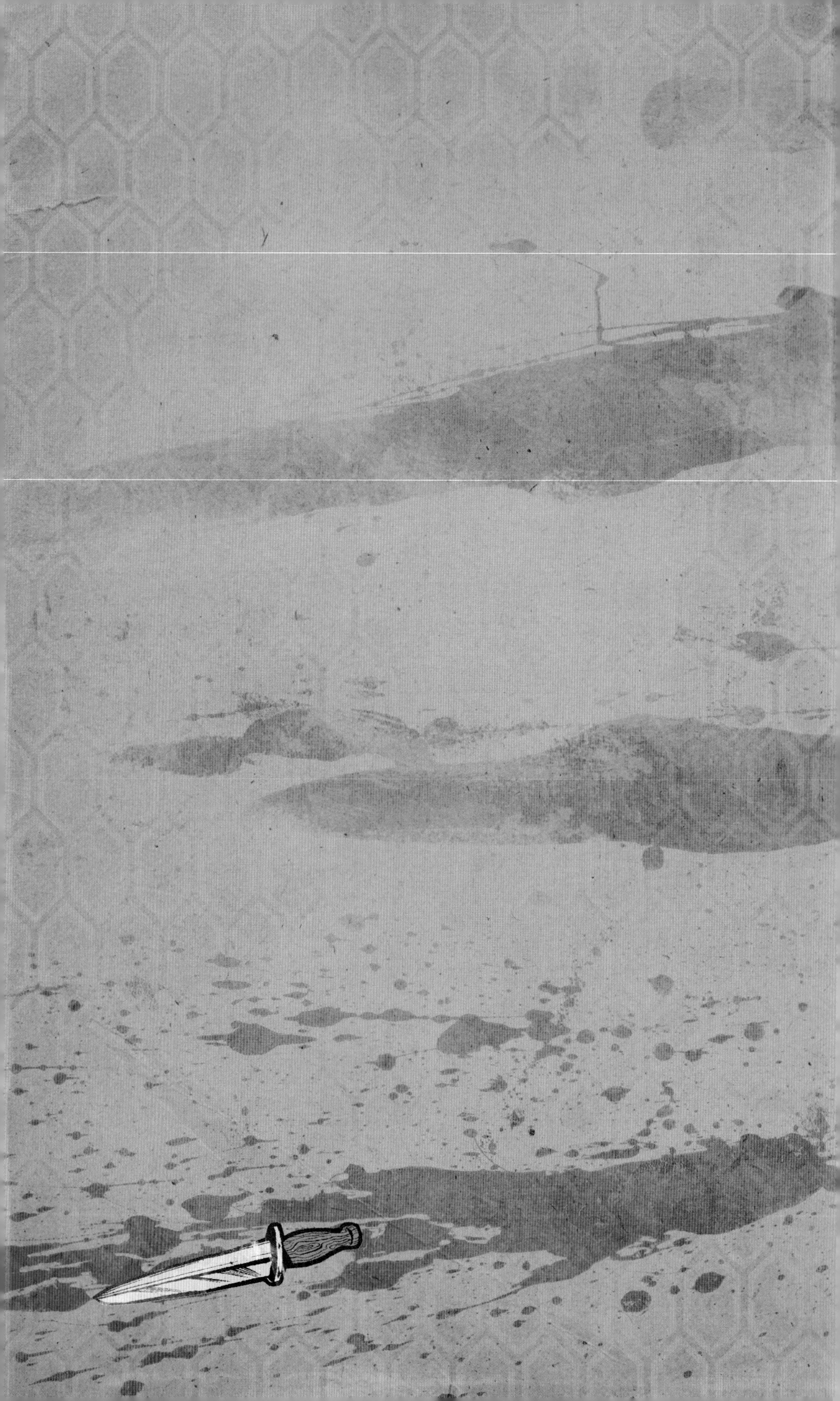

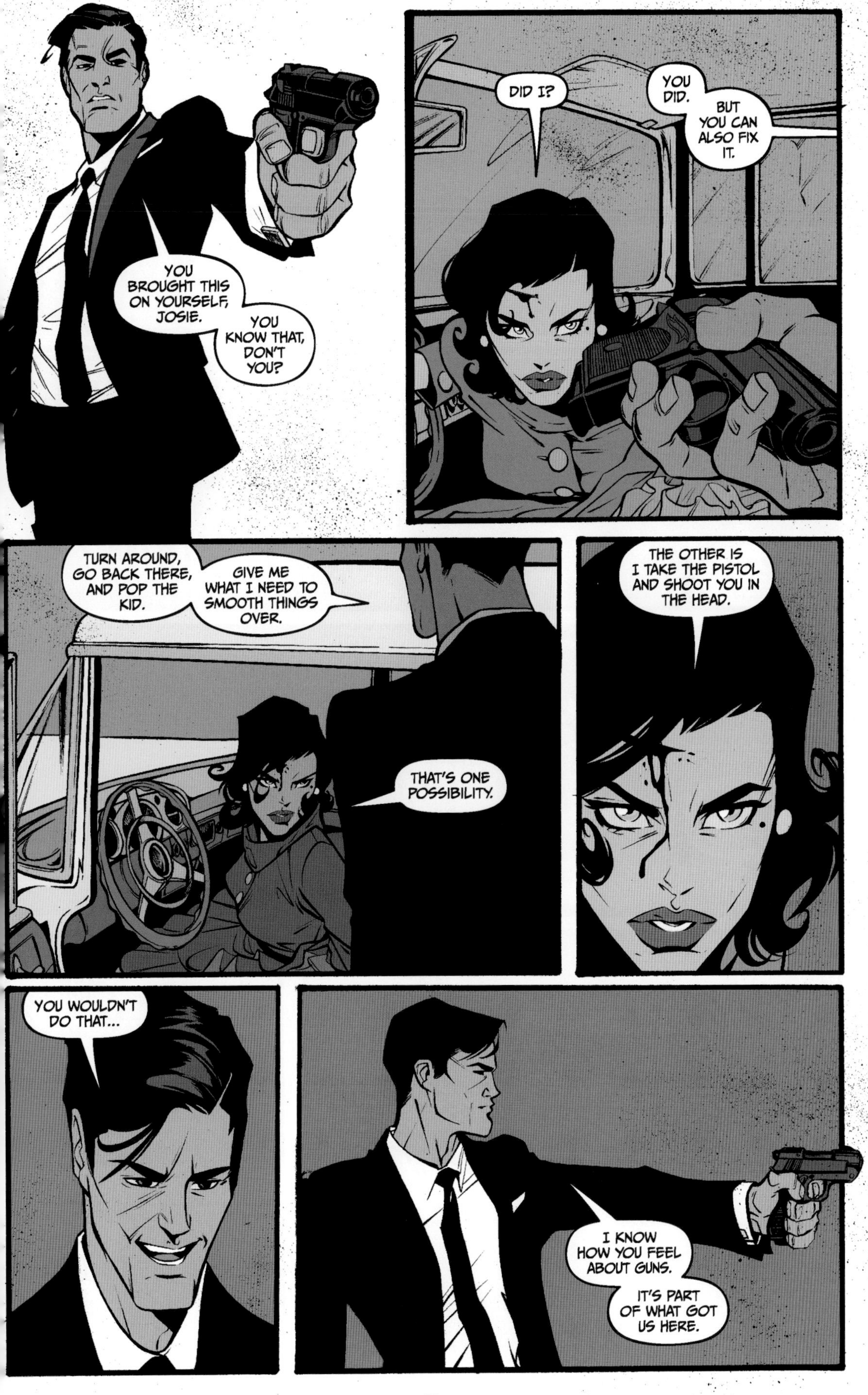

YOU BROUGHT THIS ON YOURSELF, JOSIE.
YOU KNOW THAT, DON'T YOU?
DID I?
YOU DID.
BUT YOU CAN ALSO FIX IT.
TURN AROUND, GO BACK THERE, AND POP THE KID.
GIVE ME WHAT I NEED TO SMOOTH THINGS OVER.
THAT'S ONE POSSIBILITY.
THE OTHER IS I TAKE THE PISTOL AND SHOOT YOU IN THE HEAD.
YOU WOULDN'T DO THAT...
I KNOW HOW YOU FEEL ABOUT GUNS.
IT'S PART OF WHAT GOT US HERE.

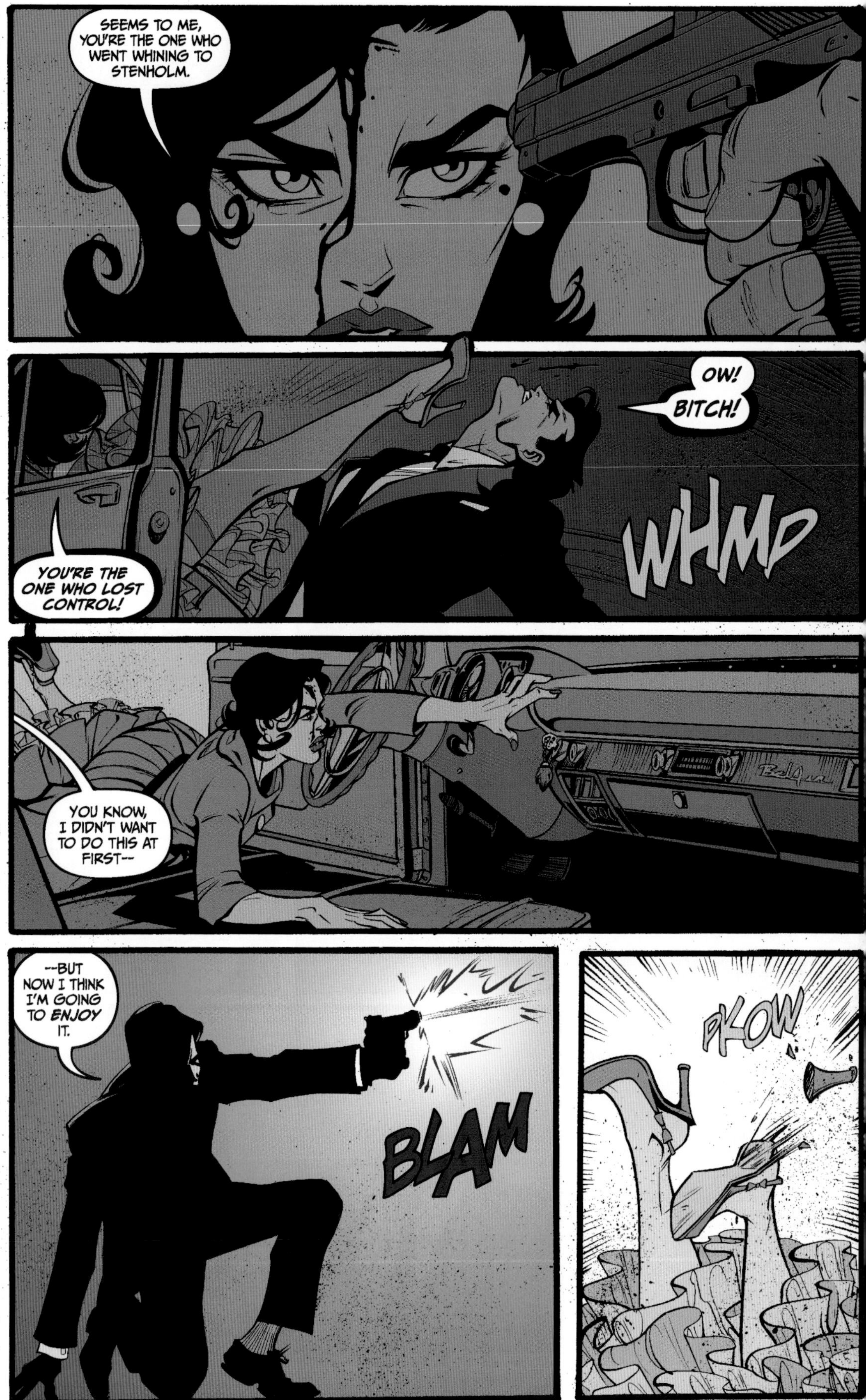
SEEMS TO ME, YOU'RE THE ONE WHO WENT WHINING TO STENHOLM.
OW! BITCH!
WHMP
YOU'RE THE ONE WHO LOST CONTROL!
YOU KNOW, I DIDN'T WANT TO DO THIS AT FIRST--
--BUT NOW I THINK I'M GOING TO *ENJOY* IT.
BLAM
PKOW

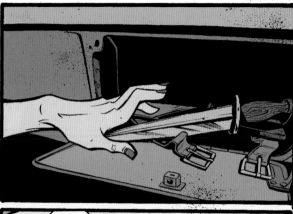

GOOD IDEA.

BETTER TO KILL YOU IN THE CAR.

MAKE IT LOOK LIKE A LOVER'S SPAT.

THE GAL WAS BEING A TEASE...

...AND GOT IN OVER HER HEAD.

DROP THE GUN AND GET OUT OF THE CAR!

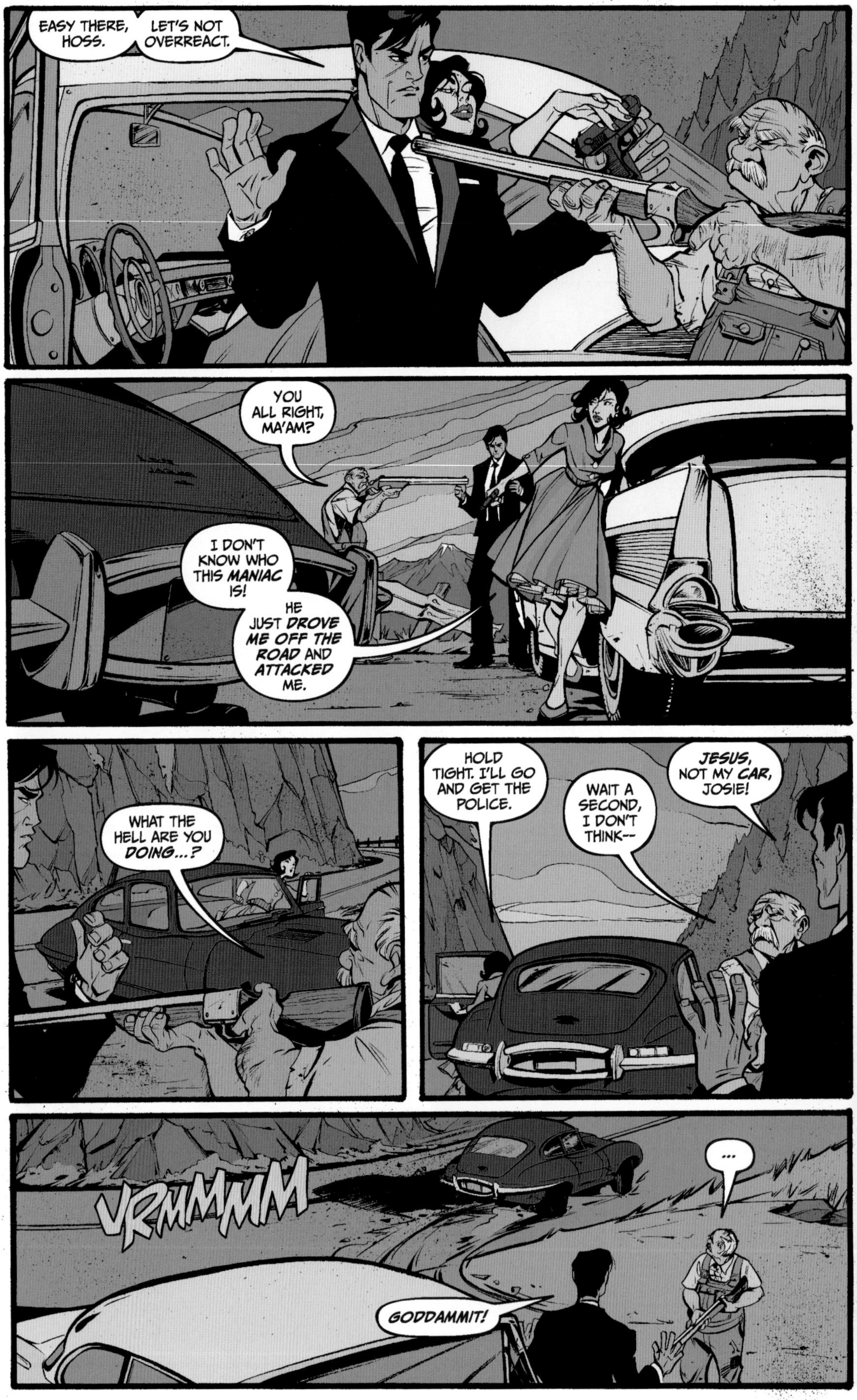
EASY THERE, HOSS.
LET'S NOT OVERREACT.
YOU ALL RIGHT, MA'AM?
I DON'T KNOW WHO THIS MANIAC IS!
HE JUST DROVE ME OFF THE ROAD AND ATTACKED ME.
WHAT THE HELL ARE YOU DOING...?
HOLD TIGHT. I'LL GO AND GET THE POLICE.
WAIT A SECOND, I DON'T THINK--
JESUS, NOT MY CAR, JOSIE!
VRMMMM
...
GODDAMMIT!

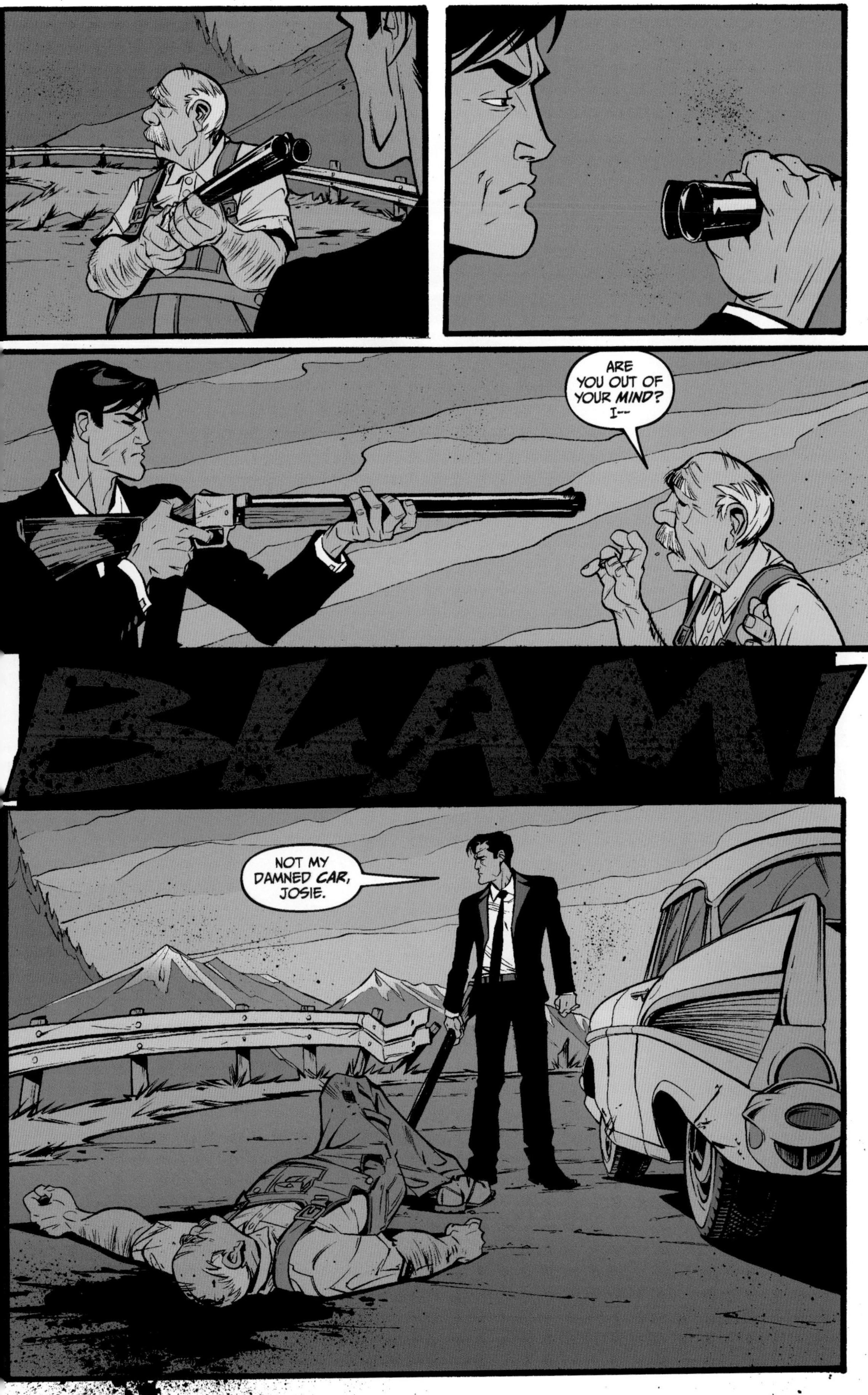
ARE YOU OUT OF YOUR *MIND*? I--
BLAM!
NOT MY DAMNED *CAR*, JOSIE.

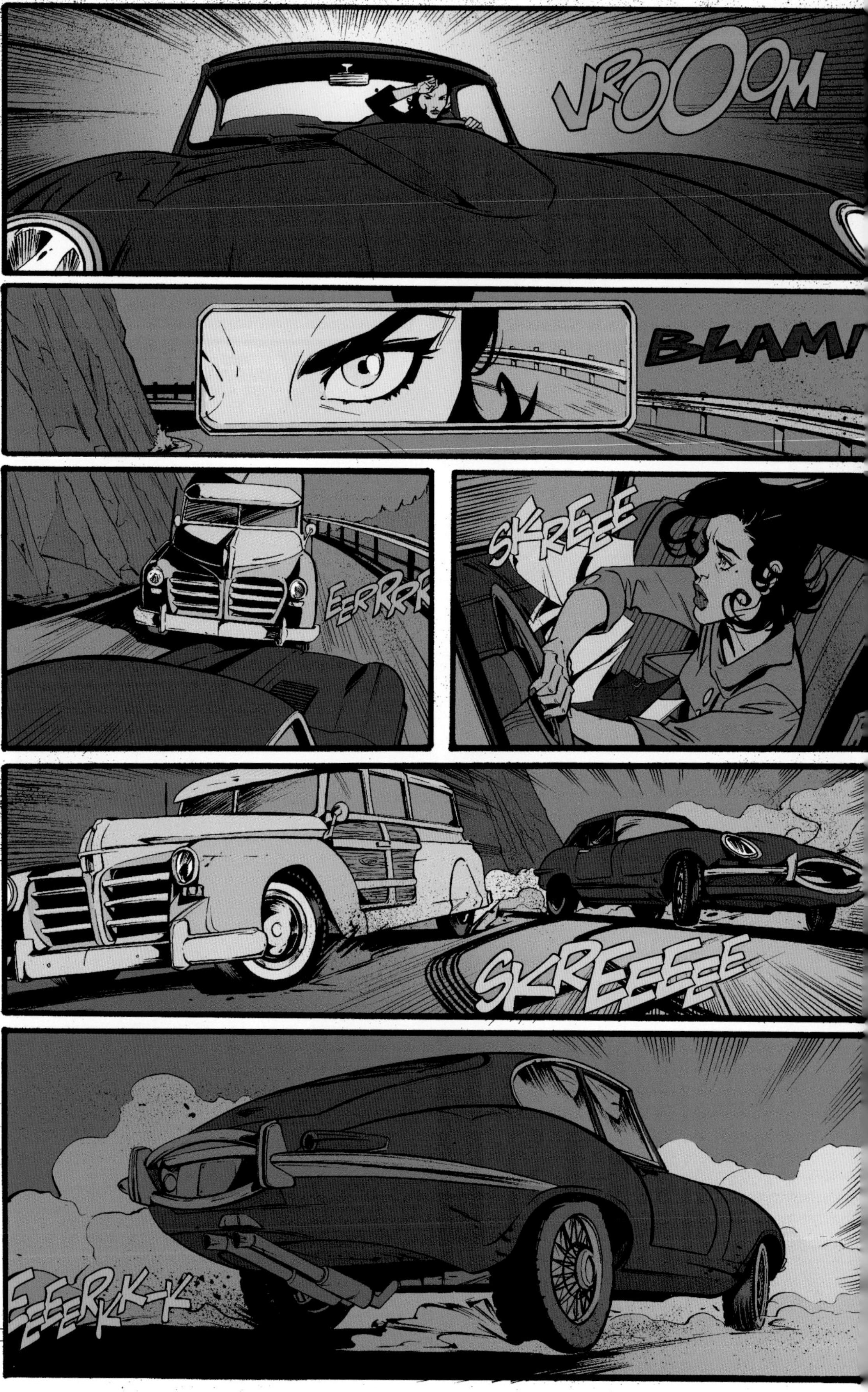
VROOOOM
BLAM!
EERRRK
SKREEE
SKREEEEEE
EEEERKK-K

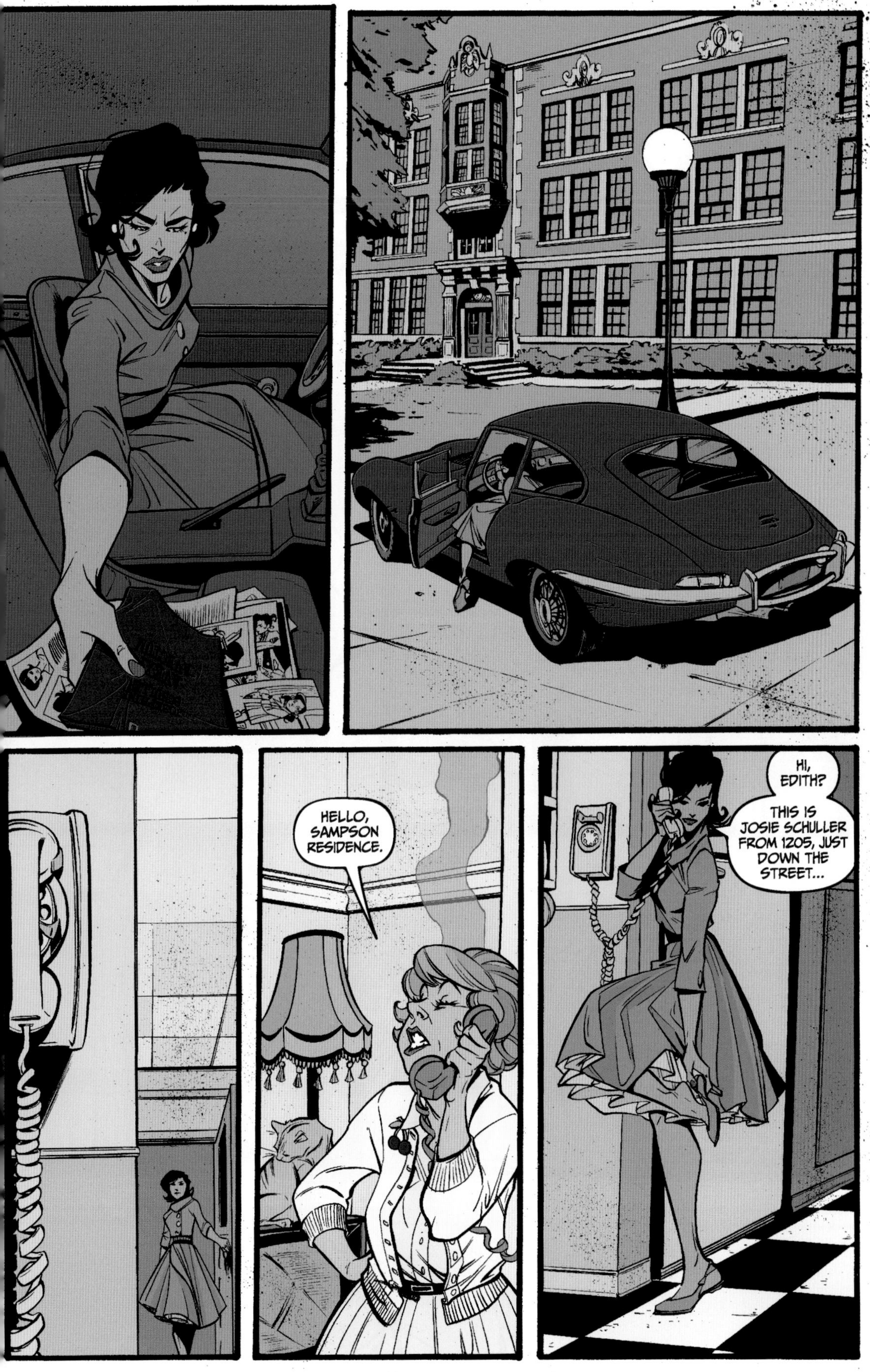
HELLO, SAMPSON RESIDENCE.
HI, EDITH?
THIS IS JOSIE SCHULLER FROM 1205, JUST DOWN THE STREET...

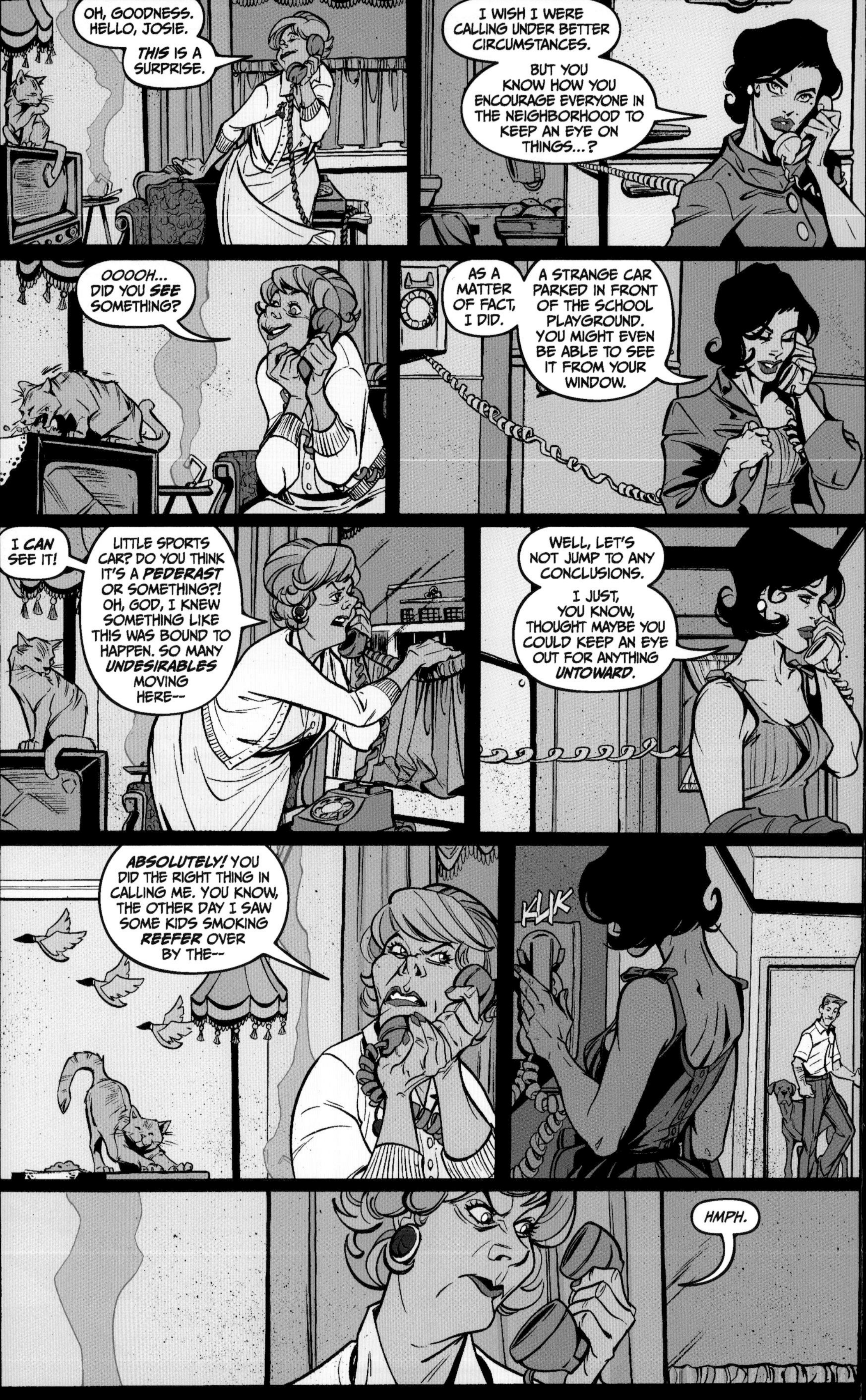
OH, GOODNESS. HELLO, JOSIE. *THIS* IS A SURPRISE.
I WISH I WERE CALLING UNDER BETTER CIRCUMSTANCES.
BUT YOU KNOW HOW YOU ENCOURAGE EVERYONE IN THE NEIGHBORHOOD TO KEEP AN EYE ON THINGS...?
OOOOH... DID YOU *SEE* SOMETHING?
AS A MATTER OF FACT, I DID.
A STRANGE CAR PARKED IN FRONT OF THE SCHOOL PLAYGROUND. YOU MIGHT EVEN BE ABLE TO SEE IT FROM YOUR WINDOW.
I *CAN* SEE IT!
LITTLE SPORTS CAR? DO YOU THINK IT'S A *PEDERAST* OR SOMETHING?! OH, GOD, I KNEW SOMETHING LIKE THIS WAS BOUND TO HAPPEN. SO MANY *UNDESIRABLES* MOVING HERE--
WELL, LET'S NOT JUMP TO ANY CONCLUSIONS.
I JUST, YOU KNOW, THOUGHT MAYBE YOU COULD KEEP AN EYE OUT FOR ANYTHING *UNTOWARD*.
ABSOLUTELY! YOU DID THE RIGHT THING IN CALLING ME. YOU KNOW, THE OTHER DAY I SAW SOME KIDS SMOKING *REEFER* OVER BY THE--
KLIK
HMPH.

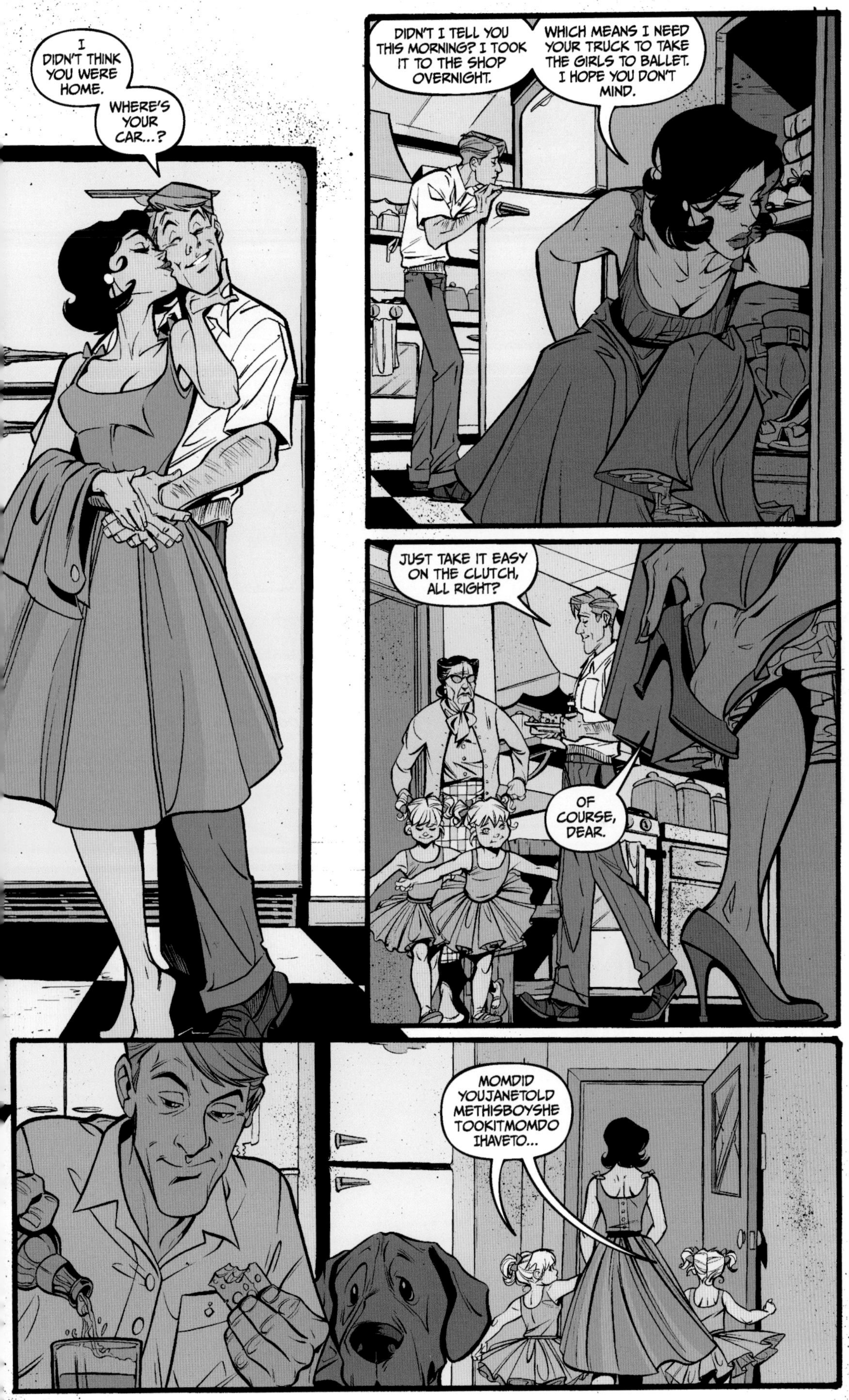
I DIDN'T THINK YOU WERE HOME.
WHERE'S YOUR CAR...?
DIDN'T I TELL YOU THIS MORNING? I TOOK IT TO THE SHOP OVERNIGHT.
WHICH MEANS I NEED YOUR TRUCK TO TAKE THE GIRLS TO BALLET. I HOPE YOU DON'T MIND.
JUST TAKE IT EASY ON THE CLUTCH, ALL RIGHT?
OF COURSE, DEAR.
MOMDID YOUJANETOLD METHISBOYSHE TOOKITMOMDO IHAVETO...

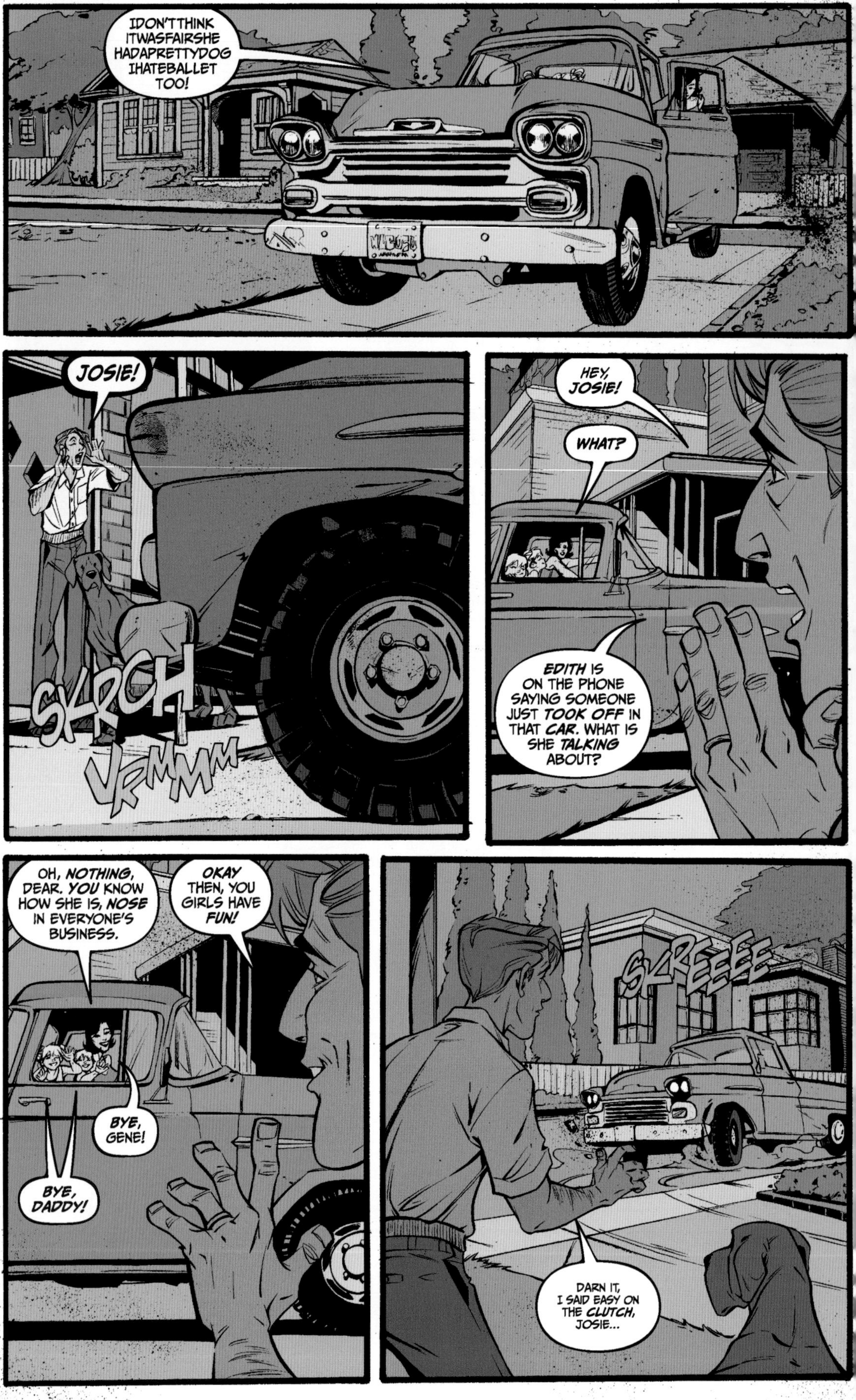
IDON'TTHINK ITWASFAIRSHE HADAPRETTYDOG IHATEBALLET TOO!
JOSIE!
SKRCH
VRMMMM
HEY, JOSIE!
WHAT?
EDITH IS ON THE PHONE SAYING SOMEONE JUST TOOK OFF IN THAT CAR. WHAT IS SHE TALKING ABOUT?
OH, NOTHING, DEAR. YOU KNOW HOW SHE IS, NOSE IN EVERYONE'S BUSINESS.
OKAY THEN, YOU GIRLS HAVE FUN!
BYE, GENE!
BYE, DADDY!
SKREEEE
DARN IT, I SAID EASY ON THE CLUTCH, JOSIE...

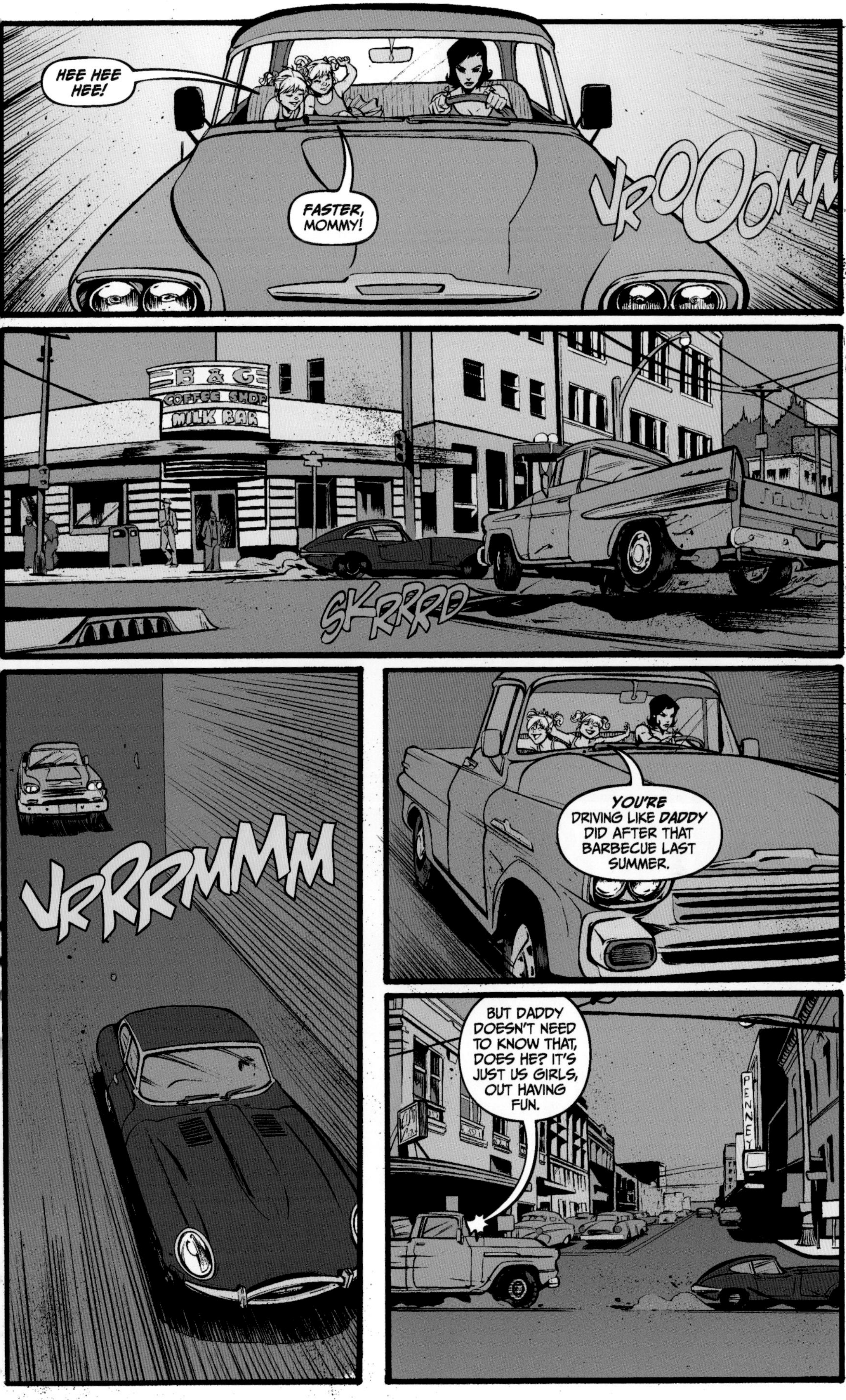
HEE HEE HEE!
FASTER, MOMMY!
VROOOOMMM
B & G
COFFEE SHOP
MILK BAR
SKRRRD
VRRRMMM
YOU'RE DRIVING LIKE DADDY DID AFTER THAT BARBECUE LAST SUMMER.
BUT DADDY DOESN'T NEED TO KNOW THAT, DOES HE? IT'S JUST US GIRLS, OUT HAVING FUN.
PENNEY

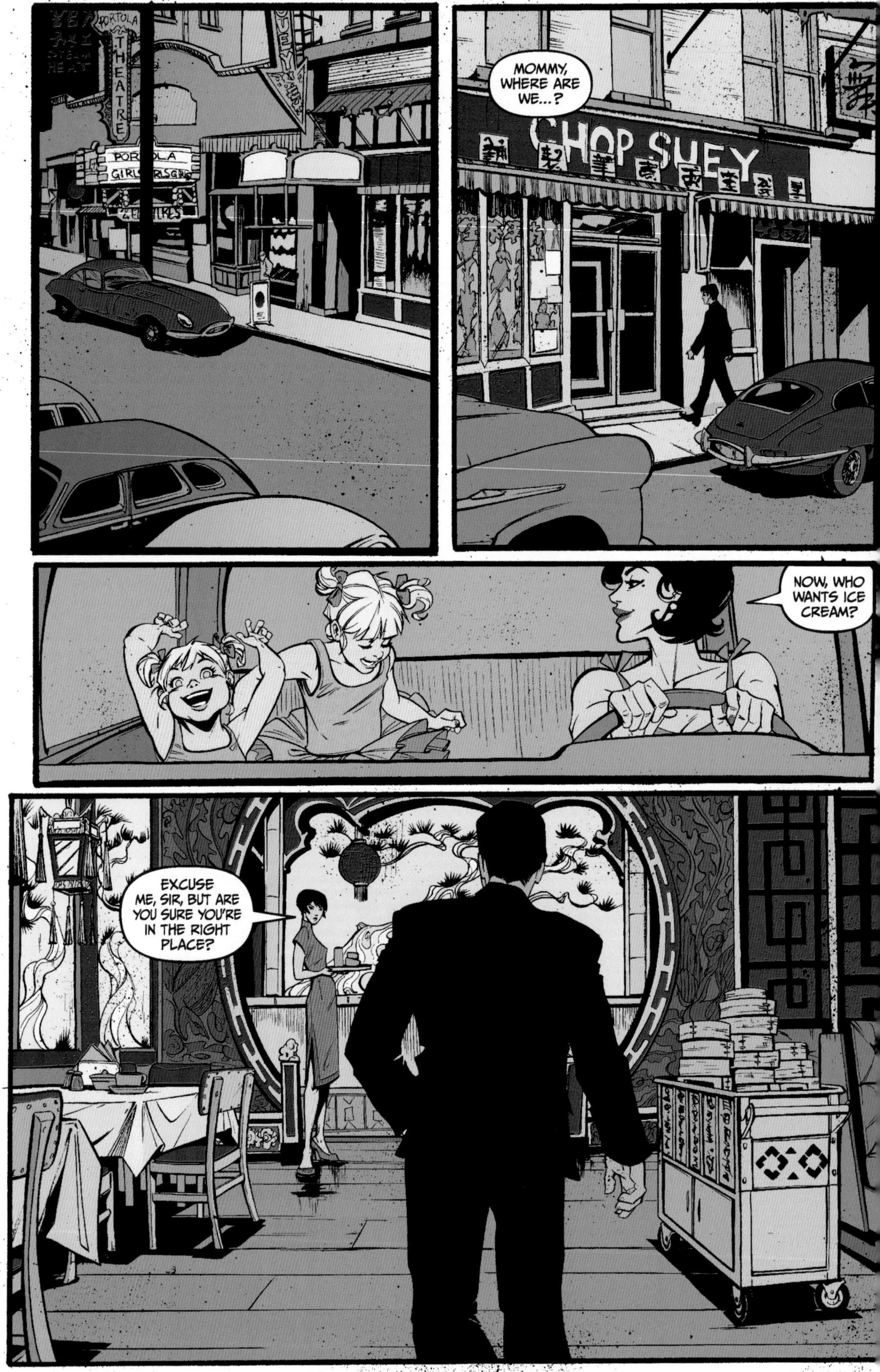
PORTOLA THEATRE
PORTOLA
GIRLS GIRLS GIRLS
SUEY
MOMMY, WHERE ARE WE...?
CHOP SUEY
NOW, WHO WANTS ICE CREAM?
EXCUSE ME, SIR, BUT ARE YOU SURE YOU'RE IN THE RIGHT PLACE?

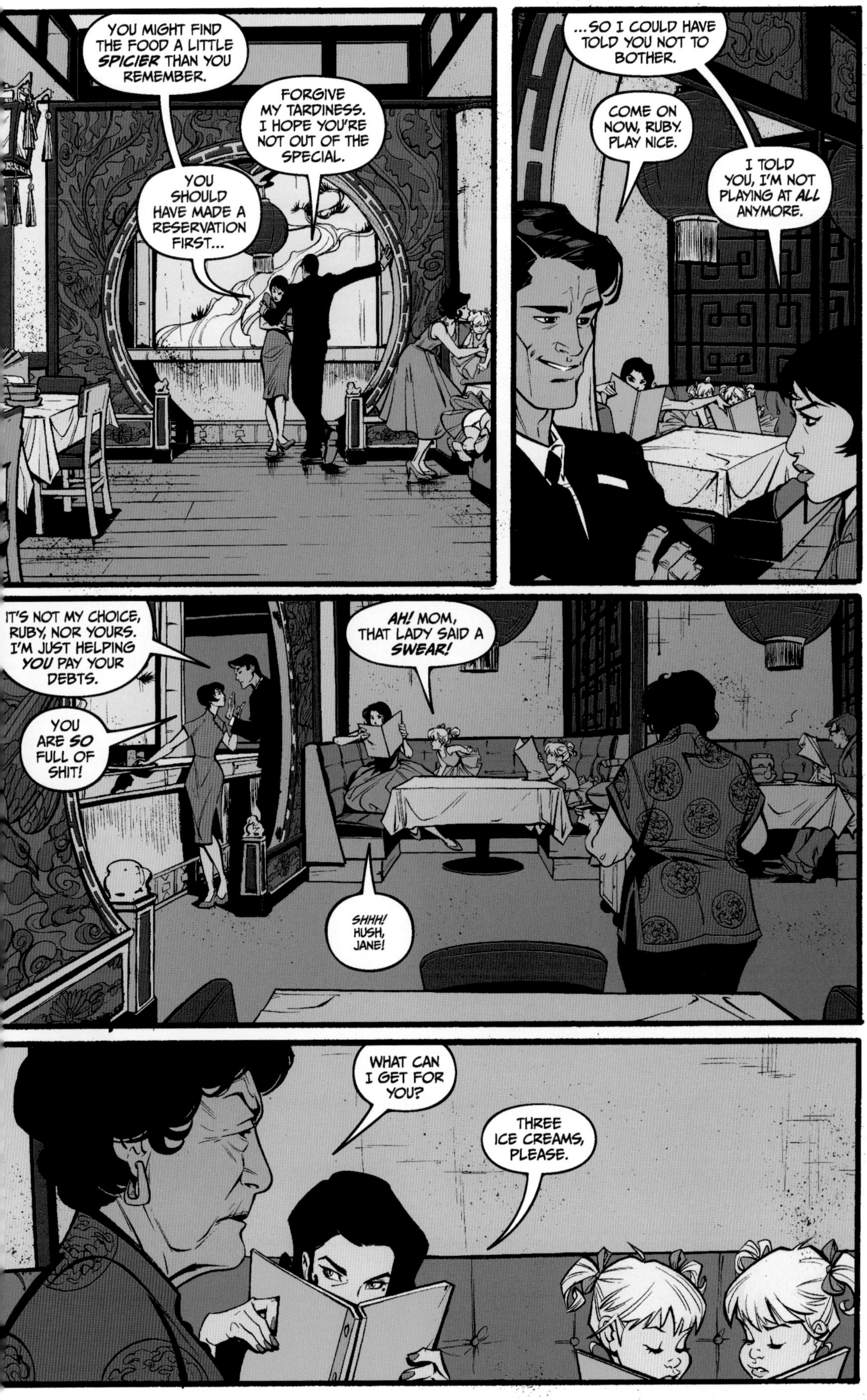

YOU MIGHT FIND THE FOOD A LITTLE SPICIER THAN YOU REMEMBER.
FORGIVE MY TARDINESS. I HOPE YOU'RE NOT OUT OF THE SPECIAL.
YOU SHOULD HAVE MADE A RESERVATION FIRST...
...SO I COULD HAVE TOLD YOU NOT TO BOTHER.
COME ON NOW, RUBY. PLAY NICE.
I TOLD YOU, I'M NOT PLAYING AT ALL ANYMORE.
IT'S NOT MY CHOICE, RUBY, NOR YOURS. I'M JUST HELPING YOU PAY YOUR DEBTS.
YOU ARE SO FULL OF SHIT!
AH! MOM, THAT LADY SAID A SWEAR!
SHHH! HUSH, JANE!
WHAT CAN I GET FOR YOU?
THREE ICE CREAMS, PLEASE.

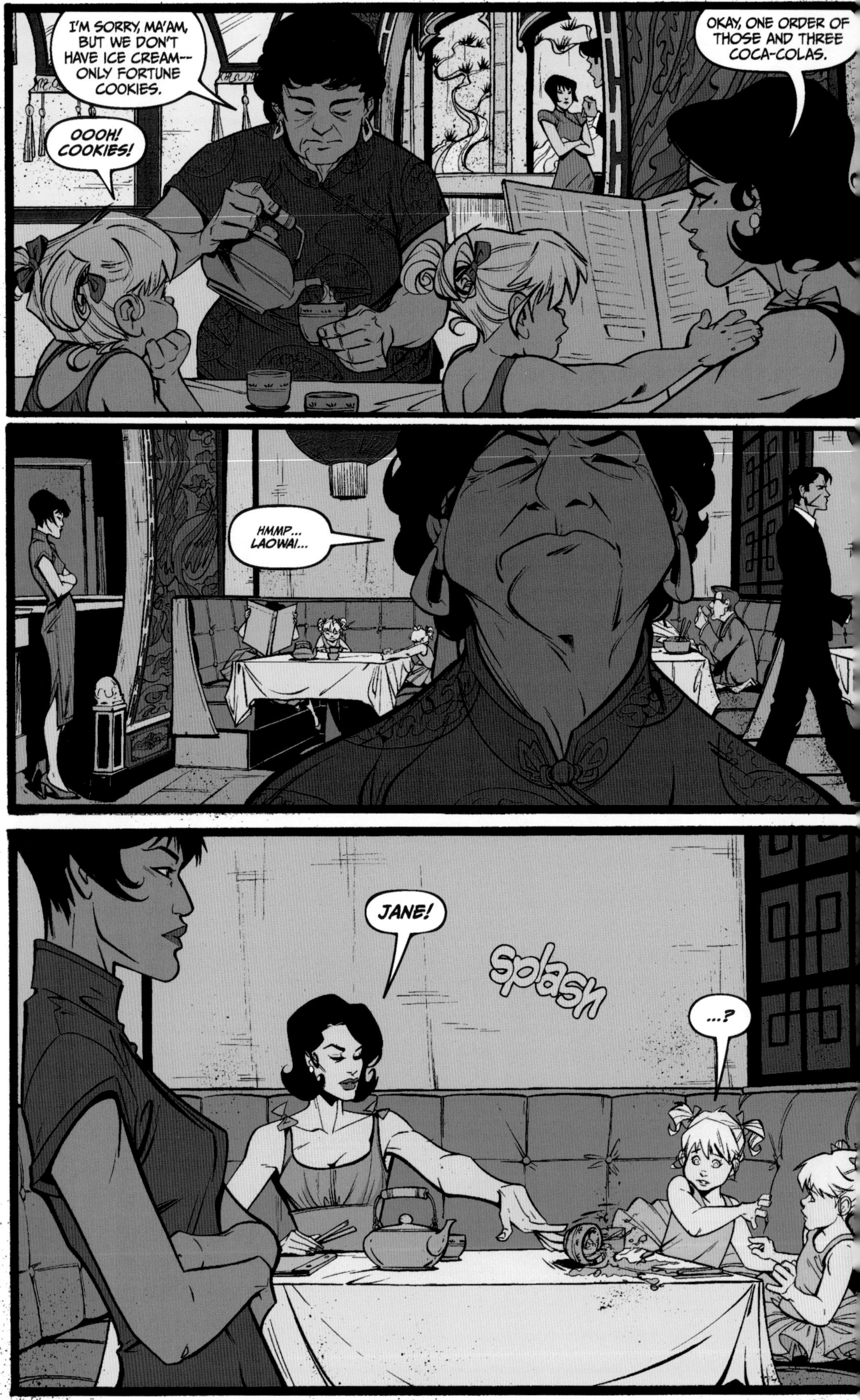
I'M SORRY, MA'AM, BUT WE DON'T HAVE ICE CREAM--ONLY FORTUNE COOKIES.
OOOH! COOKIES!
OKAY, ONE ORDER OF THOSE AND THREE COCA-COLAS.
HMMP... LAOWAI...
JANE!
splash
...?

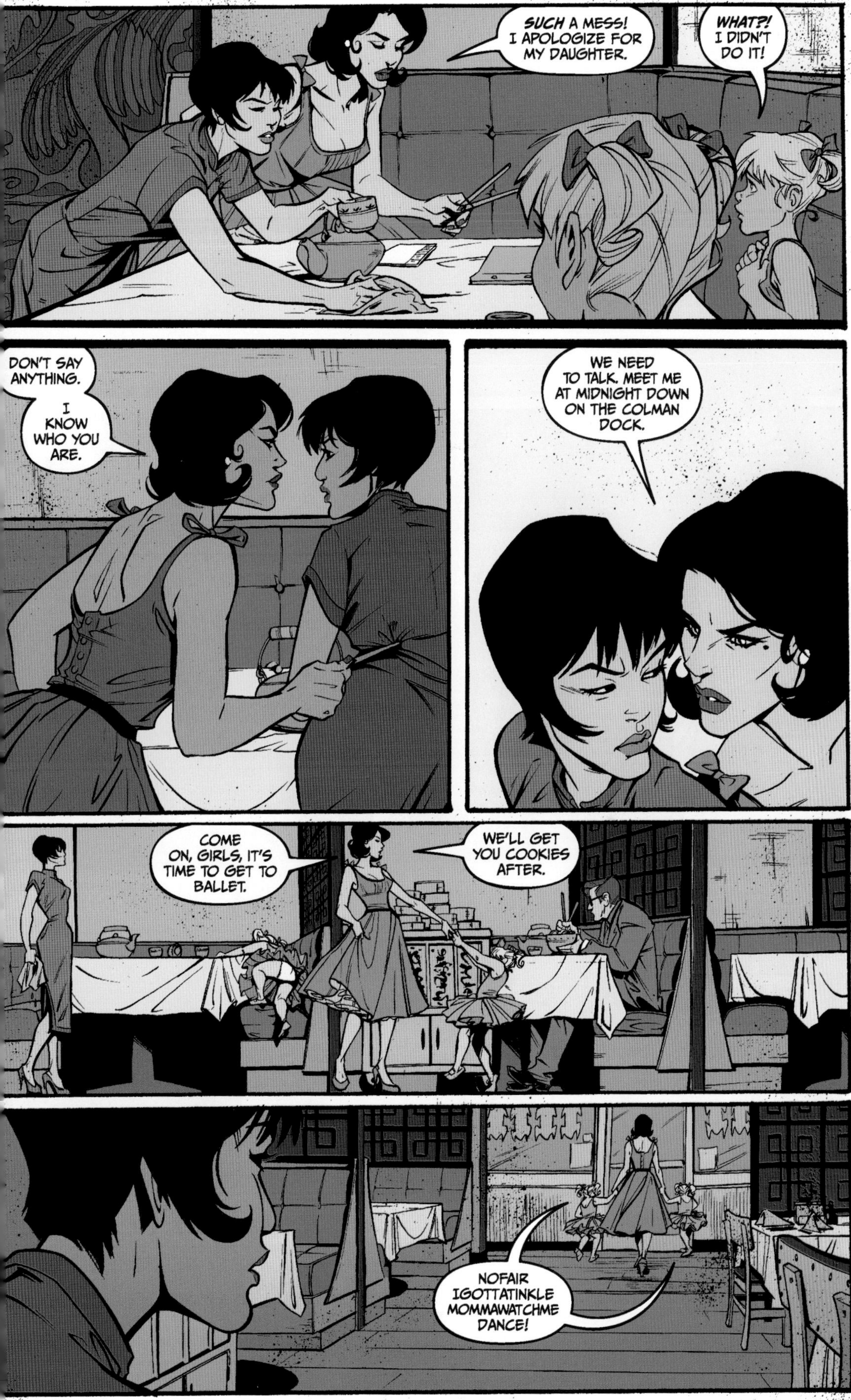
SUCH A MESS! I APOLOGIZE FOR MY DAUGHTER.
WHAT?! I DIDN'T DO IT!
DON'T SAY ANYTHING.
I KNOW WHO YOU ARE.
WE NEED TO TALK. MEET ME AT MIDNIGHT DOWN ON THE COLMAN DOCK.
COME ON, GIRLS, IT'S TIME TO GET TO BALLET.
WE'LL GET YOU COOKIES AFTER.
NOFAIR IGOTTATINKLE MOMMAWATCHME DANCE!

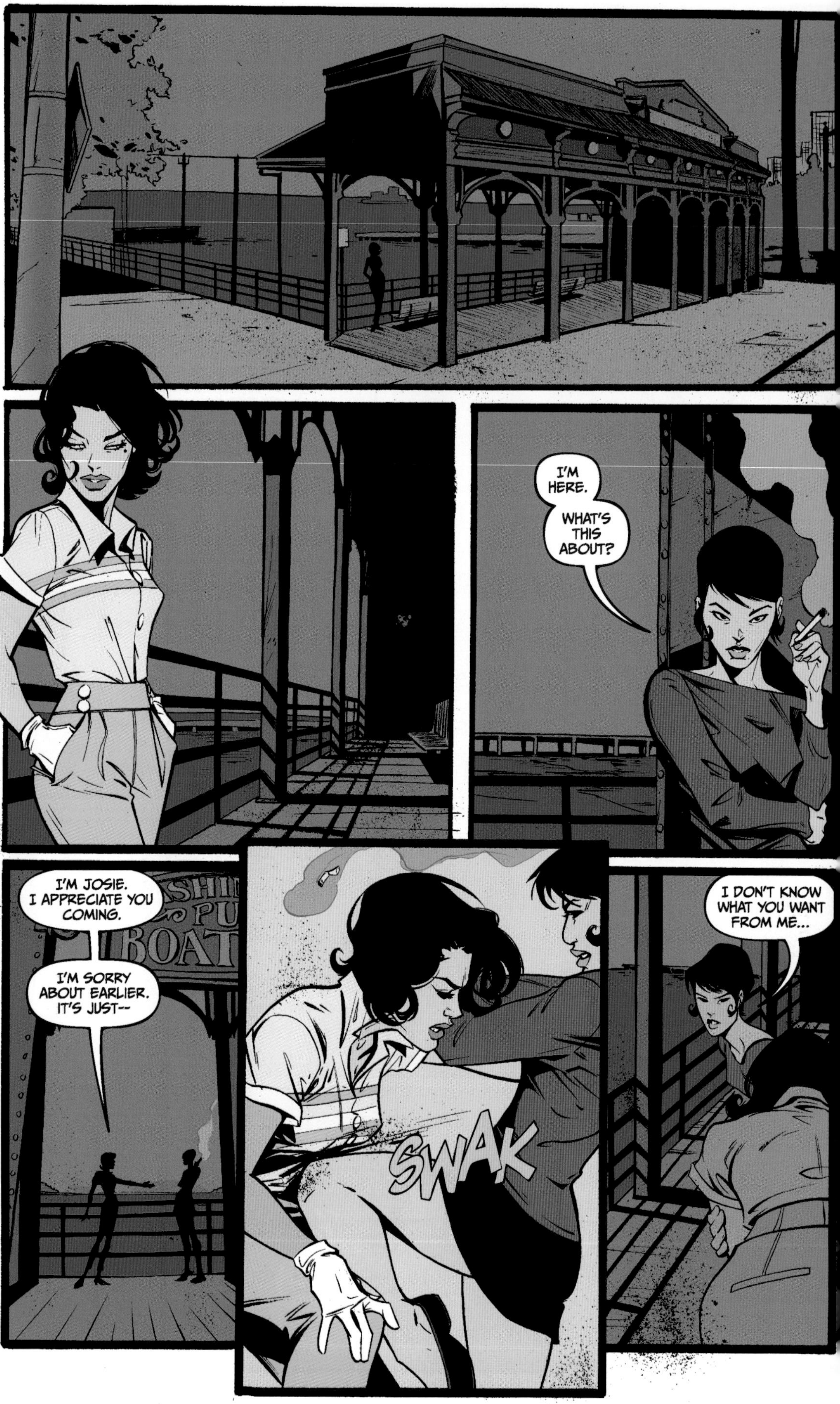
I'M HERE.
WHAT'S THIS ABOUT?
SHI PU BOAT
I'M JOSIE. I APPRECIATE YOU COMING.
I'M SORRY ABOUT EARLIER. IT'S JUST--
SWAK
I DON'T KNOW WHAT YOU WANT FROM ME...

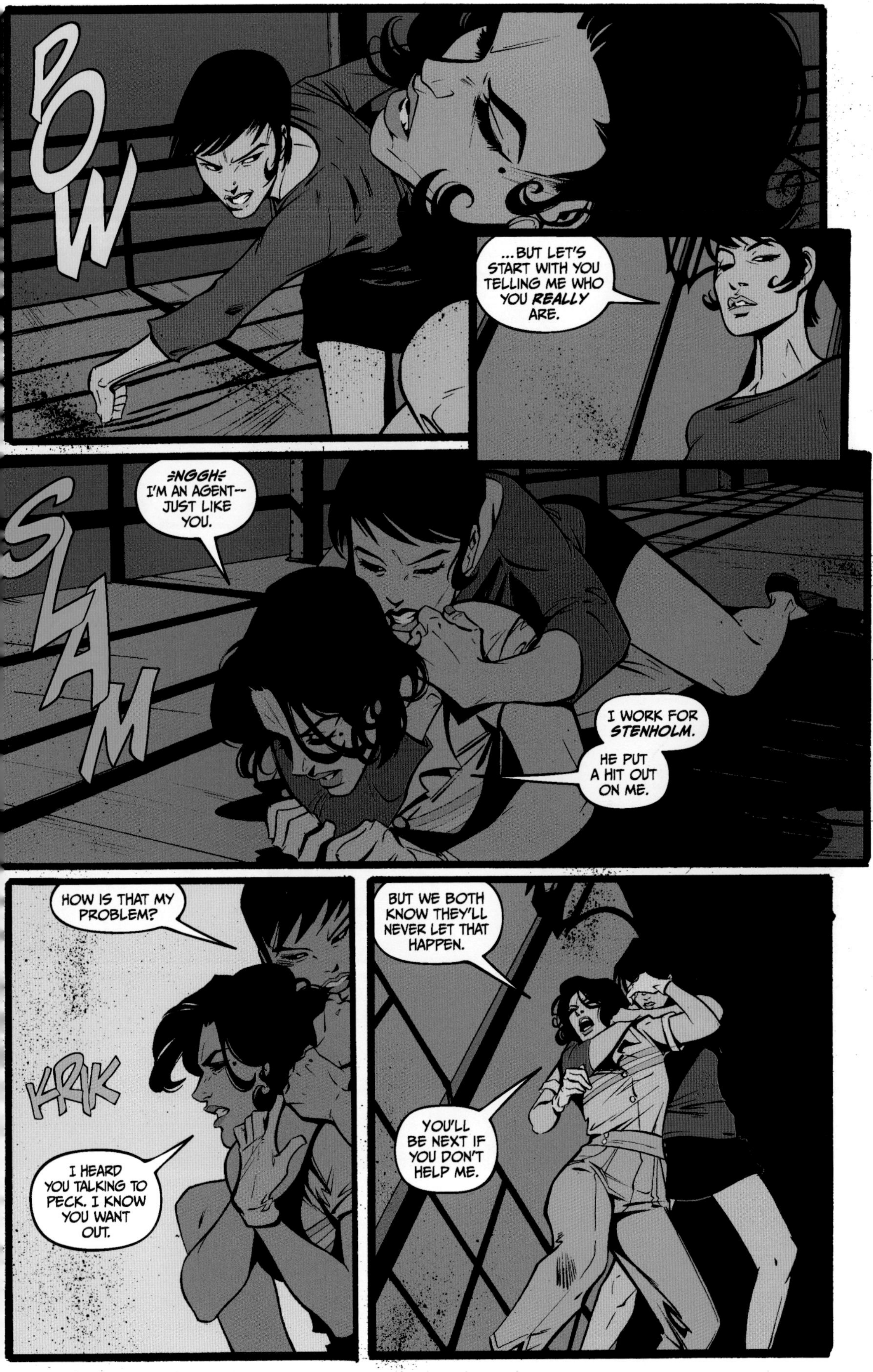
POW
...BUT LET'S START WITH YOU TELLING ME WHO YOU *REALLY* ARE.
SLAM
=NGGH= I'M AN AGENT-- JUST LIKE YOU.
I WORK FOR **STENHOLM**.
HE PUT A HIT OUT ON ME.
HOW IS THAT MY PROBLEM?
KRIK
I HEARD YOU TALKING TO PECK. I KNOW YOU WANT OUT.
BUT WE BOTH KNOW THEY'LL NEVER LET THAT HAPPEN.
YOU'LL BE NEXT IF YOU DON'T HELP ME.

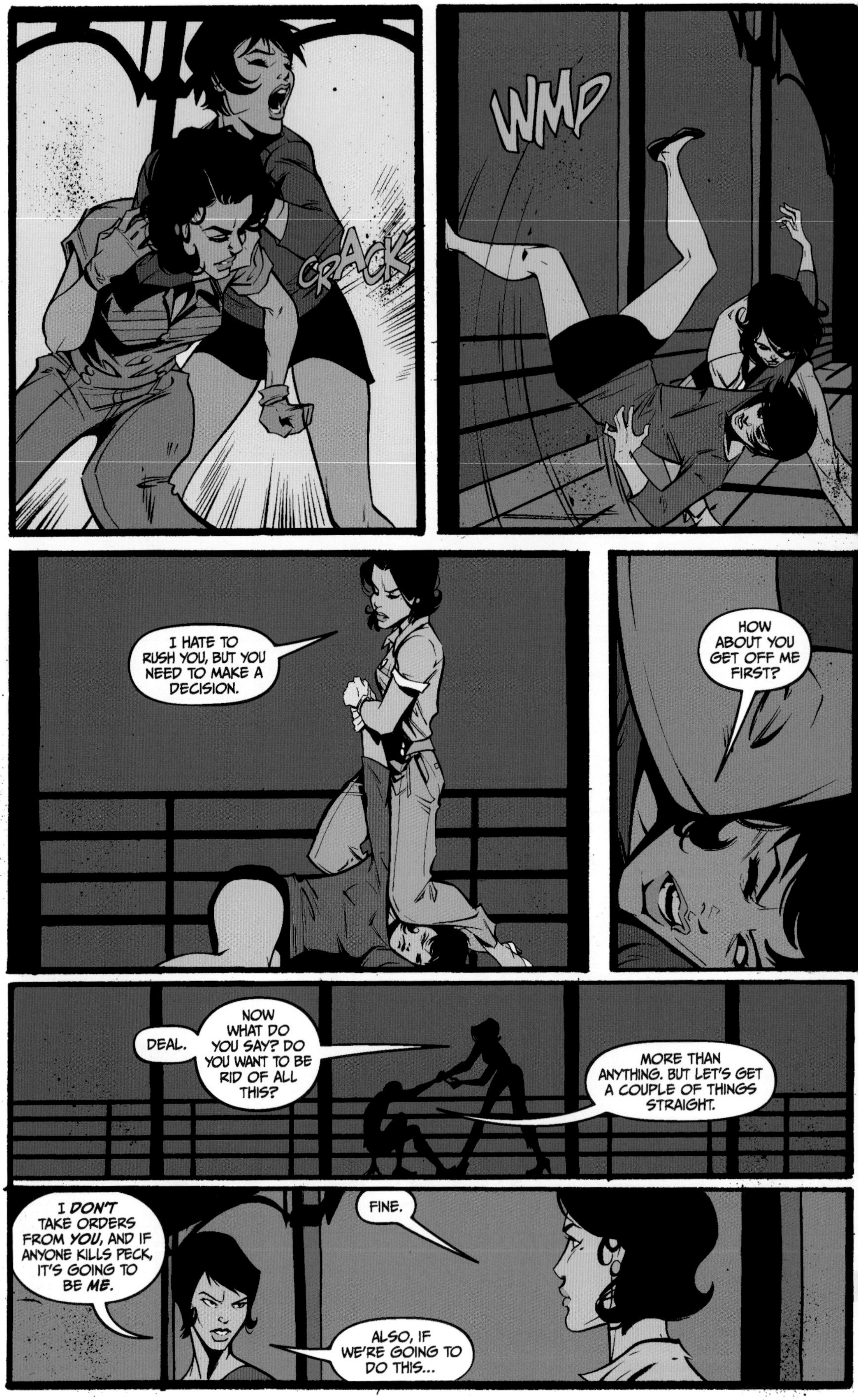
CRACK
WMP
I HATE TO RUSH YOU, BUT YOU NEED TO MAKE A DECISION.
HOW ABOUT YOU GET OFF ME FIRST?
DEAL.
NOW WHAT DO YOU SAY? DO YOU WANT TO BE RID OF ALL THIS?
MORE THAN ANYTHING. BUT LET'S GET A COUPLE OF THINGS STRAIGHT.
I DON'T TAKE ORDERS FROM YOU, AND IF ANYONE KILLS PECK, IT'S GOING TO BE ME.
FINE.
ALSO, IF WE'RE GOING TO DO THIS...

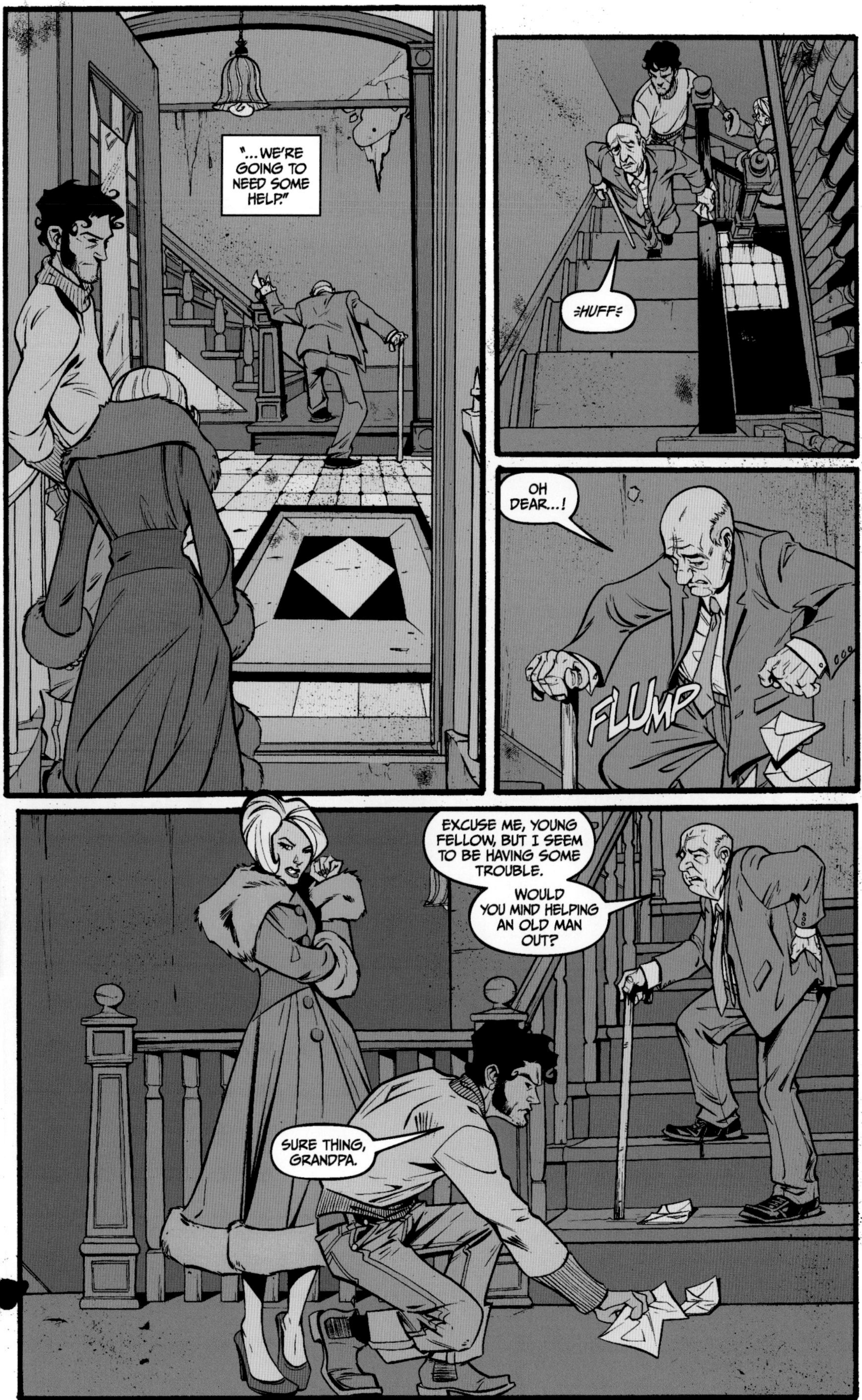
"...WE'RE GOING TO NEED SOME HELP."
HUFF
OH DEAR...!
FLUMP
EXCUSE ME, YOUNG FELLOW, BUT I SEEM TO BE HAVING SOME TROUBLE.
WOULD YOU MIND HELPING AN OLD MAN OUT?
SURE THING, GRANDPA.

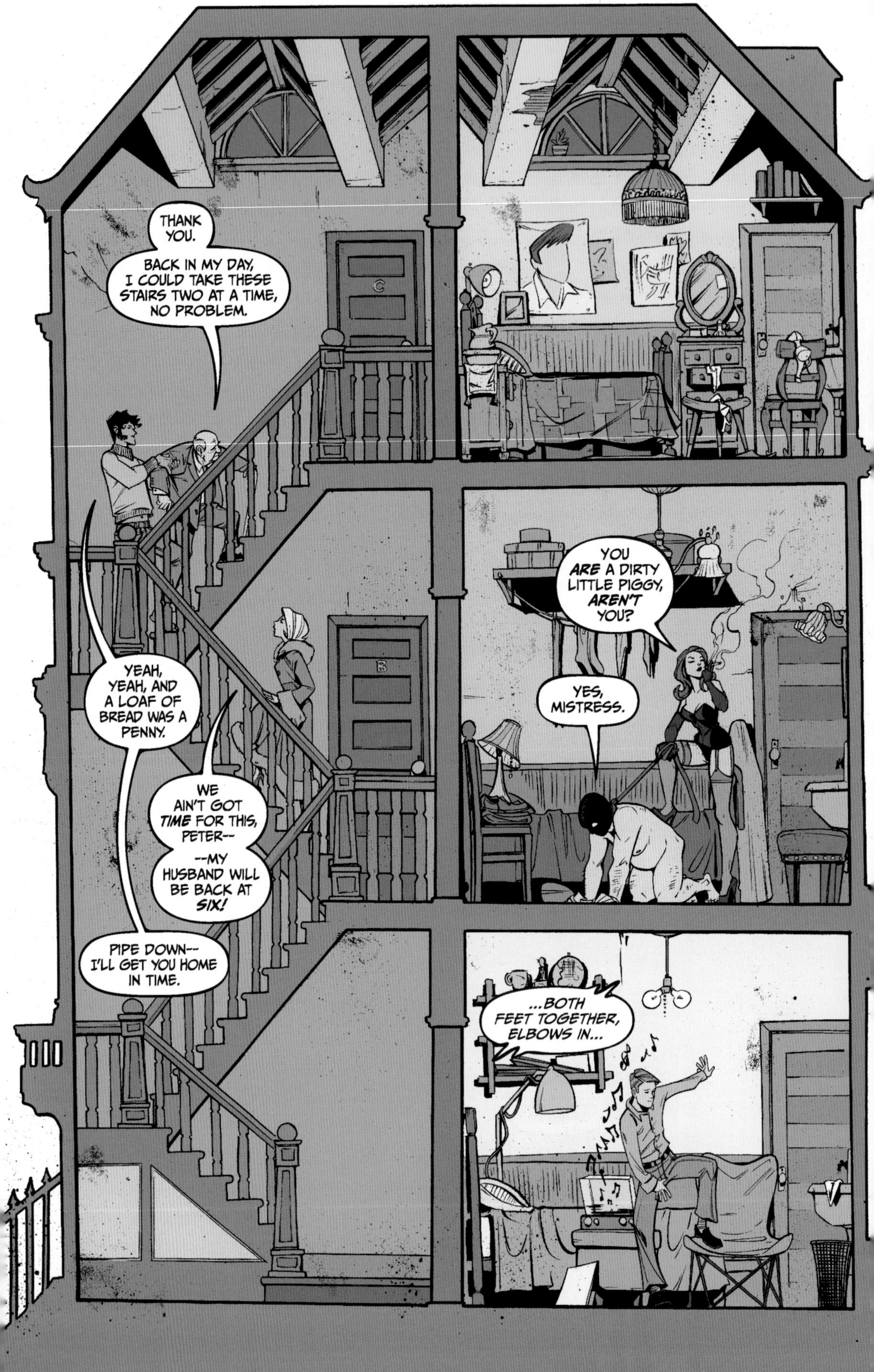
THANK YOU.
BACK IN MY DAY, I COULD TAKE THESE STAIRS TWO AT A TIME, NO PROBLEM.
YEAH, YEAH, AND A LOAF OF BREAD WAS A PENNY.
WE AIN'T GOT TIME FOR THIS, PETER--
--MY HUSBAND WILL BE BACK AT SIX!
PIPE DOWN-- I'LL GET YOU HOME IN TIME.
YOU ARE A DIRTY LITTLE PIGGY, AREN'T YOU?
YES, MISTRESS.
...BOTH FEET TOGETHER, ELBOWS IN...

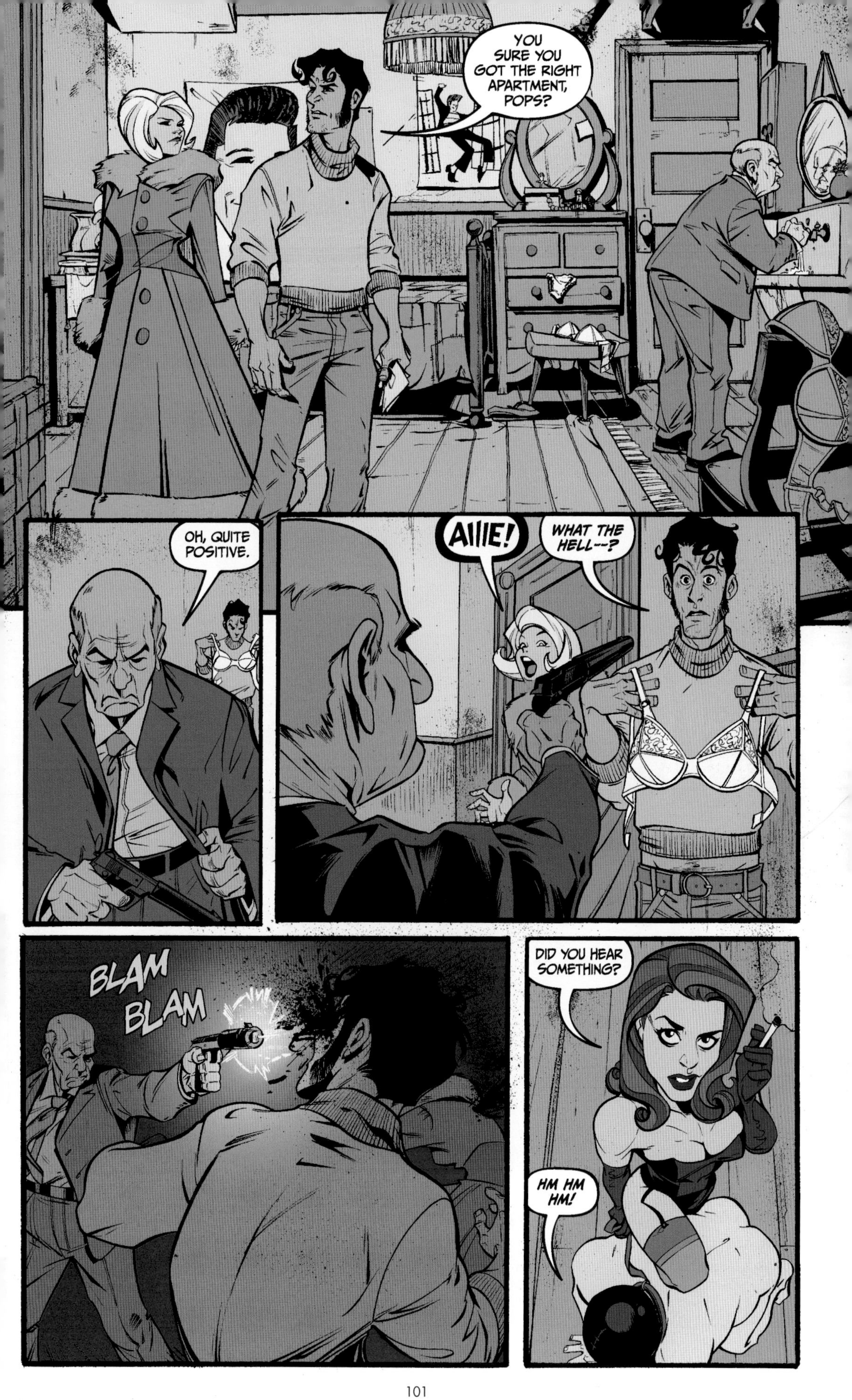
YOU SURE YOU GOT THE RIGHT APARTMENT, POPS?
OH, QUITE POSITIVE.
AIIIE!
WHAT THE HELL--?
BLAM BLAM
DID YOU HEAR SOMETHING?
HM HM HM!

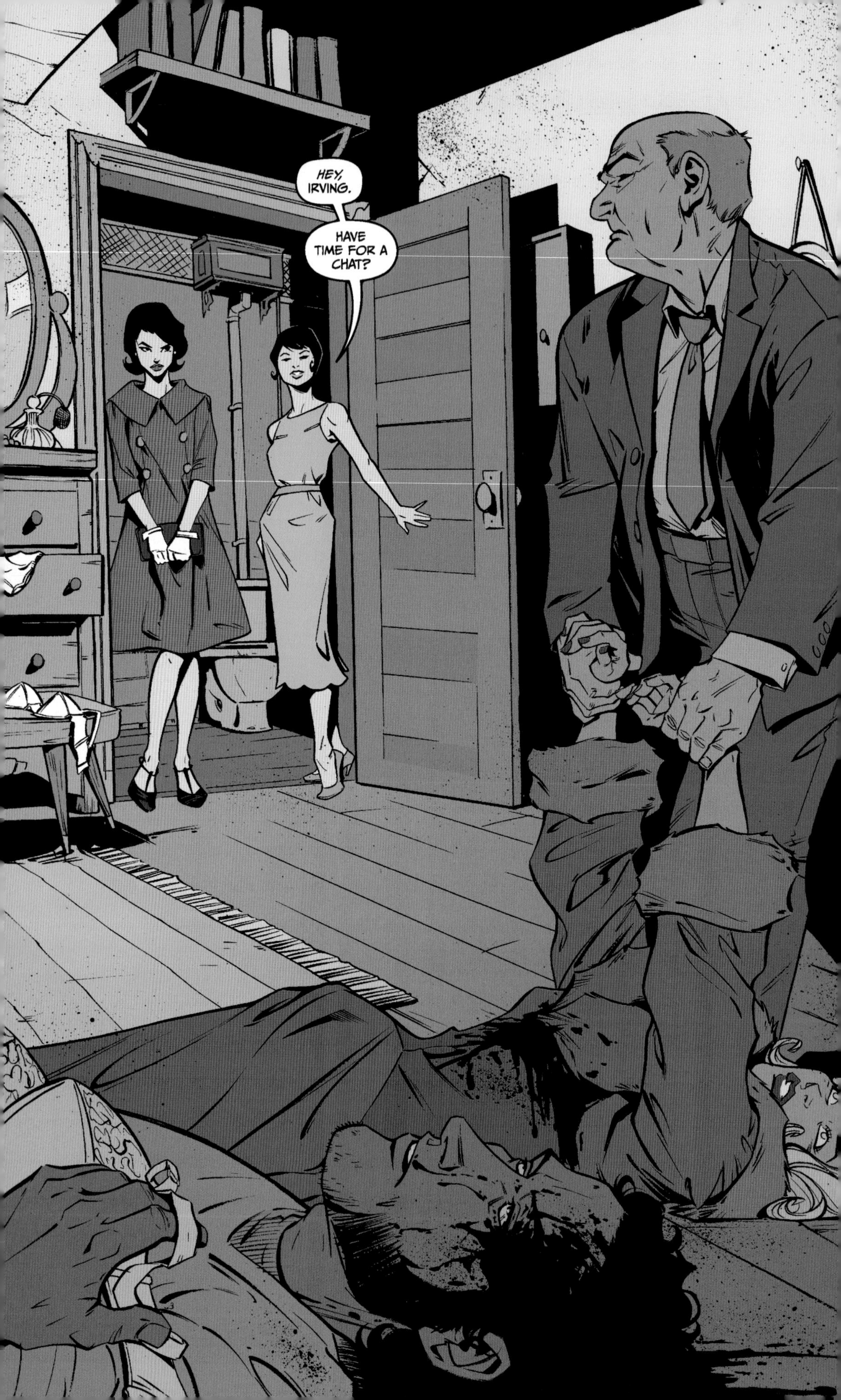
HEY, IRVING.
HAVE TIME FOR A CHAT?

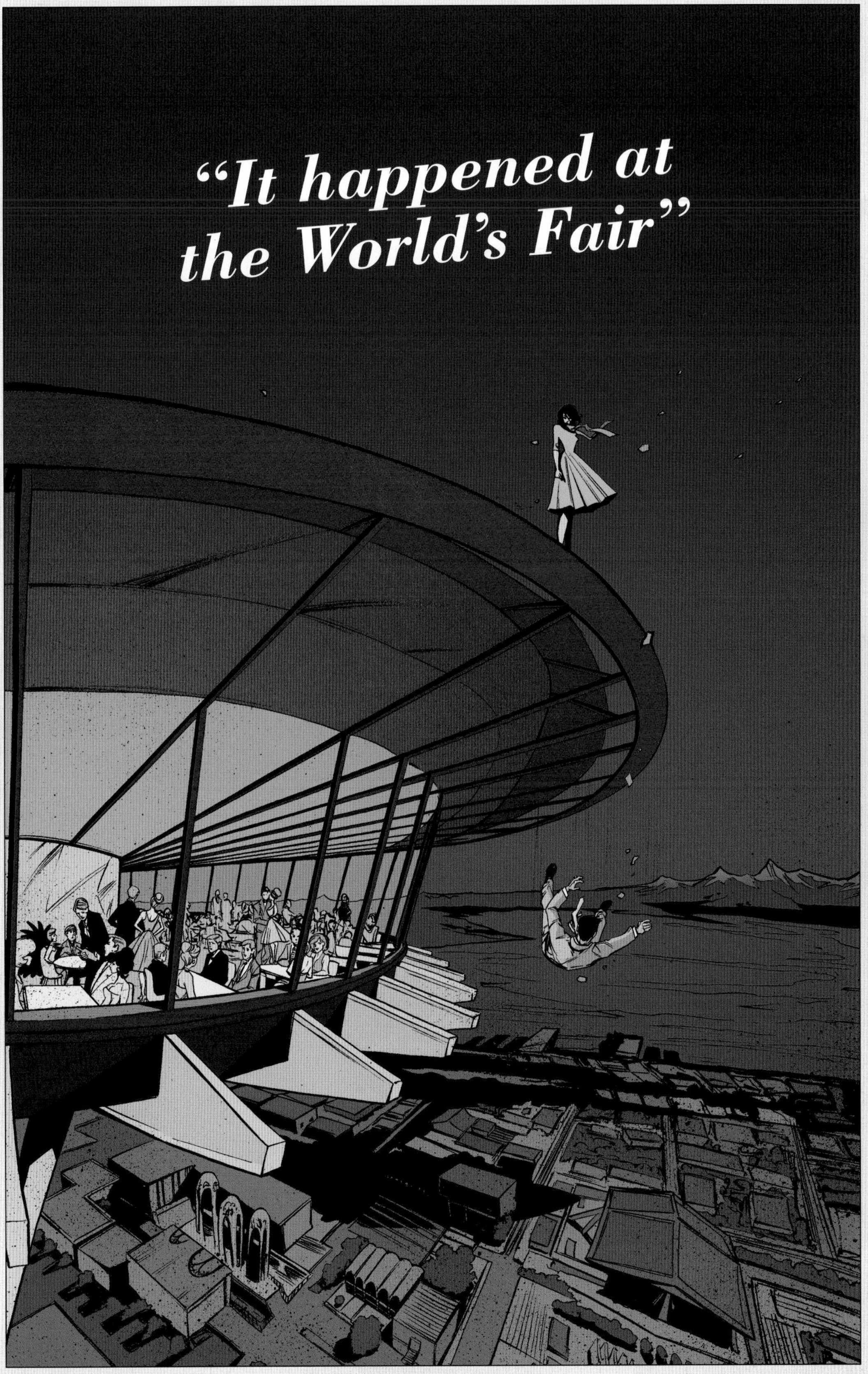
"It happened at the World's Fair"

CHAPTER FIVE

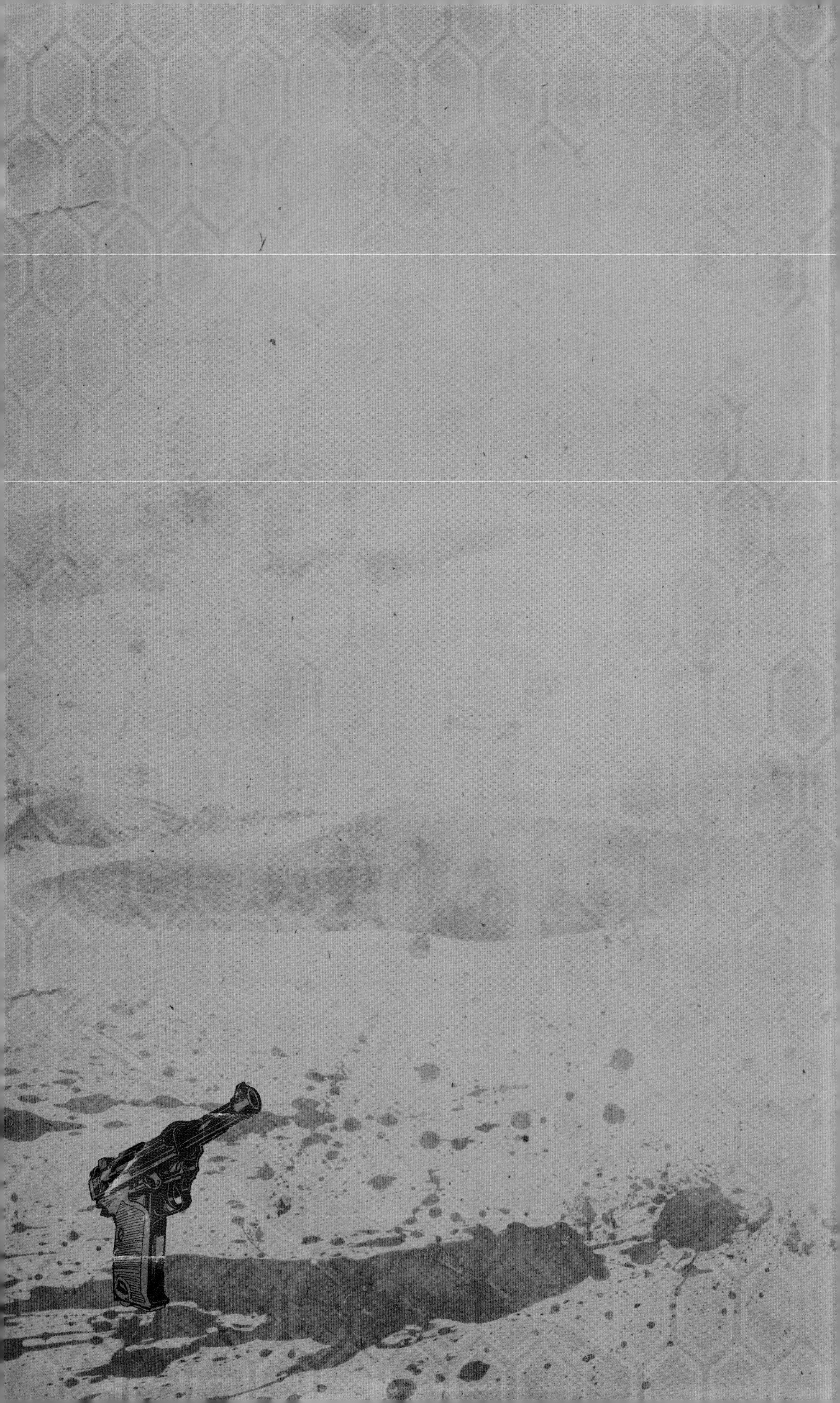

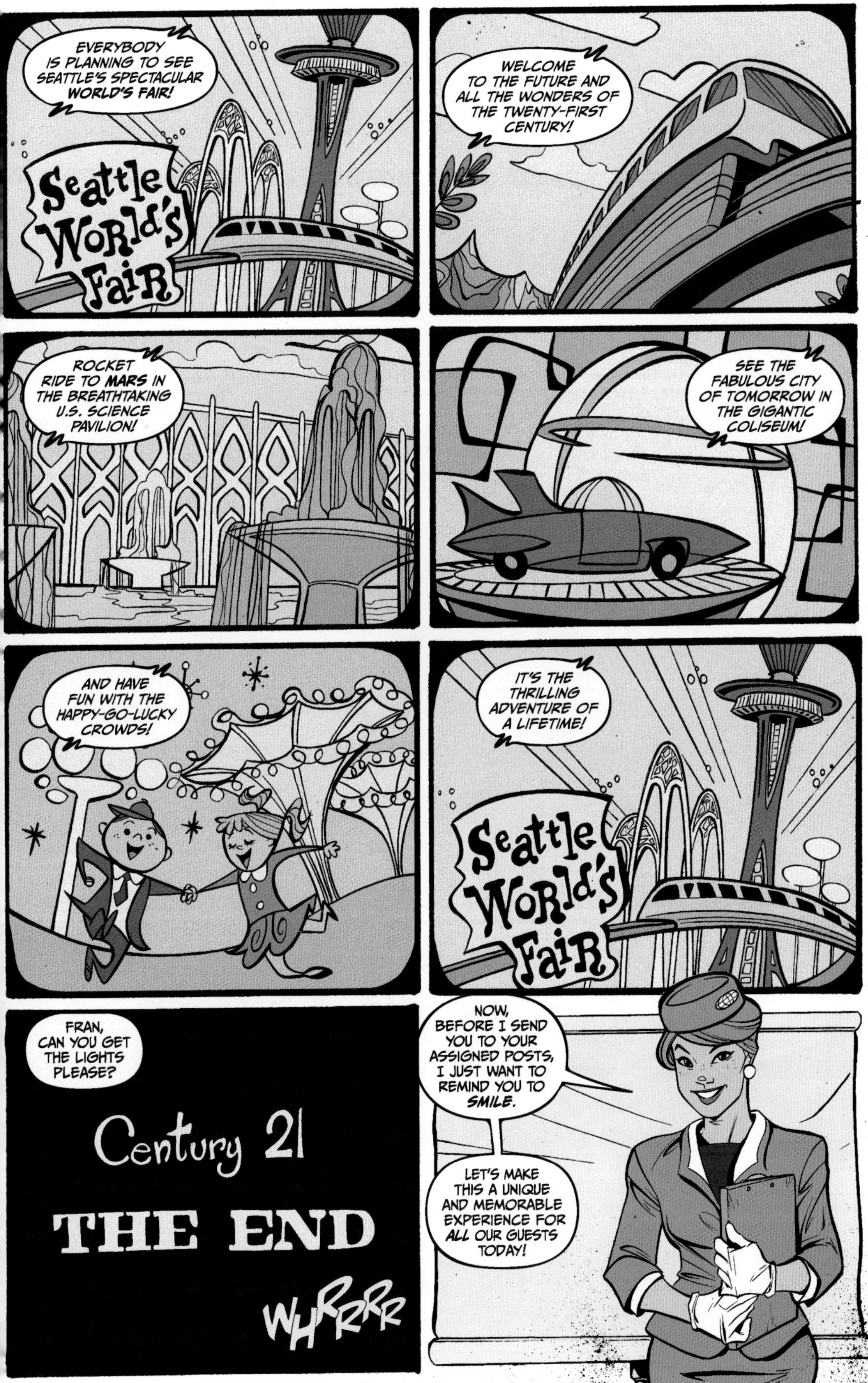
EVERYBODY IS PLANNING TO SEE SEATTLE'S SPECTACULAR WORLD'S FAIR!
Seattle World's Fair
WELCOME TO THE FUTURE AND ALL THE WONDERS OF THE TWENTY-FIRST CENTURY!
ROCKET RIDE TO MARS IN THE BREATHTAKING U.S. SCIENCE PAVILION!
SEE THE FABULOUS CITY OF TOMORROW IN THE GIGANTIC COLISEUM!
AND HAVE FUN WITH THE HAPPY-GO-LUCKY CROWDS!
IT'S THE THRILLING ADVENTURE OF A LIFETIME!
Seattle World's Fair
FRAN, CAN YOU GET THE LIGHTS PLEASE?
Century 21
THE END
WHRRRR
NOW, BEFORE I SEND YOU TO YOUR ASSIGNED POSTS, I JUST WANT TO REMIND YOU TO SMILE.
LET'S MAKE THIS A UNIQUE AND MEMORABLE EXPERIENCE FOR ALL OUR GUESTS TODAY!

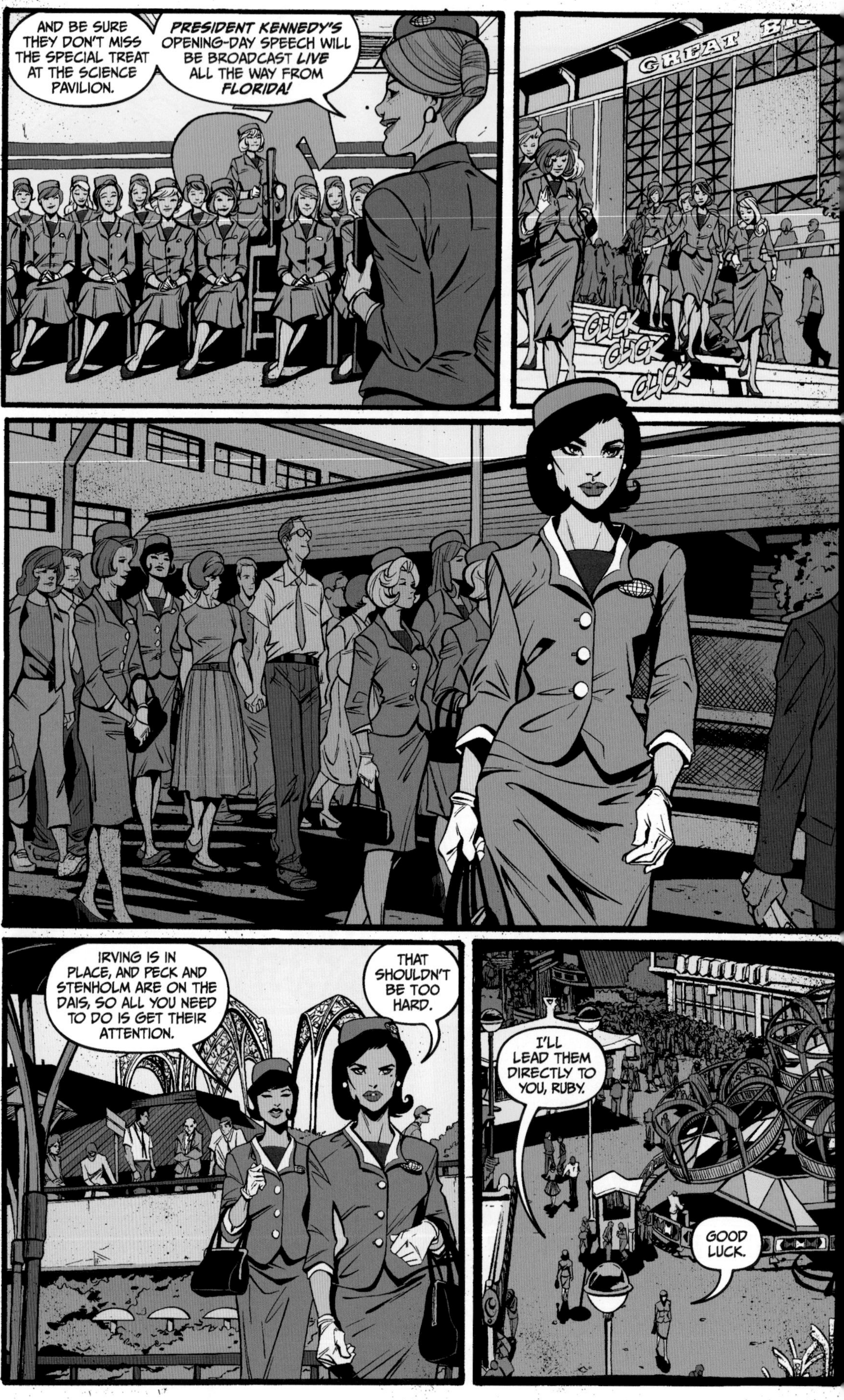
AND BE SURE THEY DON'T MISS THE SPECIAL TREAT AT THE SCIENCE PAVILION.
PRESIDENT KENNEDY'S OPENING-DAY SPEECH WILL BE BROADCAST LIVE ALL THE WAY FROM FLORIDA!
GREAT
CLICK
CLICK
CLICK
IRVING IS IN PLACE, AND PECK AND STENHOLM ARE ON THE DAIS, SO ALL YOU NEED TO DO IS GET THEIR ATTENTION.
THAT SHOULDN'T BE TOO HARD.
I'LL LEAD THEM DIRECTLY TO YOU, RUBY.
GOOD LUCK.

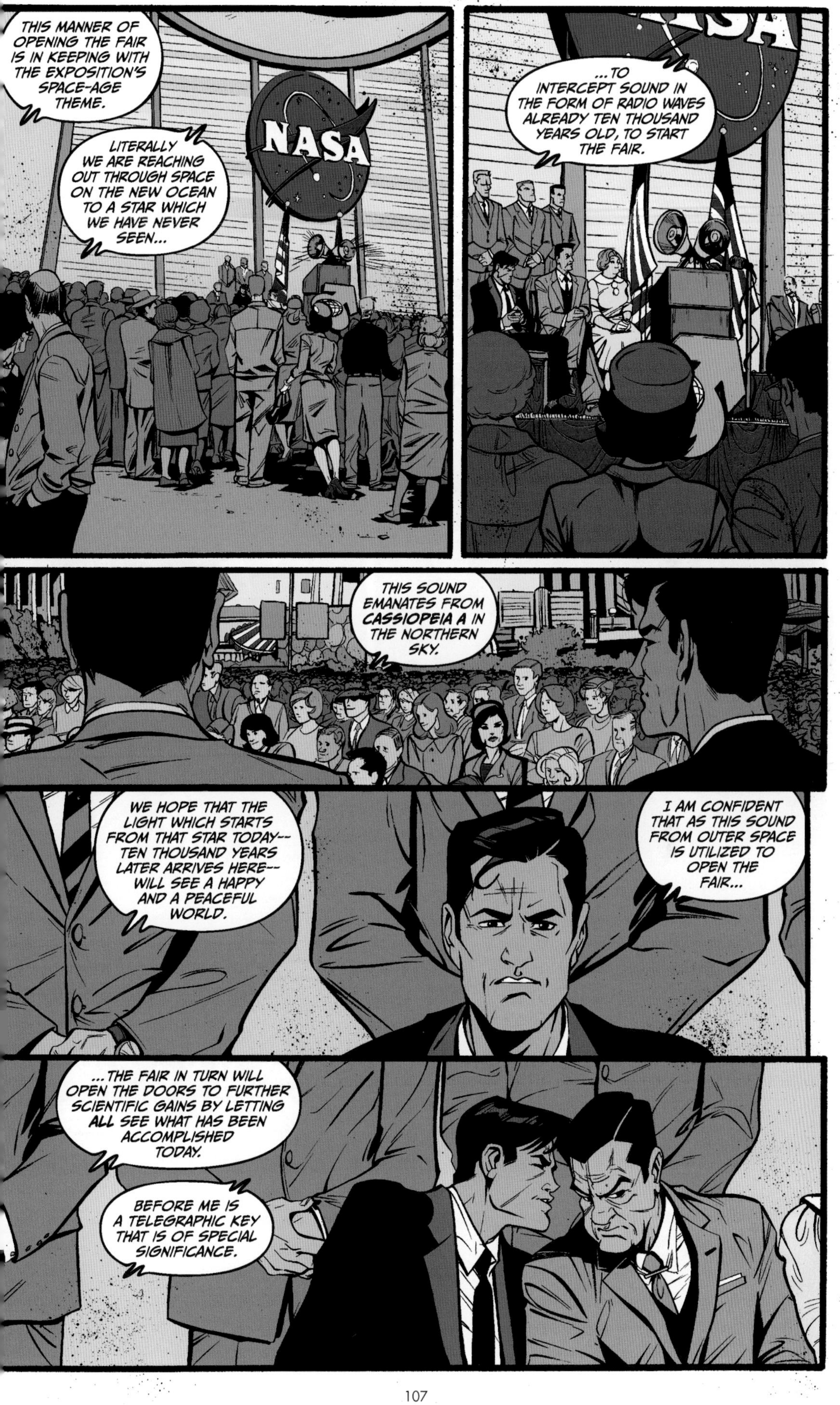
THIS MANNER OF OPENING THE FAIR IS IN KEEPING WITH THE EXPOSITION'S SPACE-AGE THEME.
LITERALLY WE ARE REACHING OUT THROUGH SPACE ON THE NEW OCEAN TO A STAR WHICH WE HAVE NEVER SEEN...
NASA
...TO INTERCEPT SOUND IN THE FORM OF RADIO WAVES ALREADY TEN THOUSAND YEARS OLD, TO START THE FAIR.
THIS SOUND EMANATES FROM CASSIOPEIA A IN THE NORTHERN SKY.
WE HOPE THAT THE LIGHT WHICH STARTS FROM THAT STAR TODAY--TEN THOUSAND YEARS LATER ARRIVES HERE--WILL SEE A HAPPY AND A PEACEFUL WORLD.
I AM CONFIDENT THAT AS THIS SOUND FROM OUTER SPACE IS UTILIZED TO OPEN THE FAIR...
...THE FAIR IN TURN WILL OPEN THE DOORS TO FURTHER SCIENTIFIC GAINS BY LETTING ALL SEE WHAT HAS BEEN ACCOMPLISHED TODAY.
BEFORE ME IS A TELEGRAPHIC KEY THAT IS OF SPECIAL SIGNIFICANCE.

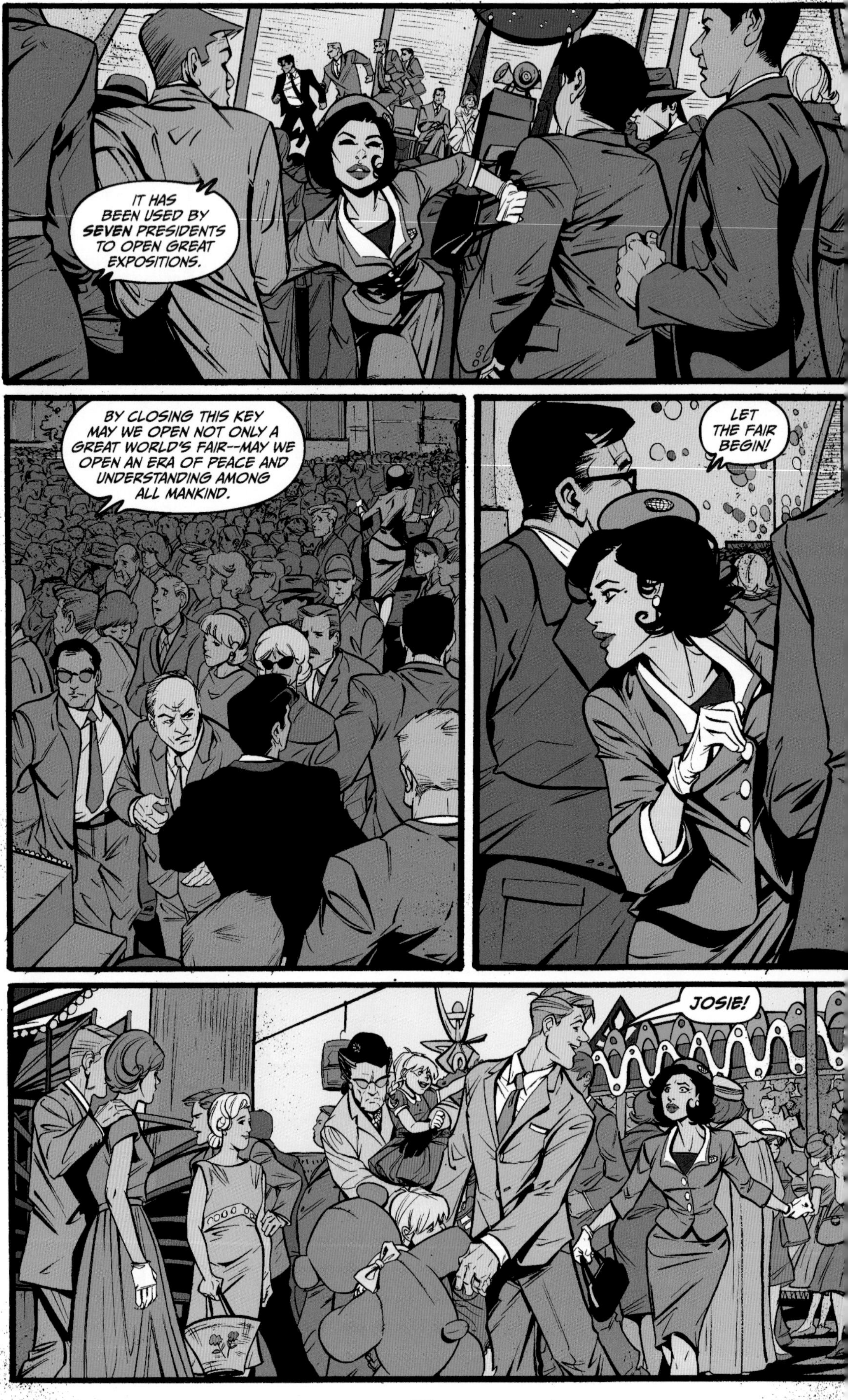

IT HAS BEEN USED BY SEVEN PRESIDENTS TO OPEN GREAT EXPOSITIONS.
BY CLOSING THIS KEY MAY WE OPEN NOT ONLY A GREAT WORLD'S FAIR--MAY WE OPEN AN ERA OF PEACE AND UNDERSTANDING AMONG ALL MANKIND.
LET THE FAIR BEGIN!
JOSIE!

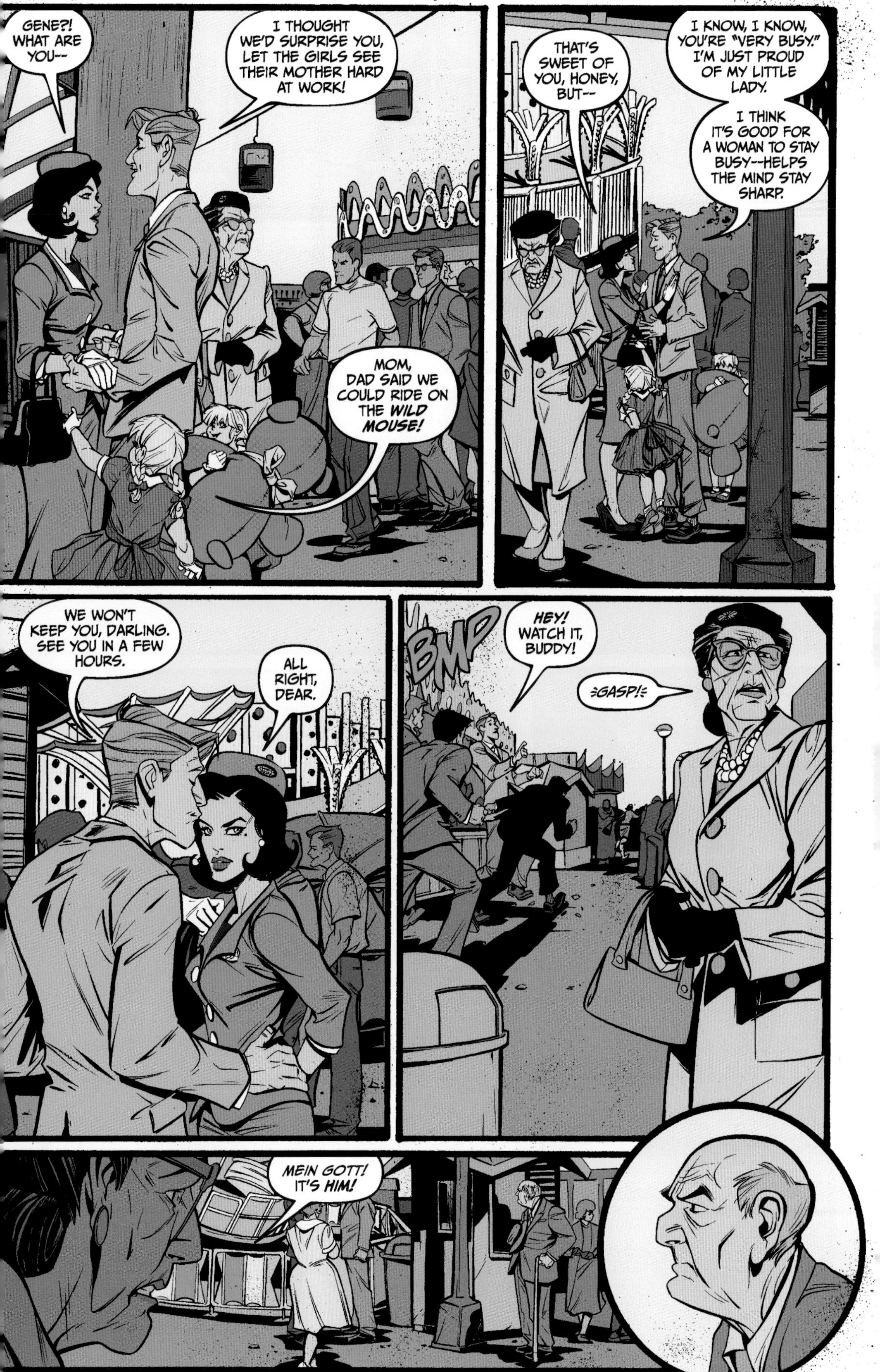
GENE?! WHAT ARE YOU--
I THOUGHT WE'D SURPRISE YOU, LET THE GIRLS SEE THEIR MOTHER HARD AT WORK!
MOM, DAD SAID WE COULD RIDE ON THE WILD MOUSE!
THAT'S SWEET OF YOU, HONEY, BUT--
I KNOW, I KNOW, YOU'RE "VERY BUSY." I'M JUST PROUD OF MY LITTLE LADY.
I THINK IT'S GOOD FOR A WOMAN TO STAY BUSY--HELPS THE MIND STAY SHARP.
WE WON'T KEEP YOU, DARLING. SEE YOU IN A FEW HOURS.
ALL RIGHT, DEAR.
BMP
HEY! WATCH IT, BUDDY!
GASP!
MEIN GOTT! IT'S HIM!

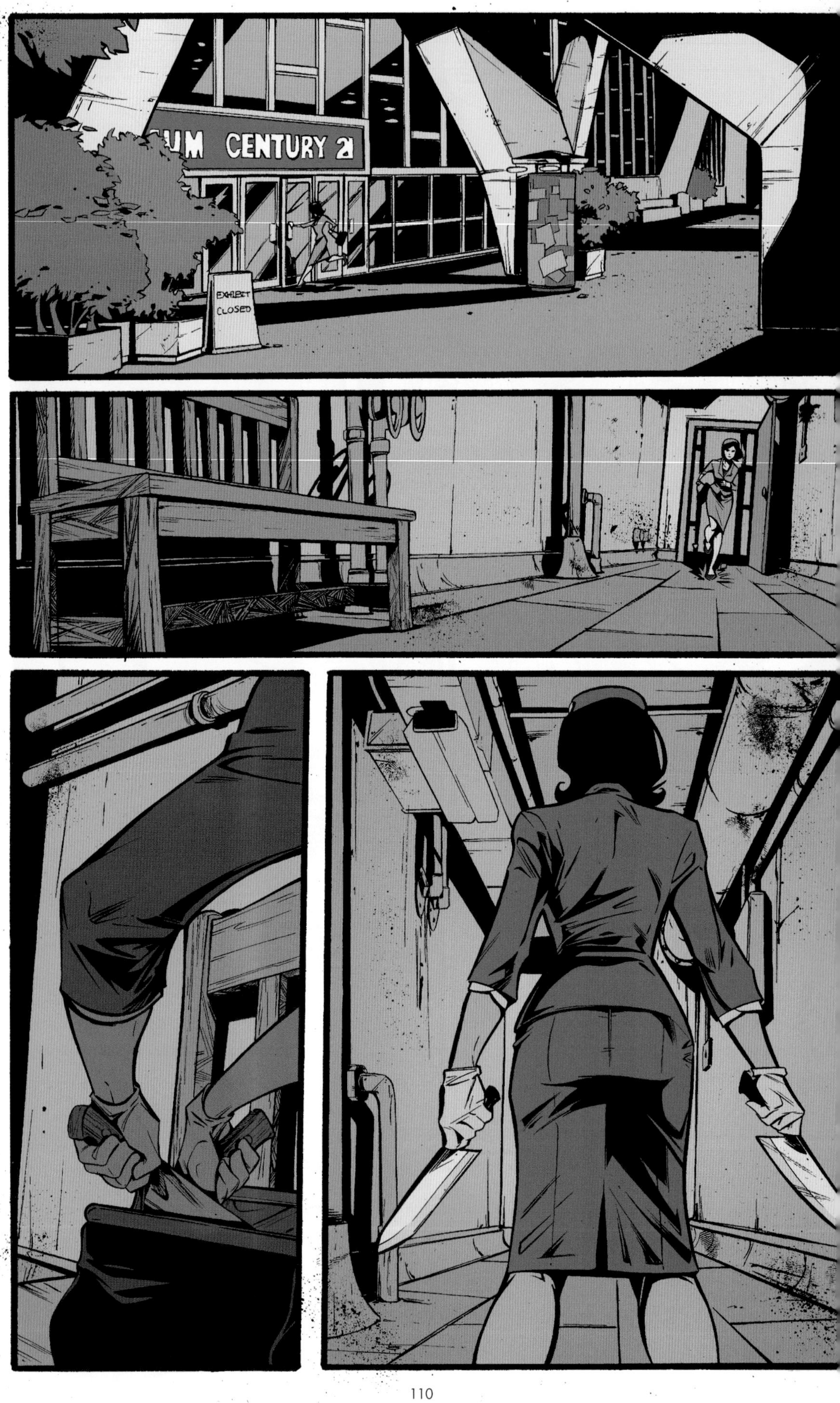
UM CENTURY 21
EXHIBIT CLOSED

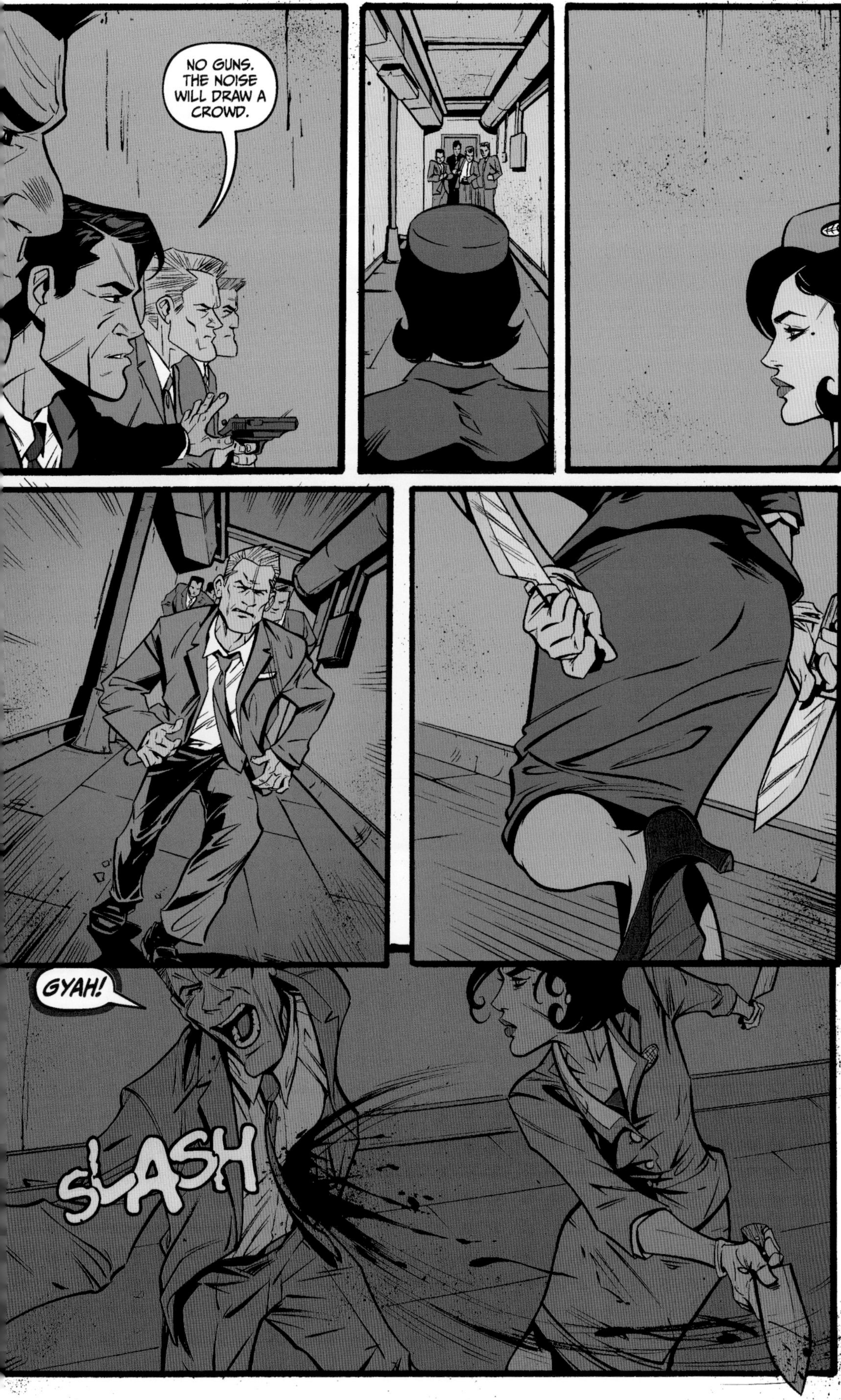
NO GUNS. THE NOISE WILL DRAW A CROWD.
GYAH!
SLASH

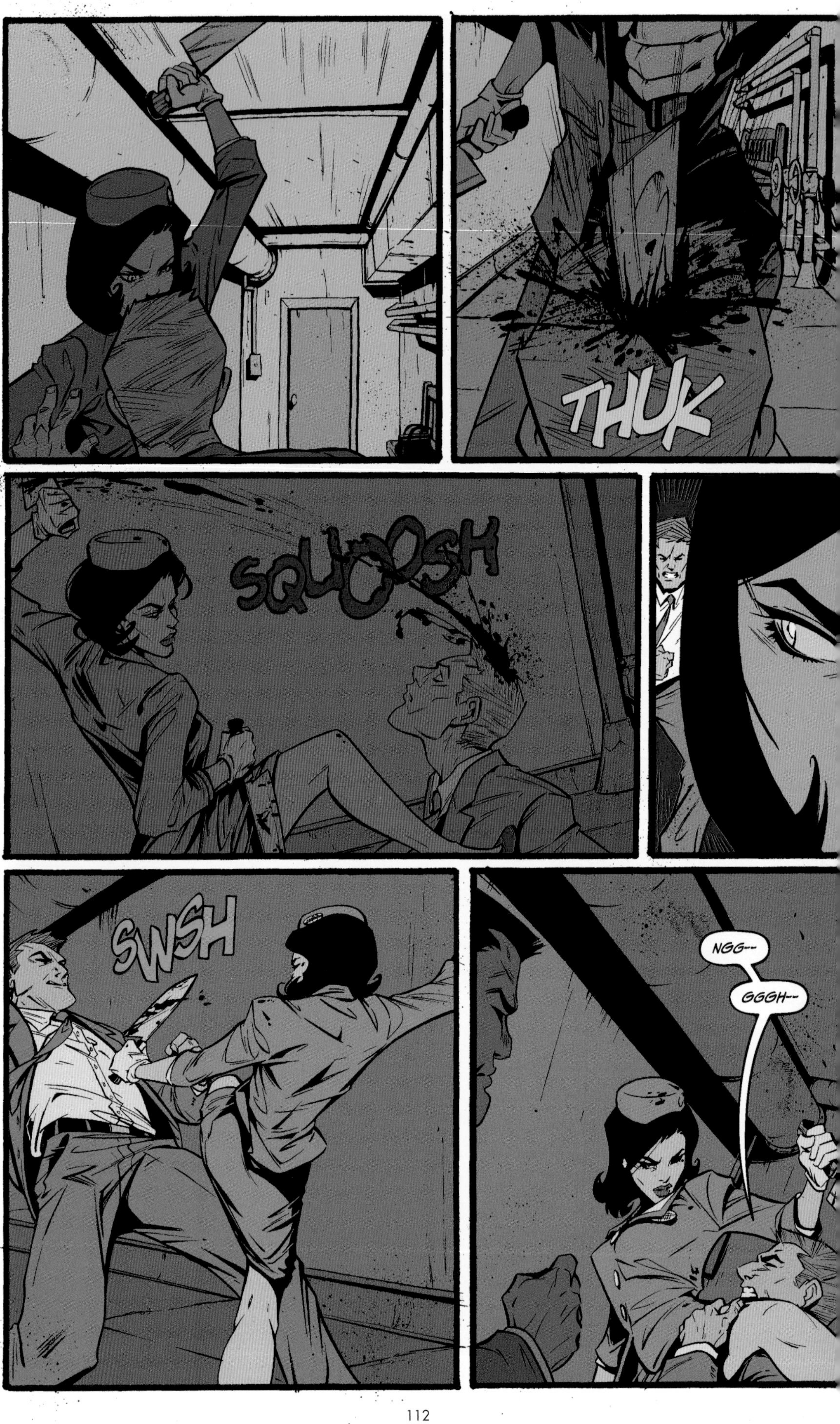
THUK
SQUOOSH
SWSH
NGG--
GGGH--

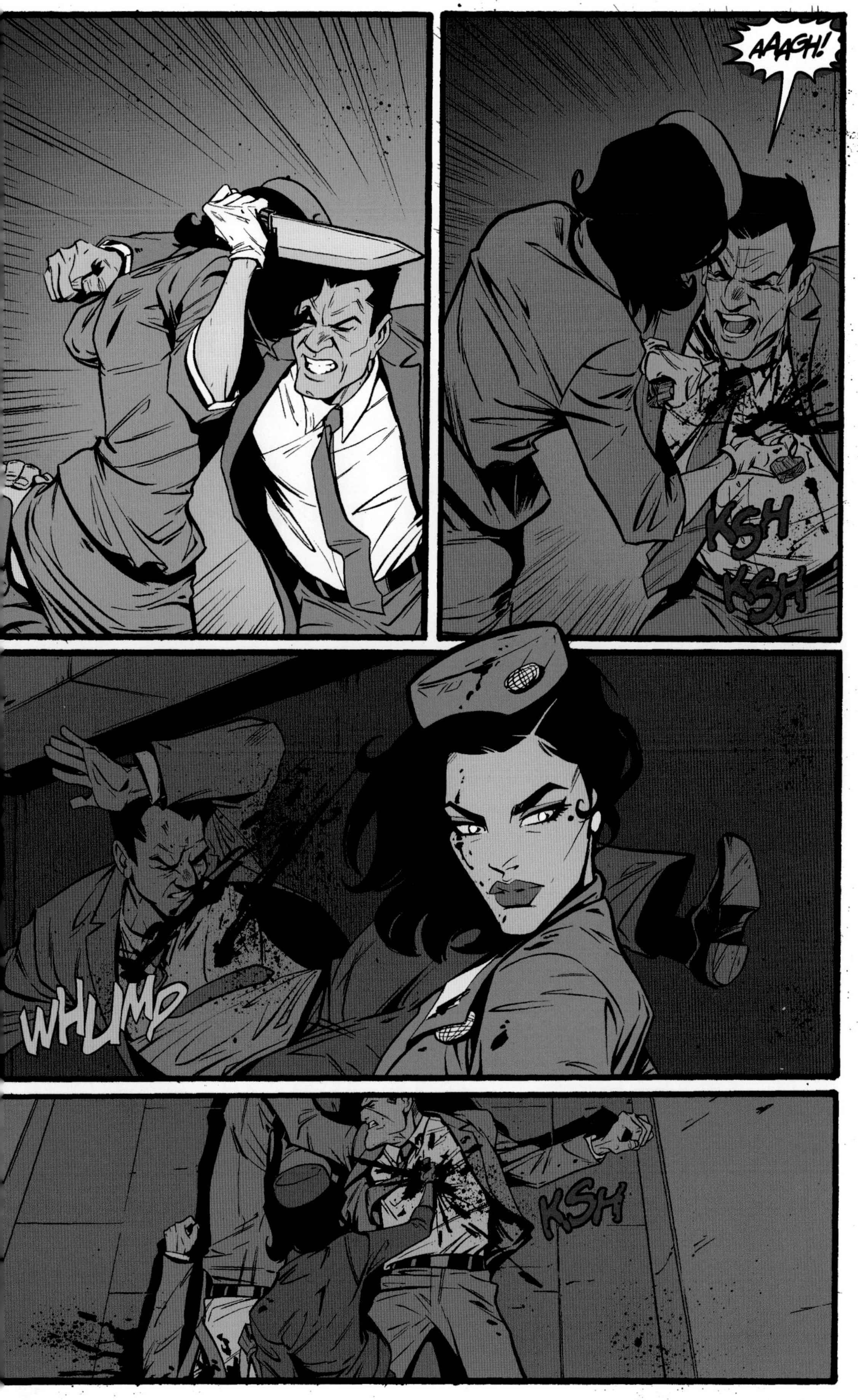
AAAGH!
KSH
KSH
WHUMP
KSH

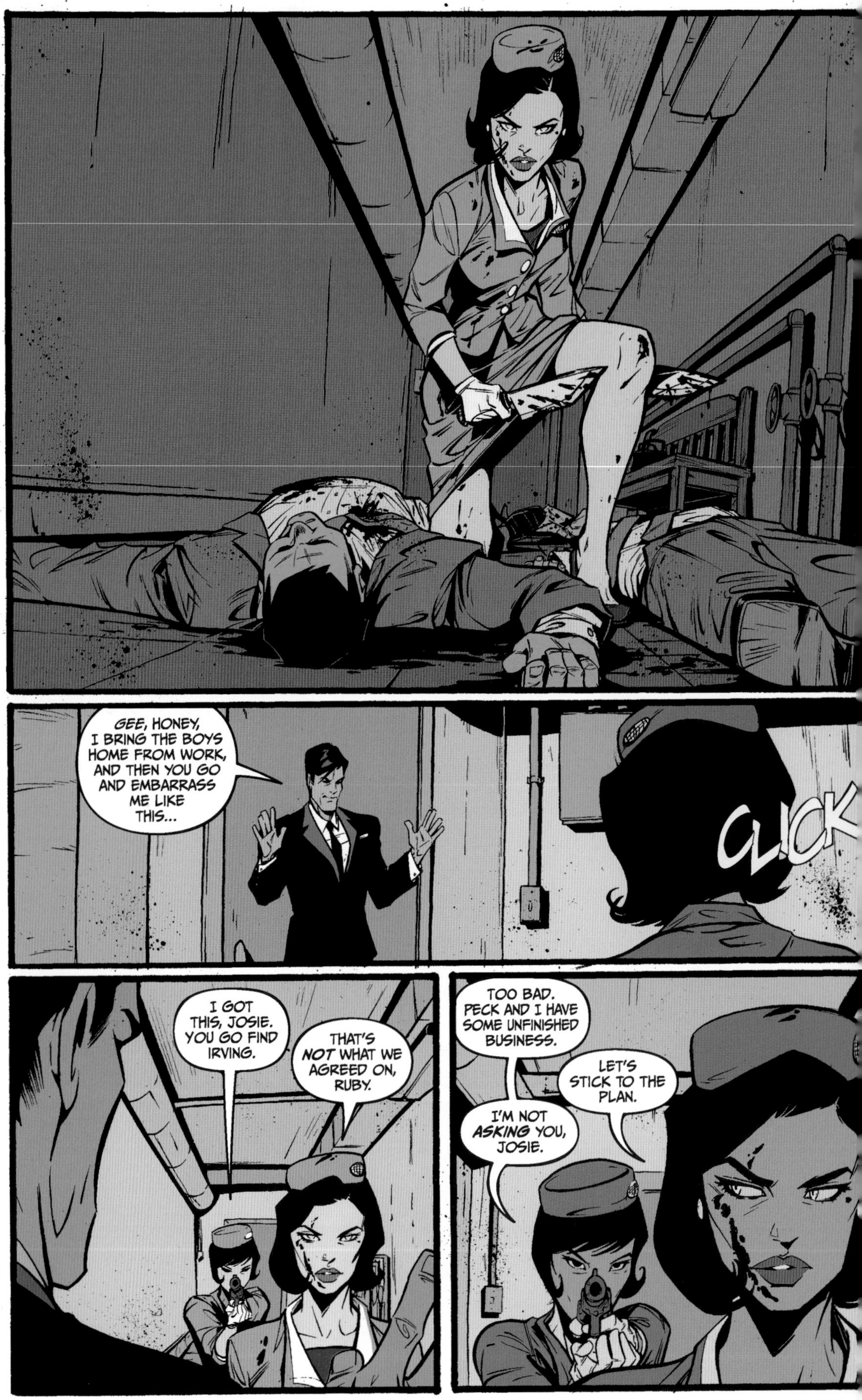
GEE, HONEY, I BRING THE BOYS HOME FROM WORK, AND THEN YOU GO AND EMBARRASS ME LIKE THIS...
CLICK
I GOT THIS, JOSIE. YOU GO FIND IRVING.
THAT'S NOT WHAT WE AGREED ON, RUBY.
TOO BAD. PECK AND I HAVE SOME UNFINISHED BUSINESS.
LET'S STICK TO THE PLAN.
I'M NOT ASKING YOU, JOSIE.

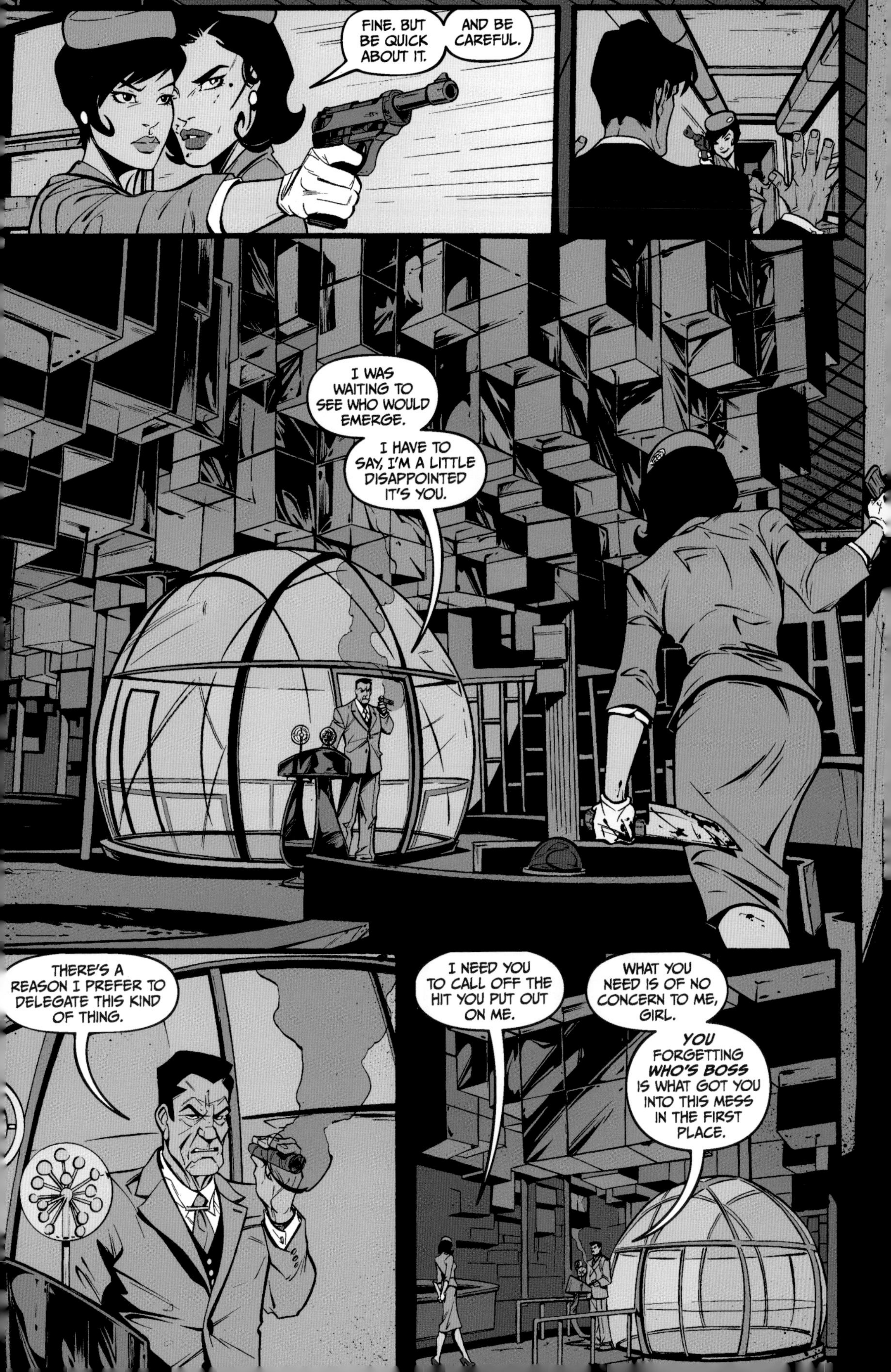
FINE. BUT BE QUICK ABOUT IT.
AND BE CAREFUL.
I WAS WAITING TO SEE WHO WOULD EMERGE.
I HAVE TO SAY, I'M A LITTLE DISAPPOINTED IT'S YOU.
THERE'S A REASON I PREFER TO DELEGATE THIS KIND OF THING.
I NEED YOU TO CALL OFF THE HIT YOU PUT OUT ON ME.
WHAT YOU NEED IS OF NO CONCERN TO ME, GIRL.
YOU FORGETTING ***WHO'S BOSS*** IS WHAT GOT YOU INTO THIS MESS IN THE FIRST PLACE.

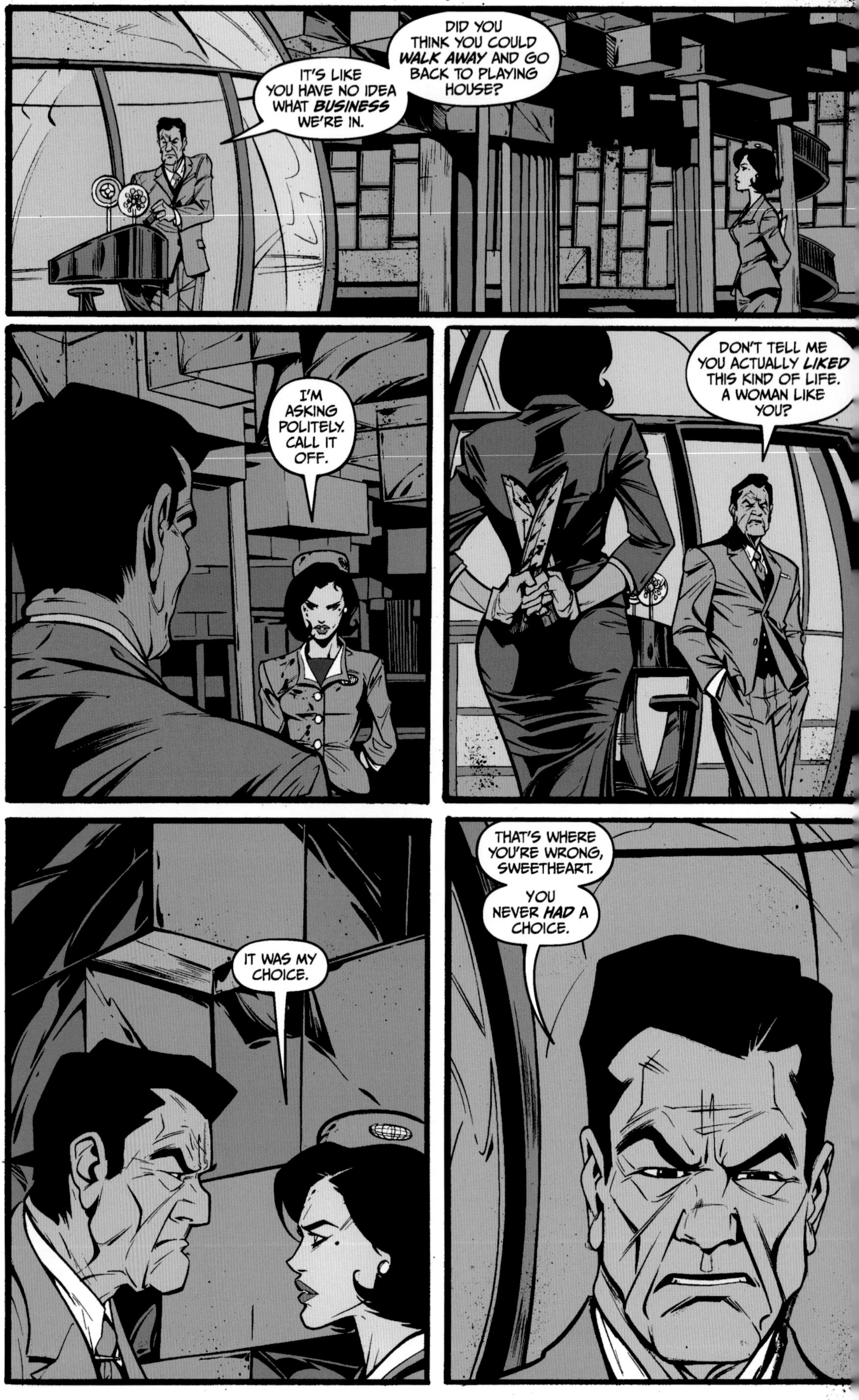
IT'S LIKE YOU HAVE NO IDEA WHAT BUSINESS WE'RE IN.
DID YOU THINK YOU COULD WALK AWAY AND GO BACK TO PLAYING HOUSE?
I'M ASKING POLITELY. CALL IT OFF.
DON'T TELL ME YOU ACTUALLY LIKED THIS KIND OF LIFE. A WOMAN LIKE YOU?
IT WAS MY CHOICE.
THAT'S WHERE YOU'RE WRONG, SWEETHEART.
YOU NEVER HAD A CHOICE.

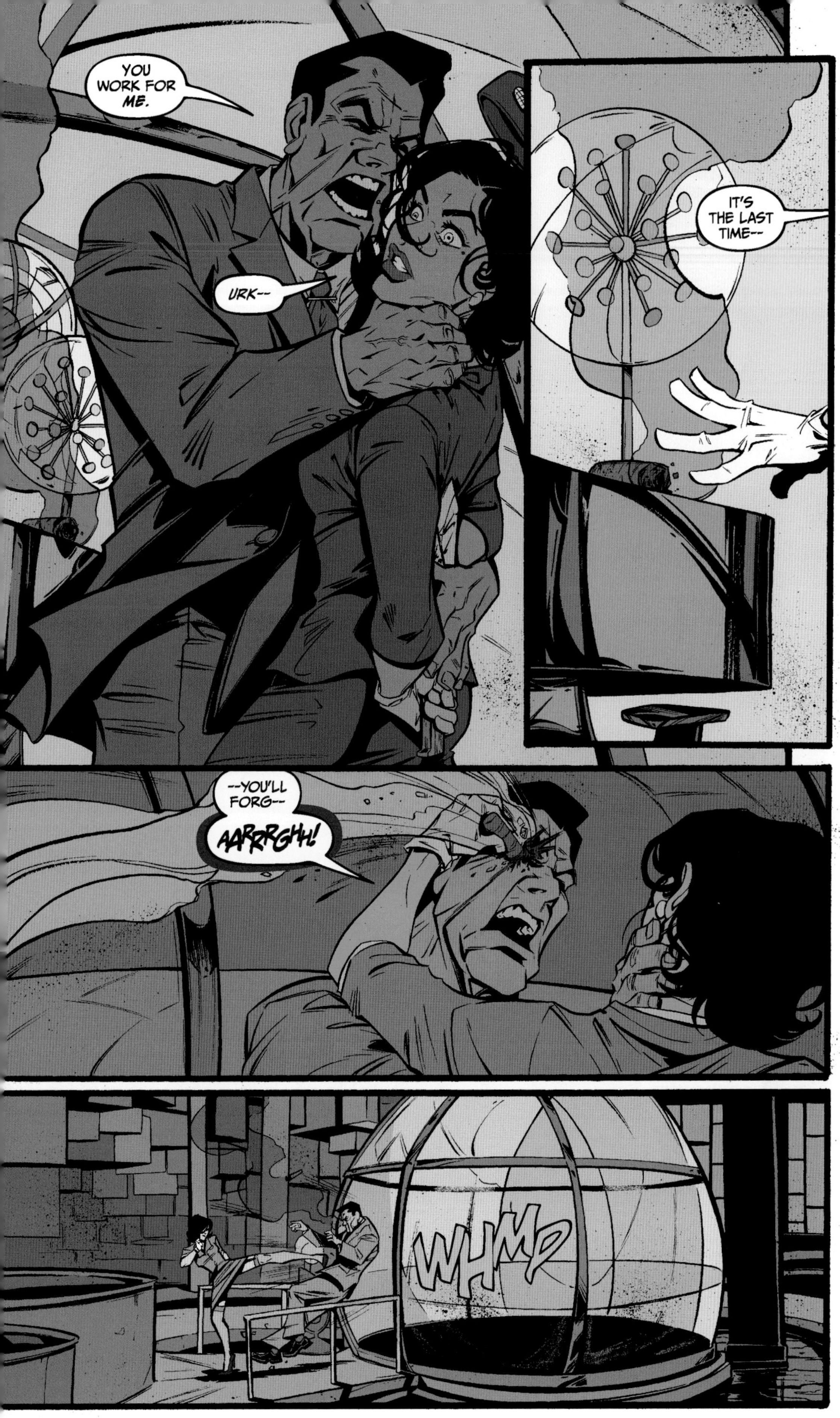
YOU WORK FOR ME.
URK--
IT'S THE LAST TIME--
--YOU'LL FORG--
AARRRGHH!
WHMP

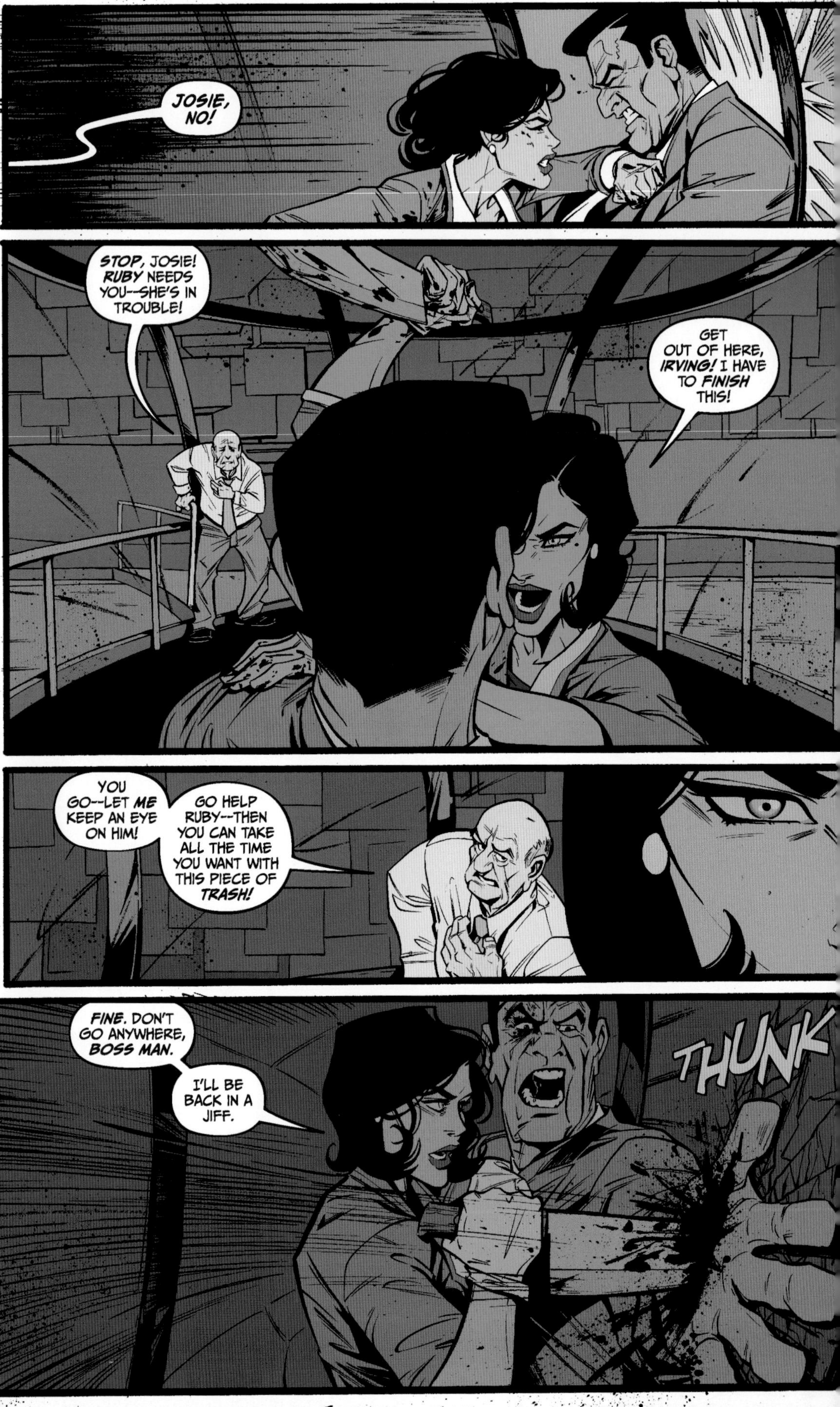
JOSIE, NO!
STOP, JOSIE! RUBY NEEDS YOU--SHE'S IN TROUBLE!
GET OUT OF HERE, IRVING! I HAVE TO FINISH THIS!
YOU GO--LET ME KEEP AN EYE ON HIM!
GO HELP RUBY--THEN YOU CAN TAKE ALL THE TIME YOU WANT WITH THIS PIECE OF TRASH!
FINE. DON'T GO ANYWHERE, BOSS MAN.
I'LL BE BACK IN A JIFF.
THUNK

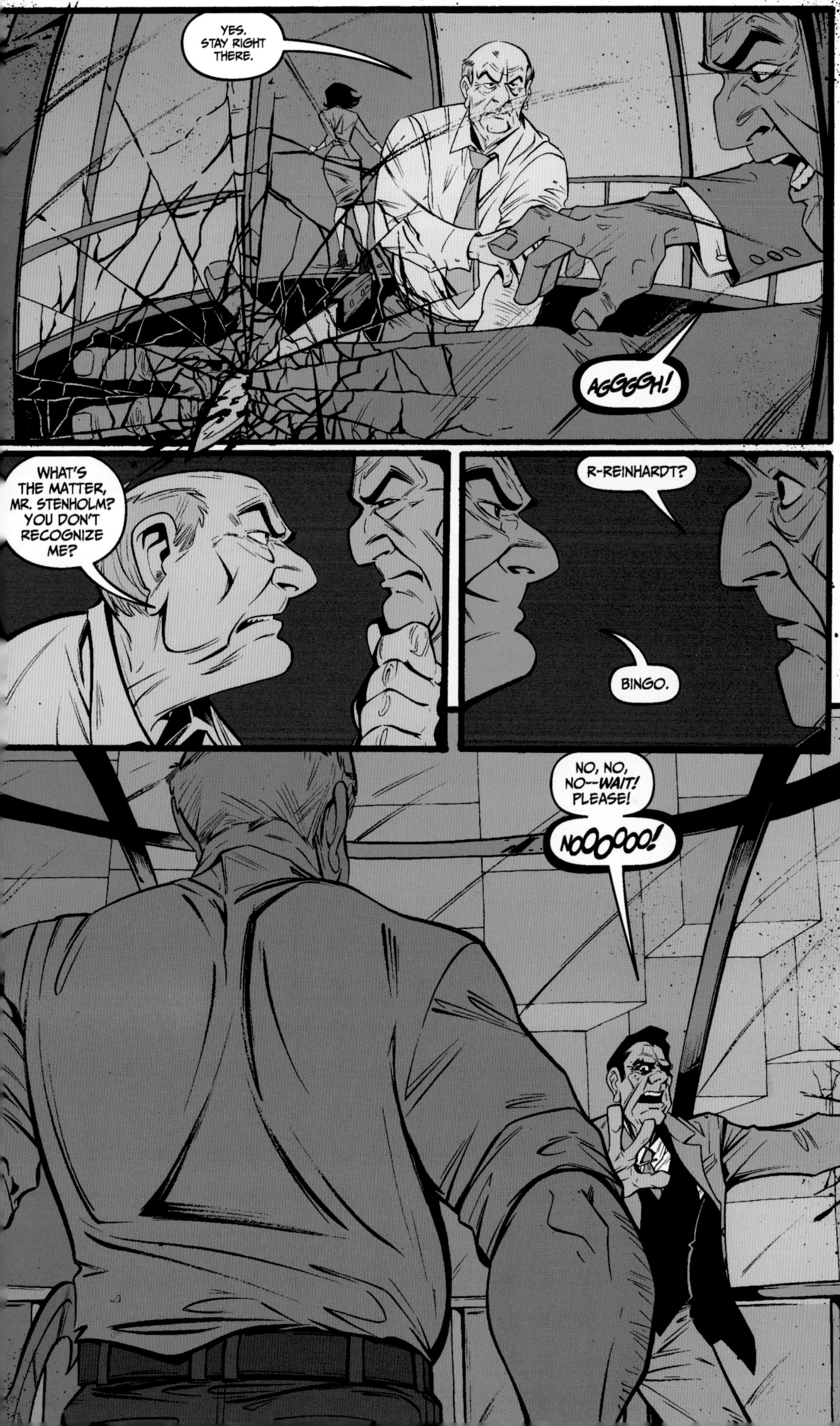
YES. STAY RIGHT THERE.
AGGGGH!
WHAT'S THE MATTER, MR. STENHOLM? YOU DON'T RECOGNIZE ME?
R-REINHARDT?
BINGO.
NO, NO, NO--WAIT! PLEASE!
NOOOOOO!

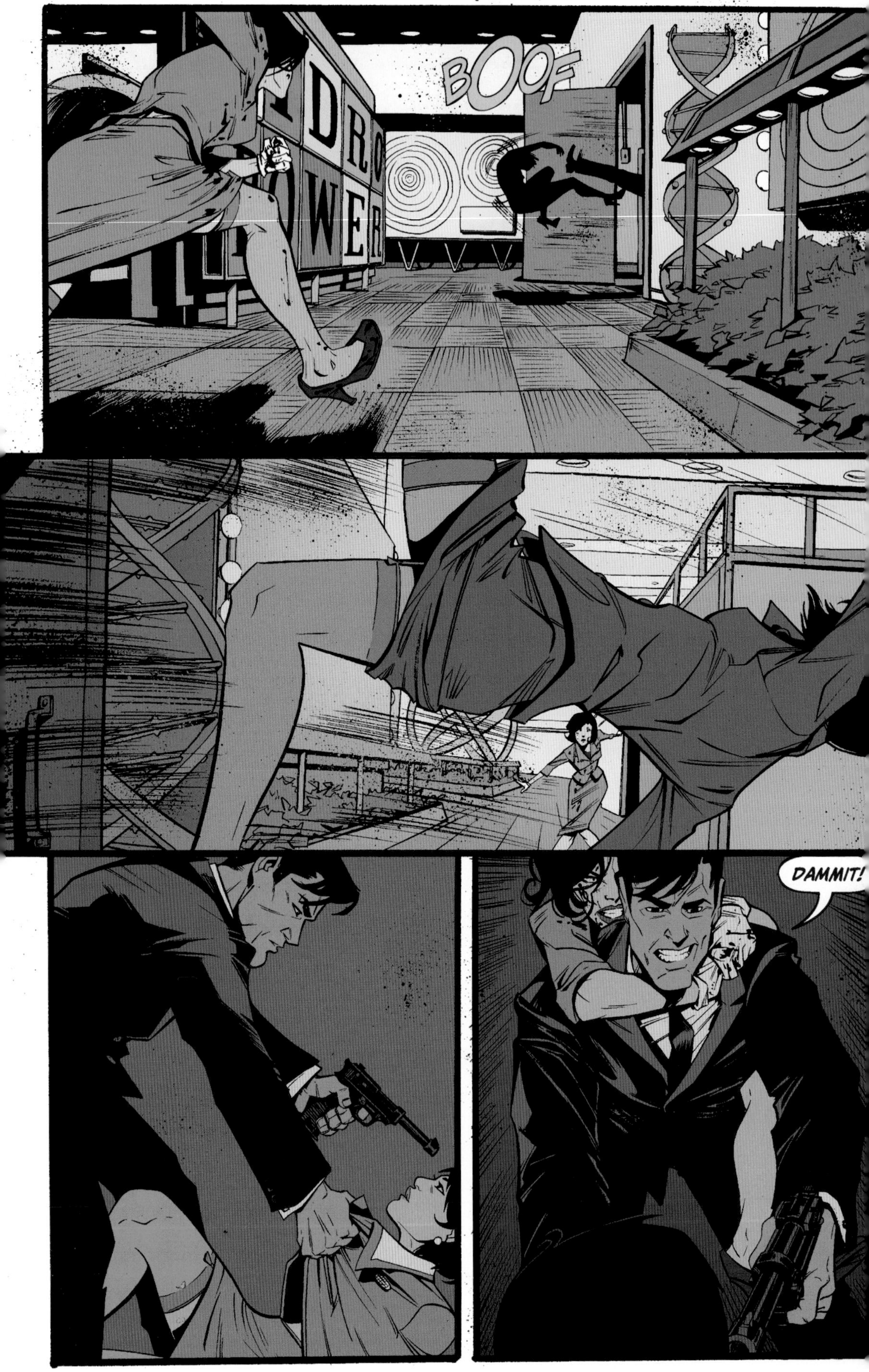
BOOF
DROWER
DAMMIT!

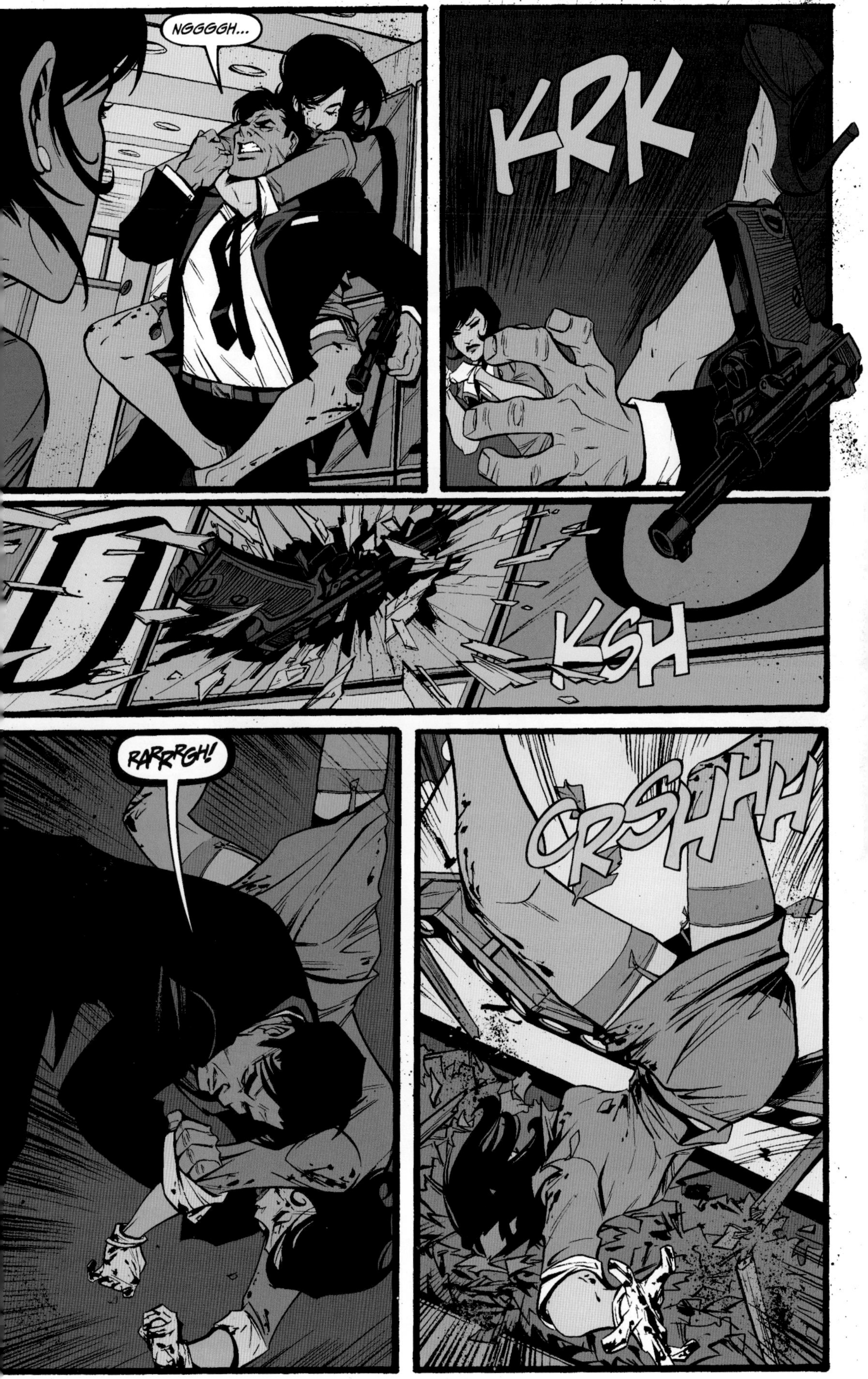
NGGGGH...
KRK
KSH
RARRRGH!
CRSHHH

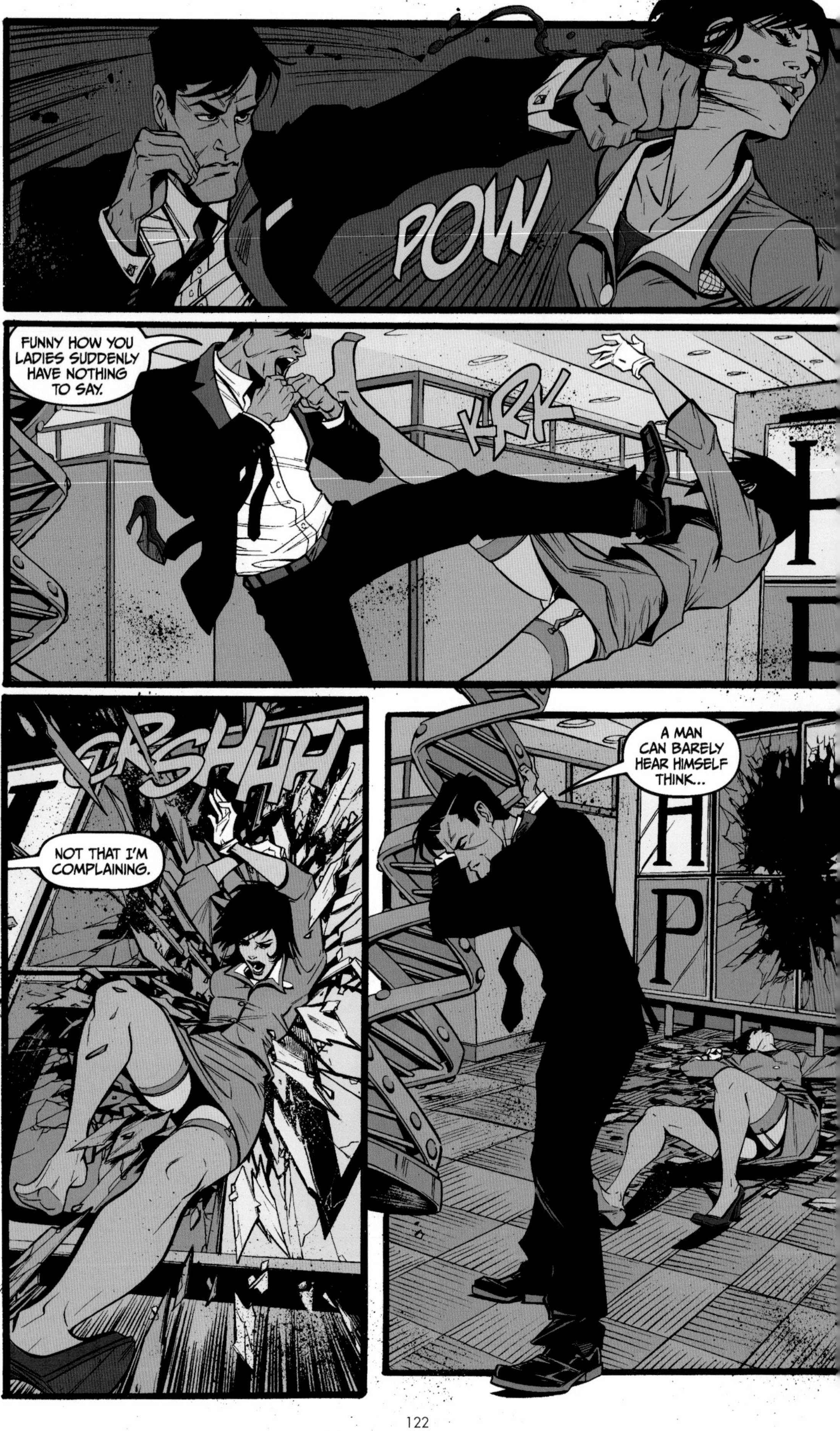
POW
FUNNY HOW YOU LADIES SUDDENLY HAVE NOTHING TO SAY.
KRK
KRSHHH
NOT THAT I'M COMPLAINING.
A MAN CAN BARELY HEAR HIMSELF THINK...

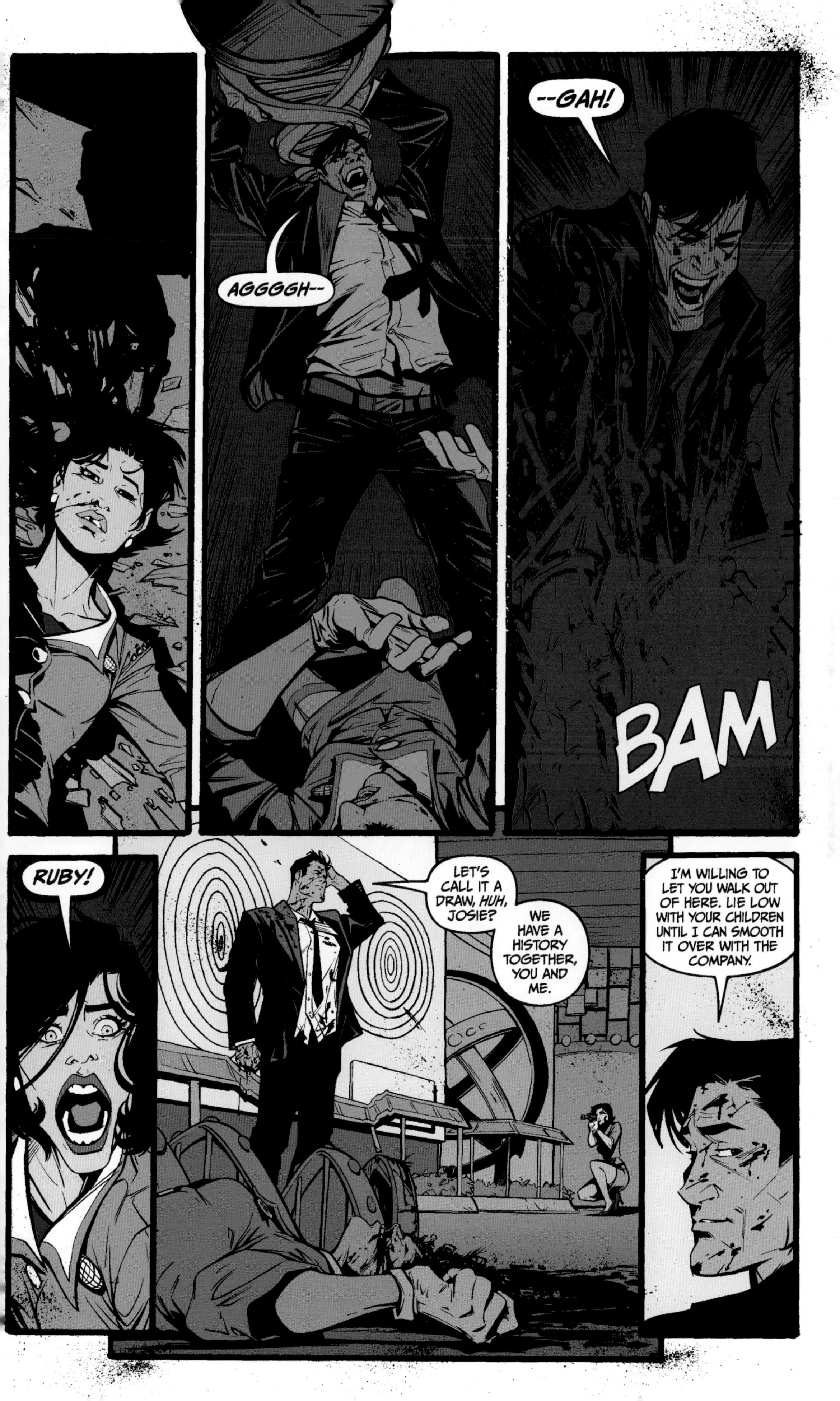
AGGGGH--
--GAH!
BAM
RUBY!
LET'S CALL IT A DRAW, *HUH*, JOSIE?
WE HAVE A HISTORY TOGETHER, YOU AND ME.
I'M WILLING TO LET YOU WALK OUT OF HERE. LIE LOW WITH YOUR CHILDREN UNTIL I CAN SMOOTH IT OVER WITH THE COMPANY.

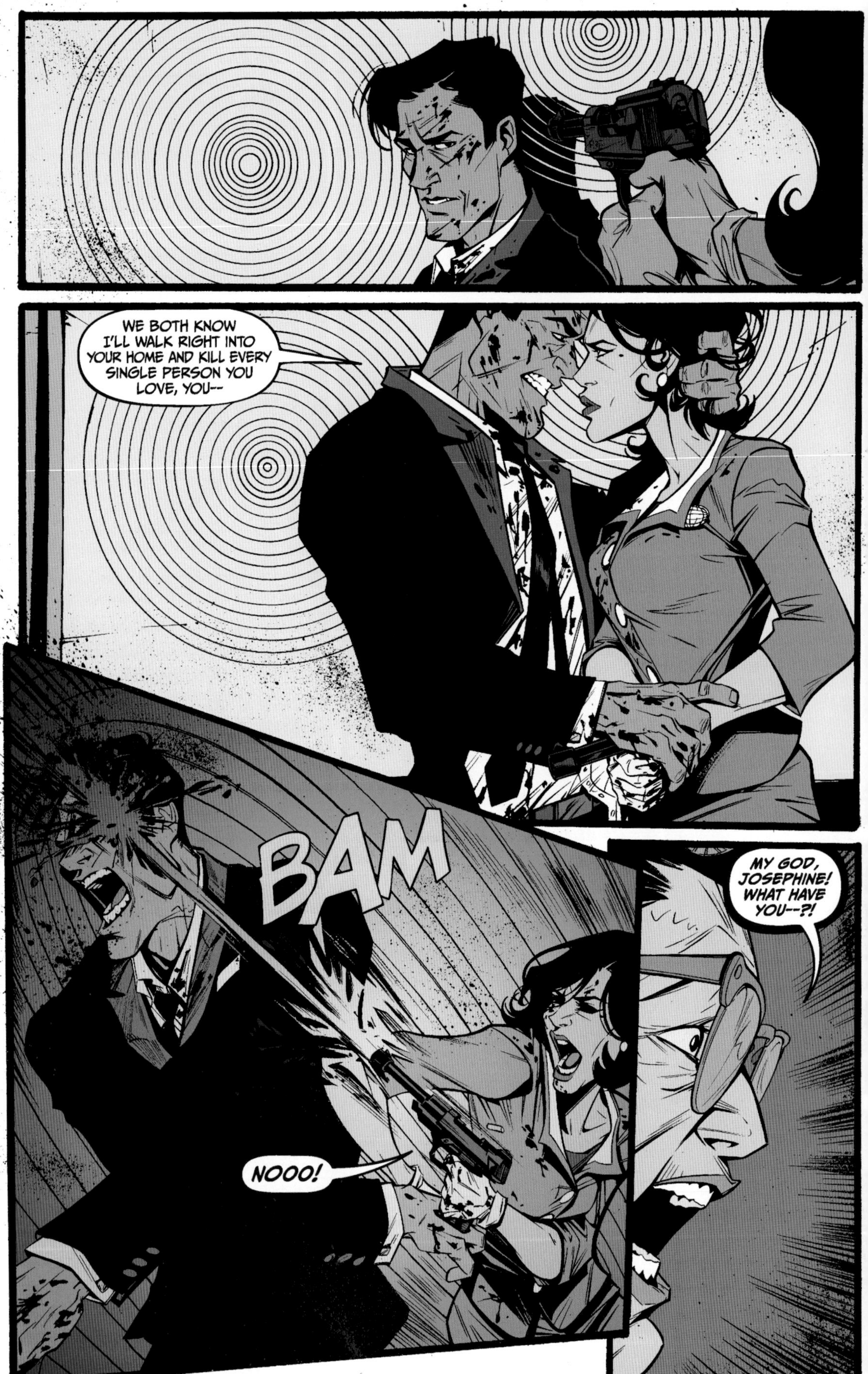
WE BOTH KNOW I'LL WALK RIGHT INTO YOUR HOME AND KILL EVERY SINGLE PERSON YOU LOVE, YOU--
BAM
NOOO!
MY GOD, JOSEPHINE! WHAT HAVE YOU--?!

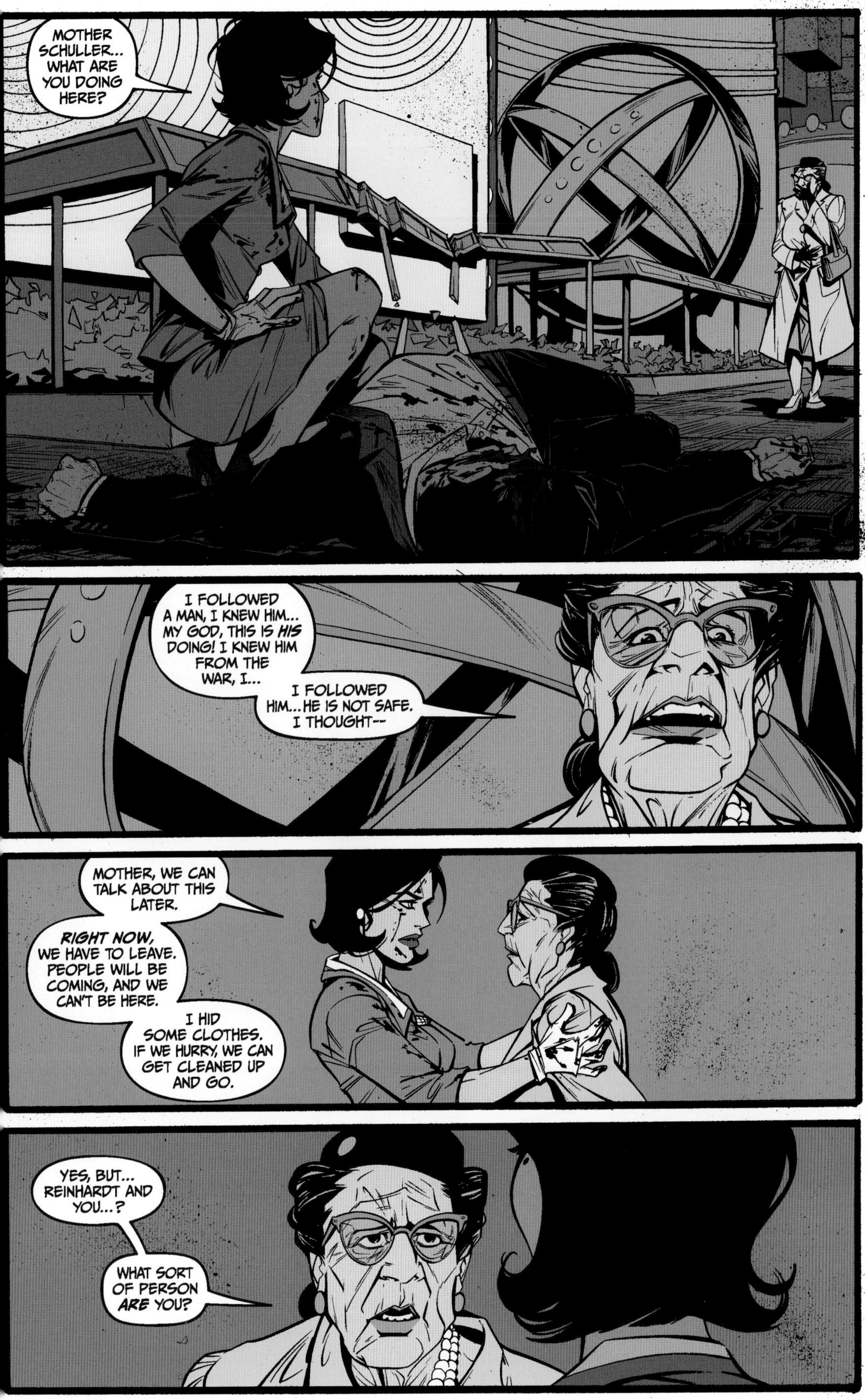
MOTHER SCHULLER... WHAT ARE YOU DOING HERE?
I FOLLOWED A MAN, I KNEW HIM... MY GOD, THIS IS *HIS* DOING! I KNEW HIM FROM THE WAR, I...
I FOLLOWED HIM... HE IS NOT SAFE. I THOUGHT--
MOTHER, WE CAN TALK ABOUT THIS LATER.
RIGHT NOW, WE HAVE TO LEAVE. PEOPLE WILL BE COMING, AND WE CAN'T BE HERE.
I HID SOME CLOTHES. IF WE HURRY, WE CAN GET CLEANED UP AND GO.
YES, BUT... REINHARDT AND YOU...?
WHAT SORT OF PERSON *ARE* YOU?

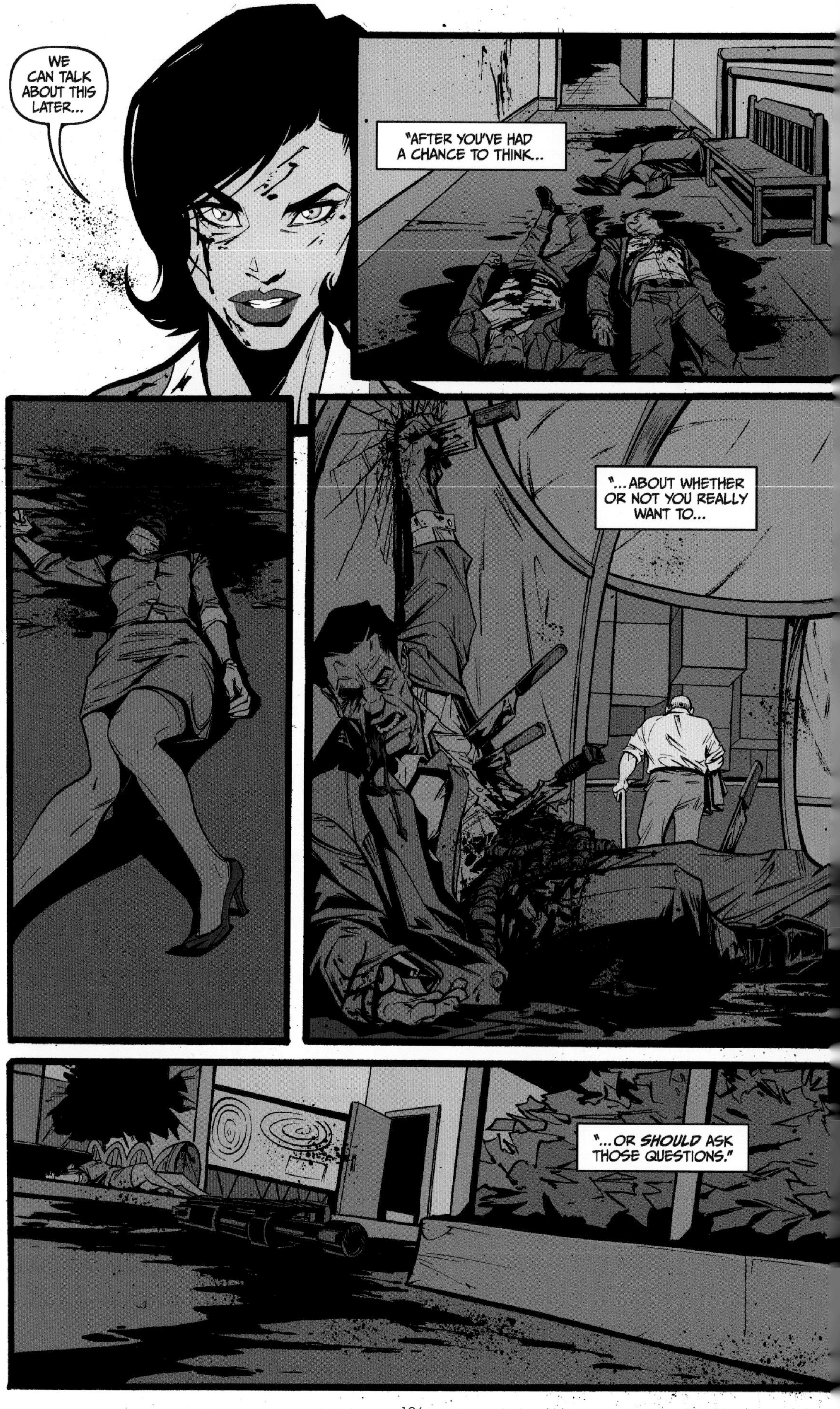
WE CAN TALK ABOUT THIS LATER...
"AFTER YOU'VE HAD A CHANCE TO THINK...
"...ABOUT WHETHER OR NOT YOU REALLY WANT TO...
"...OR SHOULD ASK THOSE QUESTIONS."

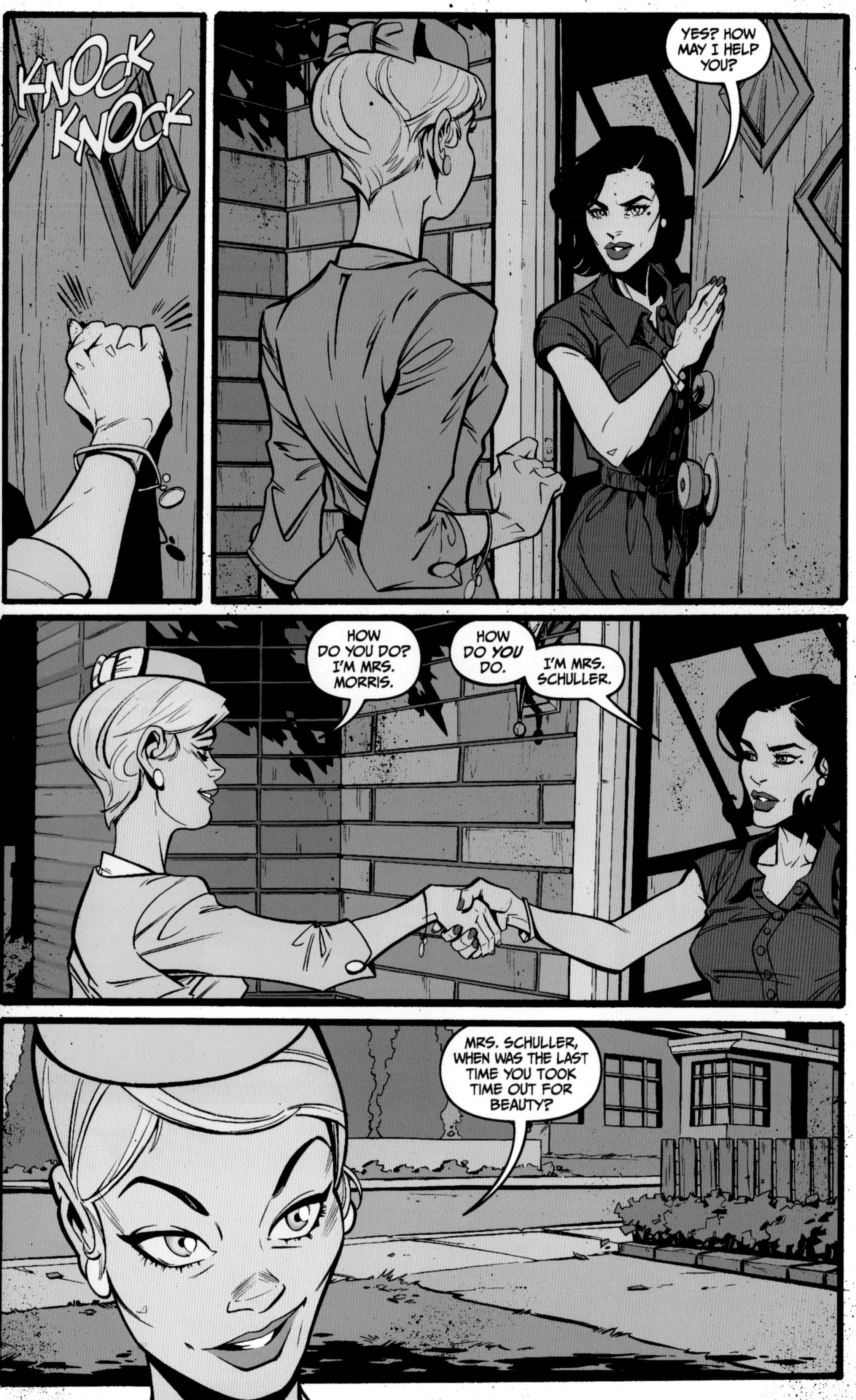
KNOCK KNOCK
YES? HOW MAY I HELP YOU?
HOW DO YOU DO? I'M MRS. MORRIS.
HOW DO YOU DO.
I'M MRS. SCHULLER.
MRS. SCHULLER, WHEN WAS THE LAST TIME YOU TOOK TIME OUT FOR BEAUTY?

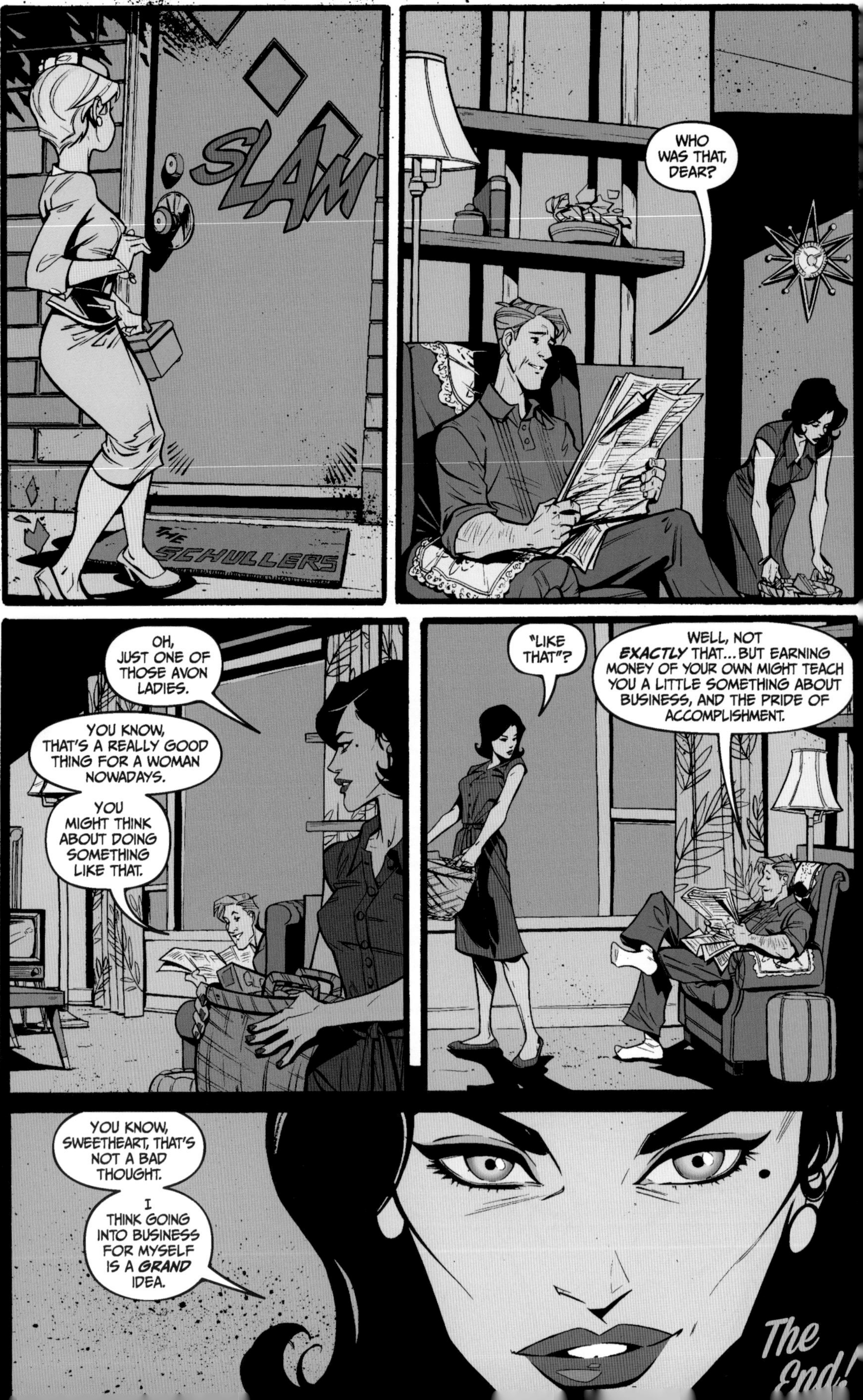
SLAM
THE SCHULLERS
WHO WAS THAT, DEAR?
OH, JUST ONE OF THOSE AVON LADIES.
YOU KNOW, THAT'S A REALLY GOOD THING FOR A WOMAN NOWADAYS.
YOU MIGHT THINK ABOUT DOING SOMETHING LIKE THAT.
"LIKE THAT"?
WELL, NOT EXACTLY THAT... BUT EARNING MONEY OF YOUR OWN MIGHT TEACH YOU A LITTLE SOMETHING ABOUT BUSINESS, AND THE PRIDE OF ACCOMPLISHMENT.
YOU KNOW, SWEETHEART, THAT'S NOT A BAD THOUGHT.
I THINK GOING INTO BUSINESS FOR MYSELF IS A GRAND IDEA.
The End!

SKETCHBOOK

NOTES BY JOËLLE JONES & JAMIE S. RICH

JOËLLE: Here are some preliminary sketches and art pieces I did prior to starting the work on the series itself. Mostly I was just playing around with colors and trying to nail down Josie's character.

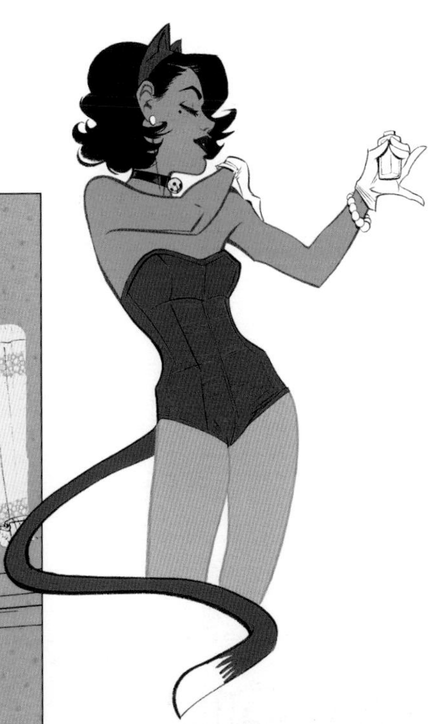

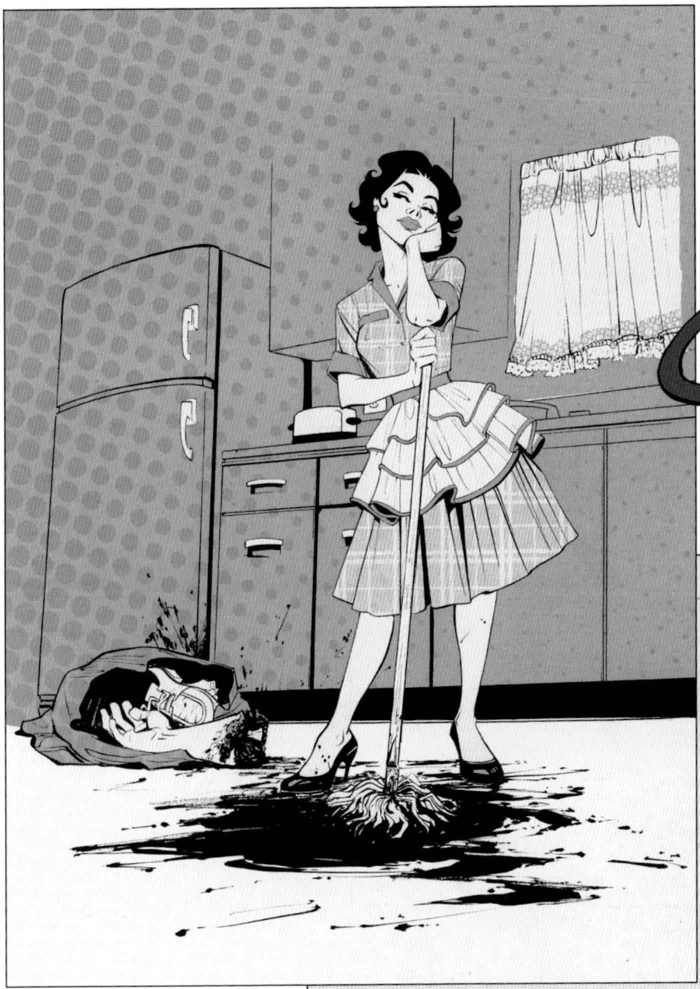

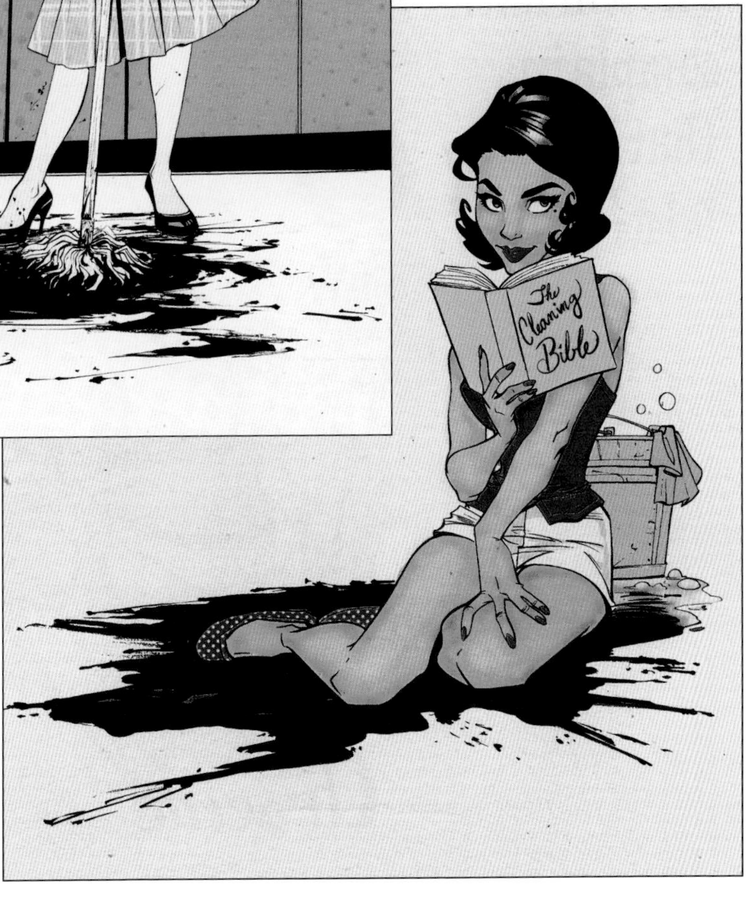
The Cleaning Bible

JAMIE: The *Cleaning Bible* image was the cover of our original pitch for the book, which actually opened with a meta television commercial that ended with a similar image.

JOËLLE: While doing research for the book I did some mock ads that I had so much fun creating. They are meant to be a spoof of ads of the period. I originally painted these quite large in gauche and hand lettered them.

Additional lettering by Crank.

JAMIE: I remember once brainstorming lines for a car advert with Joëlle, but I think she ditched it because the freezer ad worked just as well.

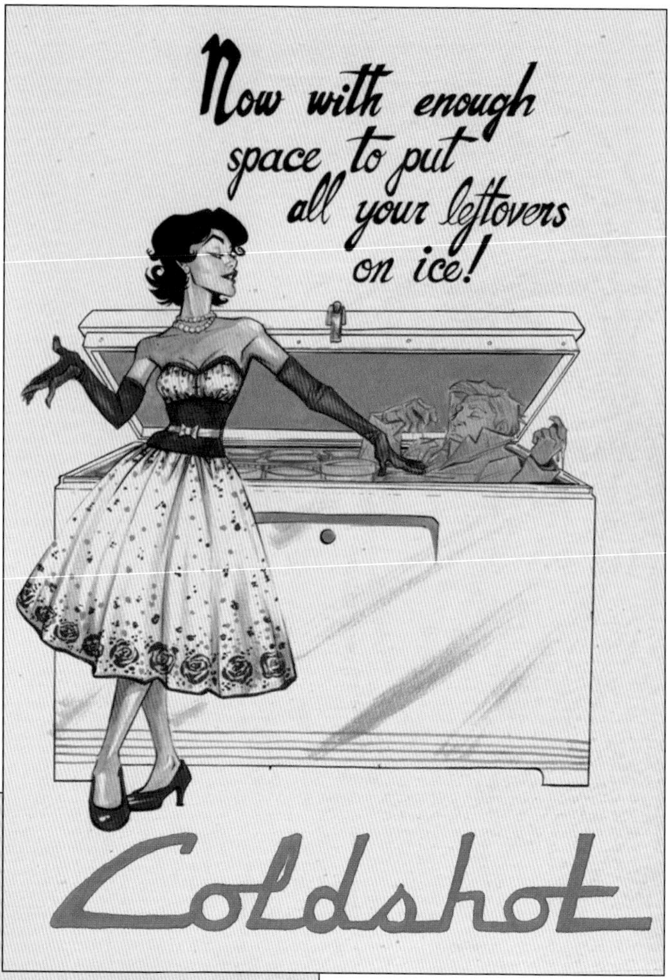
Now with enough space to put all your leftovers on ice!
Coldshot

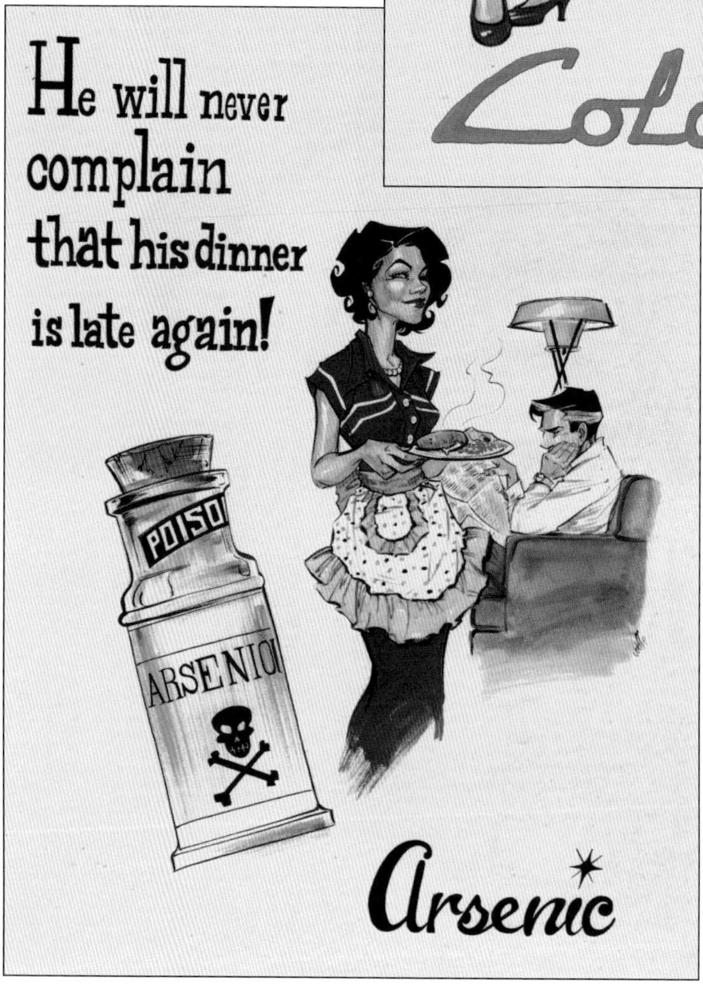
He will never complain that his dinner is late again!
POISO
ARSENIC
Arsenic

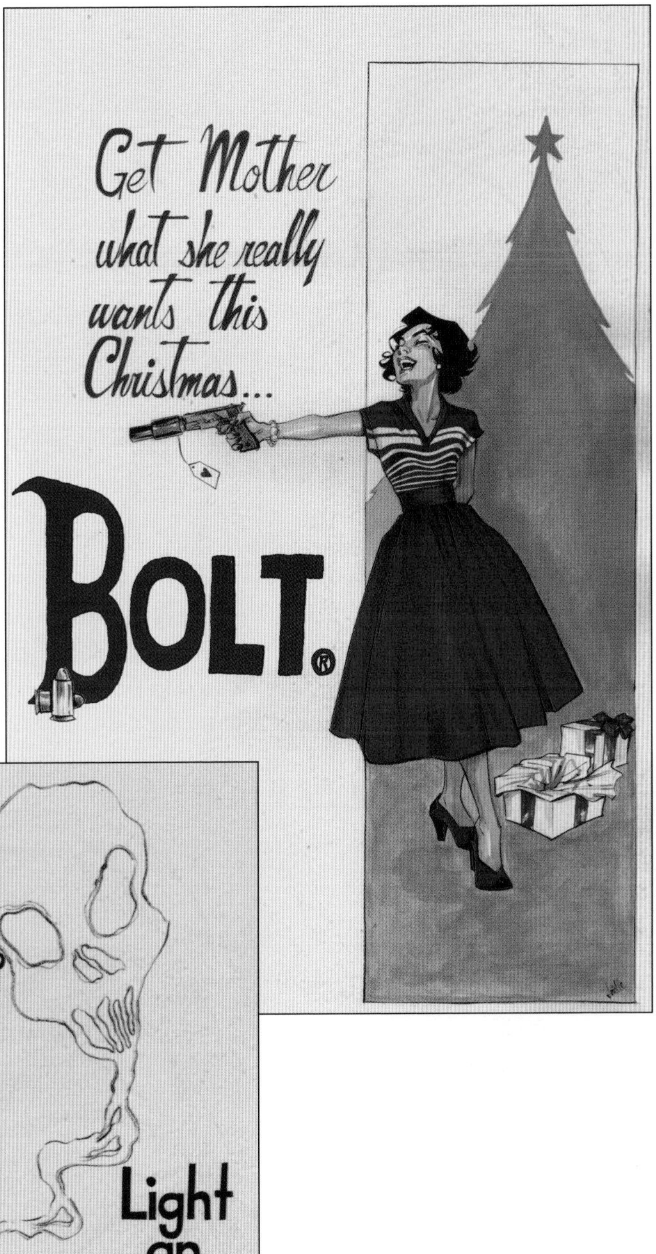
Get Mother
what she really
wants this
Christmas...
BOLT.®

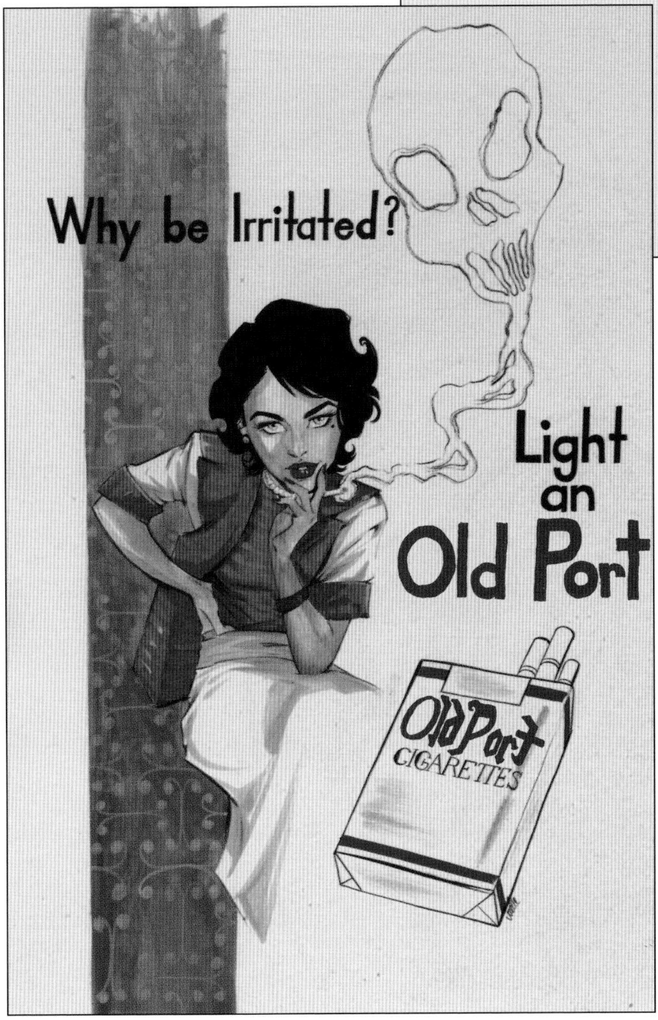
Why be Irritated?
Light
an
Old Port
Old Port
CIGARETTES

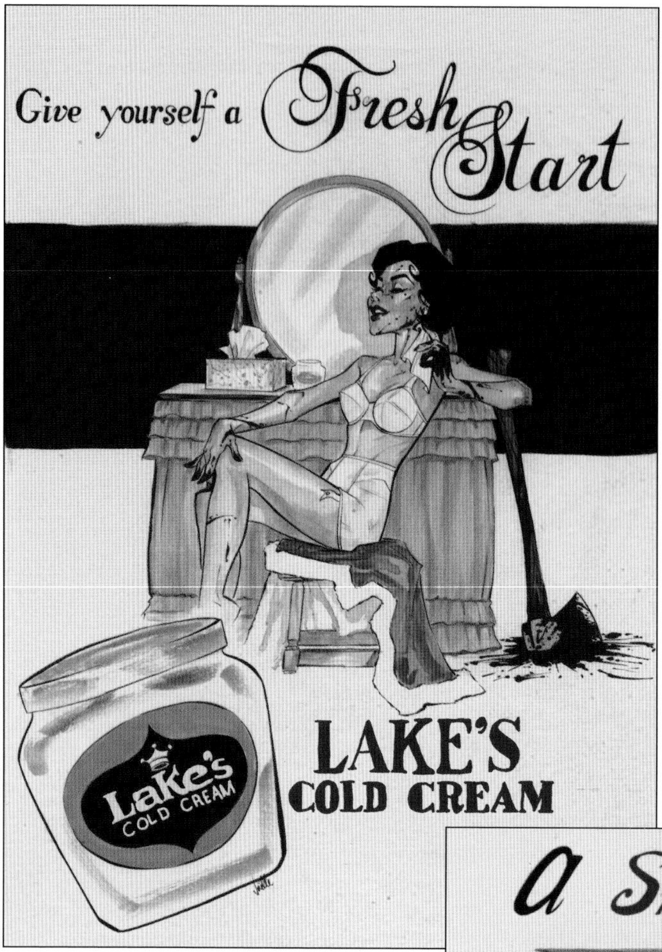
Give yourself a Fresh Start
Lake's
COLD CREAM
LAKE'S
COLD CREAM

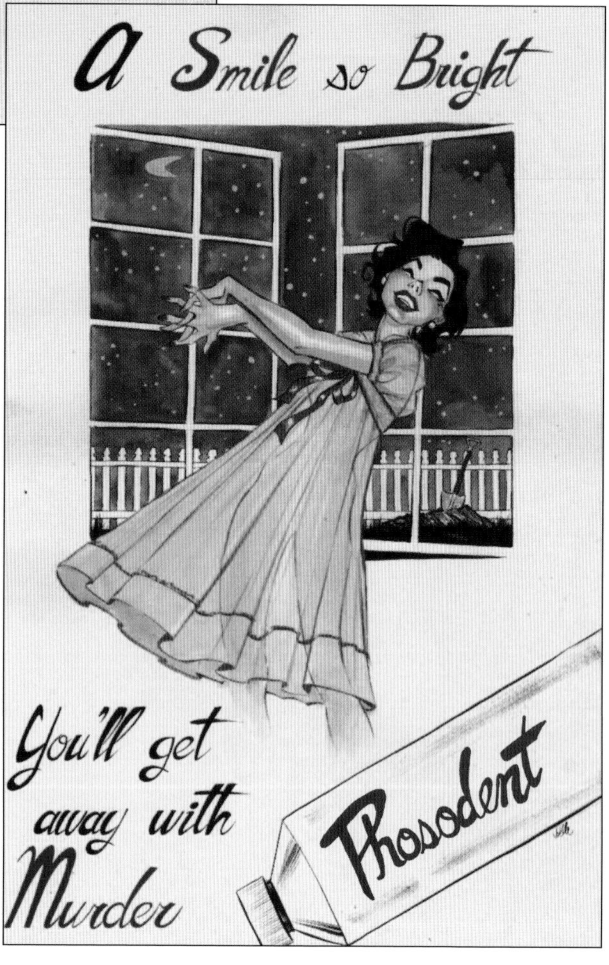
A Smile so Bright
You'll get
away with
Murder
Phosodent

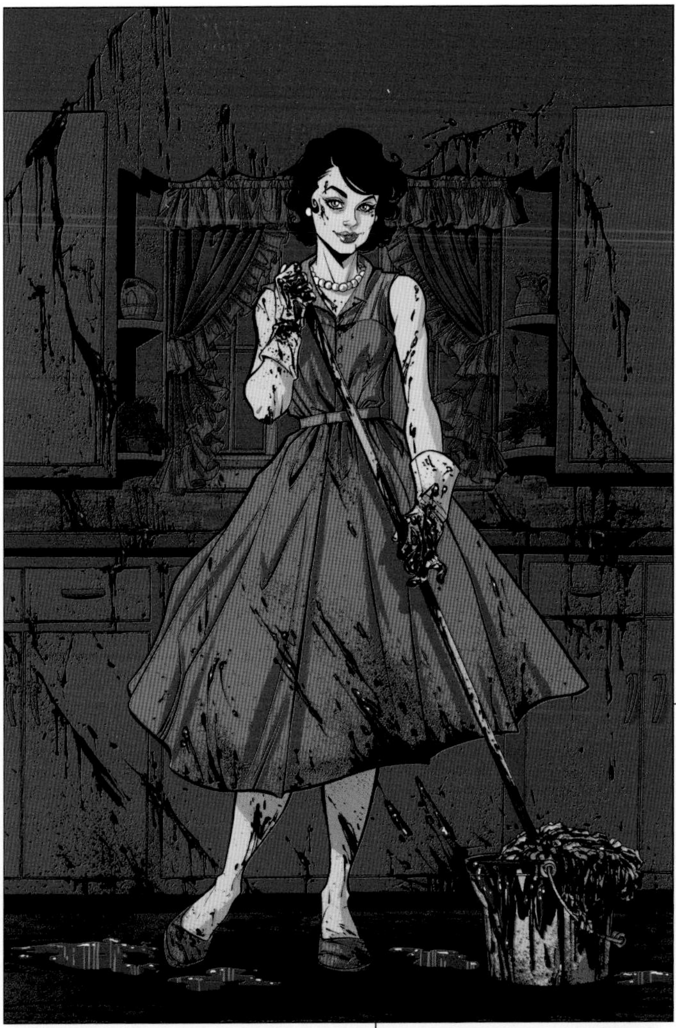

LADY KILLER #1
Second printing cover.

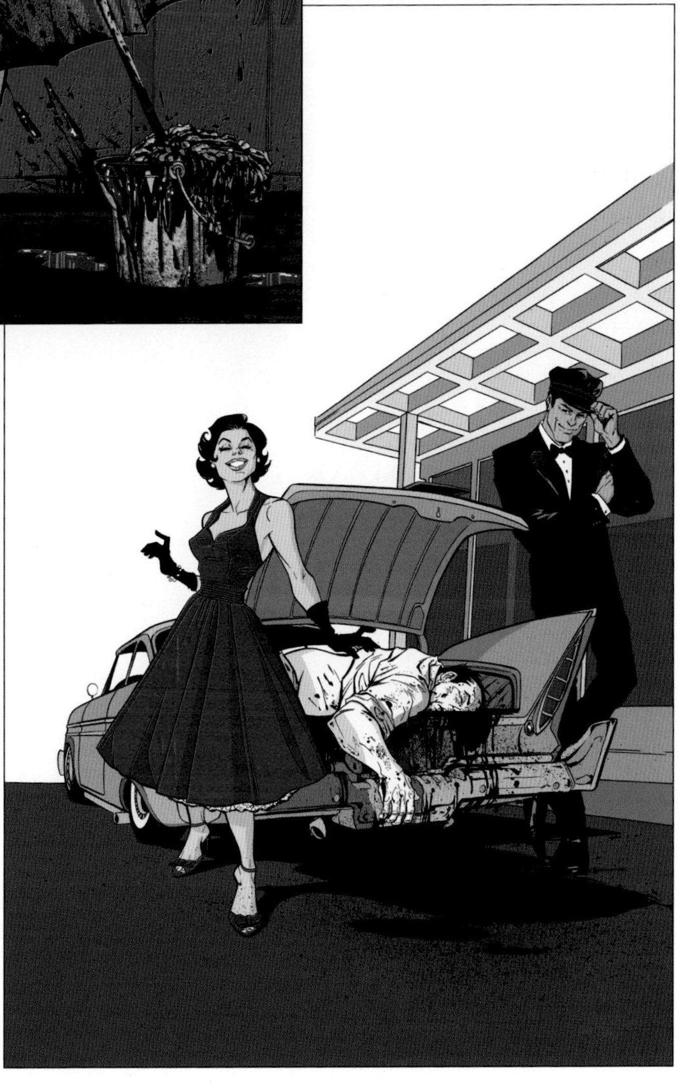

LADY KILLER #2
Second printing cover.

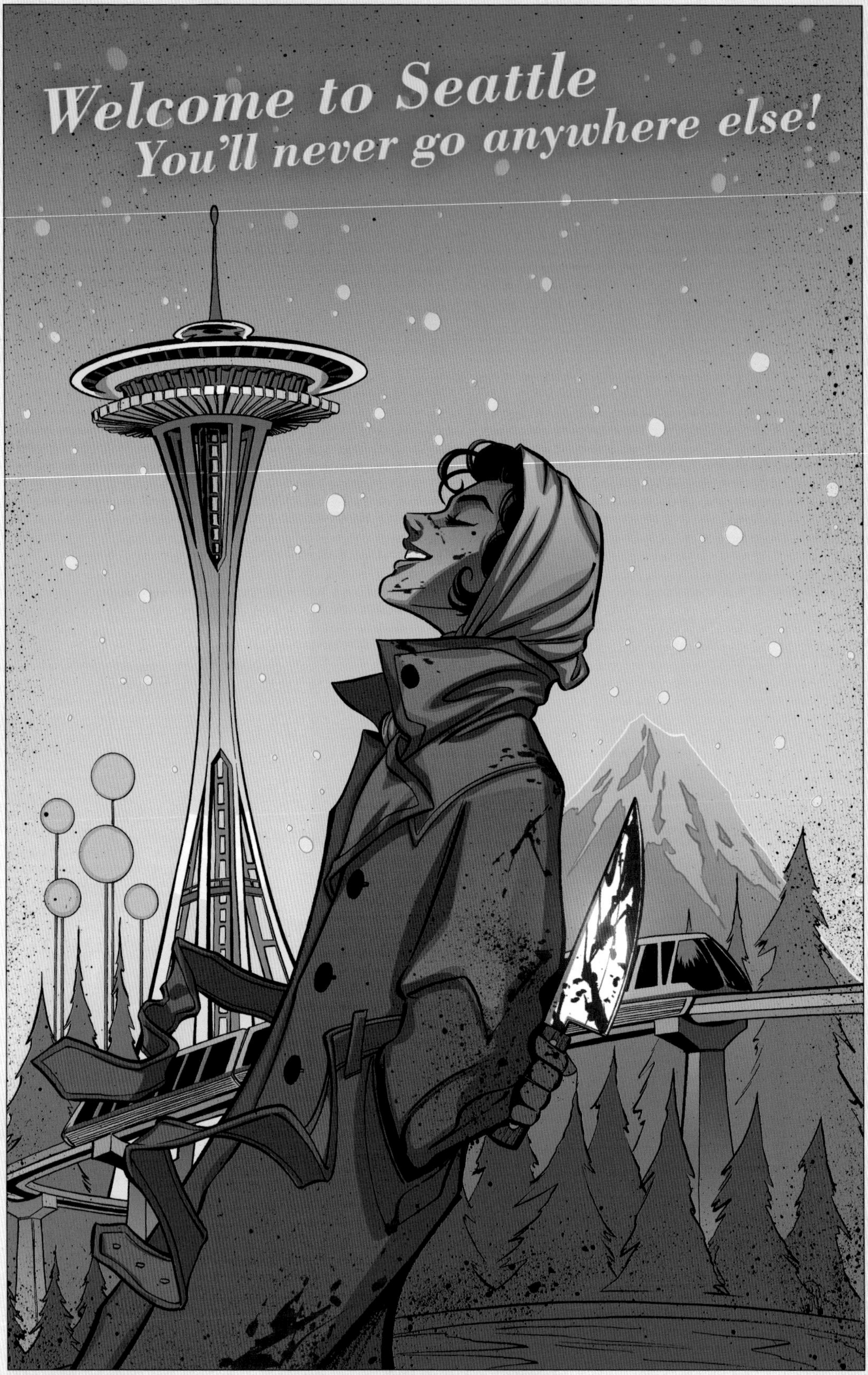
Welcome to Seattle
You'll never go anywhere else!

ISSUE #1 ECCC VARIANT COVER | *Colors by Nick Filardi*

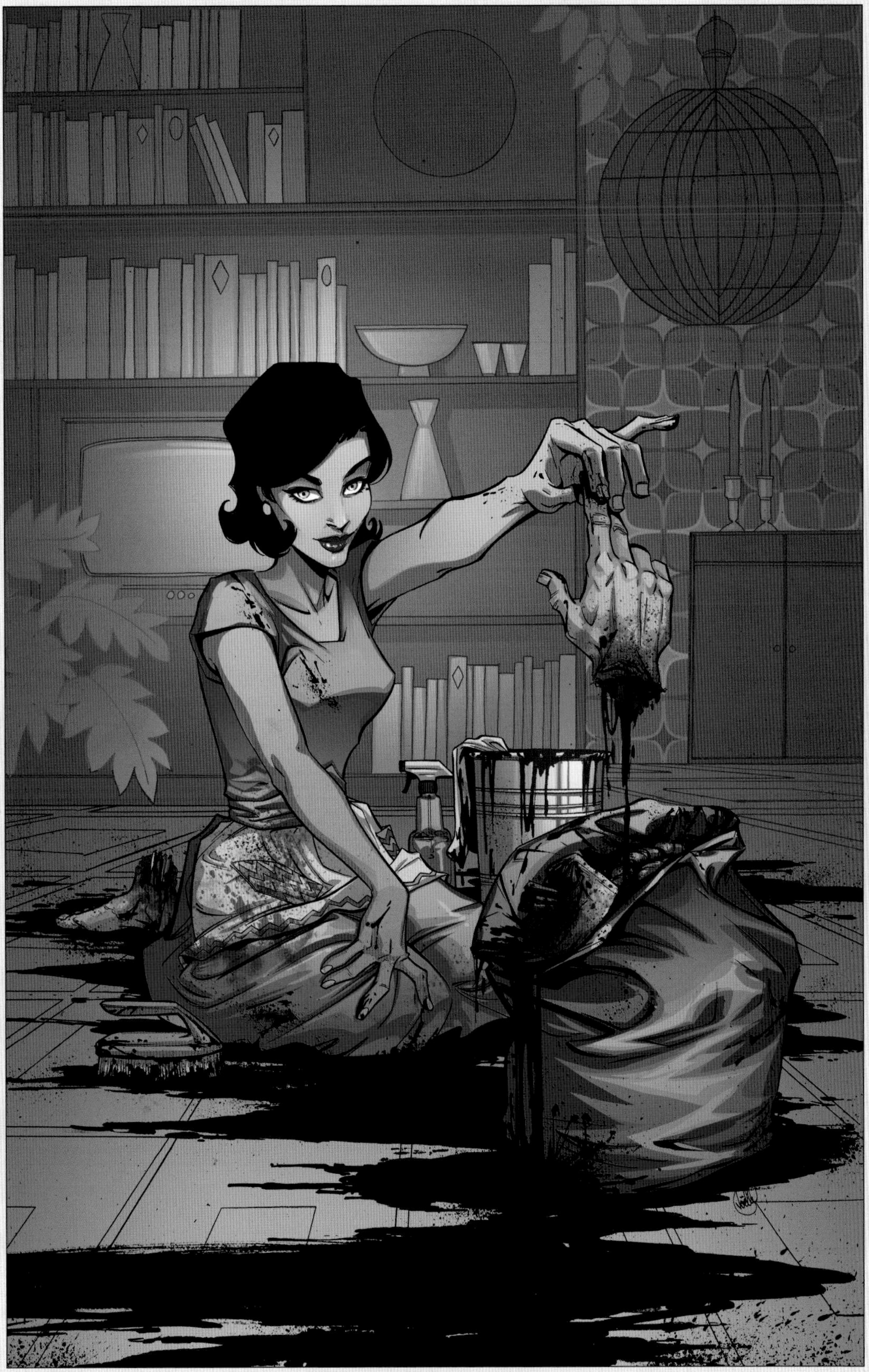

BLEEDING COOL MAGAZINE COVER | *Colors by Nick Filardi*

MORE BY JOËLLE JONES

LADY KILLER
Written by Joëlle Jones and Jamie S. Rich
Art by Joëlle Jones
ISBN 978-1-61655-757-7 | $17.99

HOUSE OF NIGHT
Written by P. C. Cast, Kristin Cast, and Kent Dalian
Art by Joëlle Jones, Jonathan Case, and others
ISBN 978-1-59582-962-7 | $14.99

TROUBLEMAKER
Written by Janet Evanovich and Alex Evanovich
Art by Joëlle Jones
VOLUME 1
ISBN 978-1-59582-488-2 | $17.99
VOLUME 2
ISBN 978-1-59582-573-5 | $17.99

DR. HORRIBLE AND OTHER HORRIBLE STORIES
Written by Zack Whedon
Art by Joëlle Jones, Eric Canete, Farel Dalrymple, Scott Hepburn, and Jim Rugg
ISBN 978-1-59582-577-3 | $9.99

"I can't wait to see more of Jones's art." —Comic Bastards

AVAILABLE AT YOUR LOCAL COMICS SHOP OR BOOKSTORE

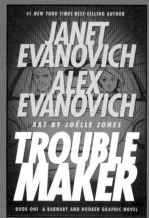

TO FIND A COMICS SHOP IN YOUR AREA, CALL 1-888-266-4226

DARKHORSE.COM
FOR MORE INFORMATION OR TO ORDER DIRECT:
ON THE WEB: DarkHorse.com E-MAIL: mailorder@darkhorse.com PHONE: 1-800-862-0052 Mon.–Fri. 9 AM to 5 PM Pacific Tim

Lady Killer™ © Joëlle Jones and Jamie S. Rich. House of Night™ & © PC Cast. Troublemaker™ © Evanovich, Inc. Dr. Horrible™ © Timescience Bloodclub LLC
Dark Horse Books® and the Dark Horse logo are registered trademarks of Dark Horse Comics, Inc. All rights reserved. (BL 6047)